Between Two Revolutions
Islandmagee, County Antrim 1798-1920

BETWEEN TWO REVOLUTIONS

Islandmagee, County Antrim 1798-1920

by
Donald Harman Akenson

1979
Archon Books
Hamden, Connecticut

First published 1979

© 1979 Donald H. Akenson

All rights reserved — no part of this book may be reproduced in any form without permission in writing from the publisher, except by a reviewer who wishes to quote brief passages in connection with a review written for inclusion in a magazine or newspaper.

First published 1979 in Canada by P.D. Meany Company Incorporated and in the U.S.A. as an Archon Book an imprint of The Shoe String Press, Inc. Hamden, Connecticut 06514.

Library of Congress Cataloguing in Publication Data

Akenson, Donald H
  Between two revolutions.

  Includes bibliographical references and index.
  1. Island-Magee, Ire. — History 1. Title.
DA990.186A38   1979   941.6'1   79-12899
ISBN 0-208-01827-1

Printed in Canada

Robert Manning Strozier Library

FEB 7 1980

Tallahassee, Florida

Acknowledgments

The author makes grateful acknowledgment for financial aid to the Institute of Irish Studies of the Queen's University of Belfast, and to Queen's University, Kingston, Ontario.

Acknowledgment for providing illustrations and permitting their reproduction is gratefully made to the Ordnance Survey of Northern Ireland, the Public Record Office of Northern Ireland, the Ulster Folk and Transport Museum, the Belfast Harbour Commissioners, and Miss Maureen Donaldson. Special acknowledgment is made to Professor Dennis Cashman of Quinnipiac College, Connecticut, who generously undertook photographic work specifically for this volume.

FOR

Bessie L. Harman

Contents

Preface	1
Chapter One. Revolution: One Try was Enough	11
Chapter Two. The Physical Framework	23
Chapter Three. A Reasonable Livelihood	31
Chapter Four. Population: A Non-Existent Problem	65
Chapter Five. The Famine that did not Happen	75
Chapter Six. Domestic Architecture: The Hearthside Order	79
Chapter Seven. Communications	91
Chapter Eight. Social Control and Social Risks	99
Chapter Nine. A Cohesive Culture—I. The Island Cosmology	119
Chapter Ten. A Cohesive Culture—II. Social Life and Institutions	145
Chapter Eleven. A Cohesive Culture—III. Conclusion	171
Notes	179
Index	215

Preface

The reason why a professional Irish historian should not do local or regional history is obvious: there is scant professional credit in it. Local studies usually are done by retired colonels, by unpromising post-graduate students (those judged too weak to be steered towards important topics) and by clergymen with antiquarian predilections. Occasionally a superannuated don engages in local research, but rarely an active professional. All that is well known. What is not so obvious is another, and I think more fundamental, reason that Irish academic historians have avoided the field: it is devilish hard work. In preparing this study I discovered that the research demanded was much more onerous, the resources more widely scattered, and finding-aids less readily available than in the research I previously had done in the fields of educational, religious, and political history. For example, whereas a scholar working, say, on the administration of the Irish poor relief system can quickly find most of the published governmental material simply by using the indexes to the parliamentary papers, a local historian has to work through literally thousands of blue books, searching, usually without the aid of index, for mentions of his particular area. Similar difficulties occur in using manuscript sources.

Initially, my reasons *for* beginning a local study were

based on scepticism about the way Irish history has been written (emphatically, I am here including my own work). Almost universally, Irish historians have been guilty of what is best termed the "fallacy of cross-grouping."* That is, almost all groups within Irish society, even deviant and dissident groups, have been studied in terms of the nation-state or the national culture. Writing two decades ago, Sean O'Faolain stated, "all histories are nationalist, patriotic, political, sentimental. I have not a single book to turn to which is not either pre-occupied with the national ego and a delusion of its self-sufficiency, or else a cursive record of political events, or a source-book of these events."* Since then a good deal of intelligent writing has appeared, especially in administrative and religious history, but almost all of it adopts the nation-state or national-culture perspective. Unfortunately, this perspective perforce has woven yet another deep-running fallacy into Irish historiography, namely an ethnomorphism wherein the entire nation has been conceptualized in the terms of the Dublin administrators. Historians of Irish life in the nineteenth century, even the most nationalistic, have taken the same viewpoint as did the former British administration in Dublin in emphasizing patterns discernible only from that imperial centre. By focusing upon national patterns of governmental and religious administration, we have wrongly projected upon local communities the belief that national concerns, not local issues, should be at the forefront of local consciousness.

Further, admirable as many of the recent studies of Irish institutional development have been, too often historians have forgotten that our categories—ecclesiastical developments, educational history, governmental administration, and so on—are matters of intellectual convenience. At their

---

*See David Hackett Fischer, *Historians' Fallacies. Toward a Logic of Historical Thought* (London: Routledge and Kegan Paul, 1971), pp. 236-42.

*Sean O'Faolain, *The Irish. A Character Study* (New York: Devin-Adair Co., 1956), p. viii.

best the categories are useful artificial devices cutting Irish history into workable segments, but at their worst they are highly misleading. In reality, the framework of life for the typical Irishman was not the nation, not the Dublin-centred administrative apparatus, and not the categories by which historians later analyzed Irish society. The framework of his life was the parish or town. He was concerned with making a living, keeping on a proper footing with his neighbours, and, perhaps, with saving his own soul. These occupations were highly time-consuming, intensely personal, and almost entirely local. And far from being segmented, Irish life at the local level was a marvellously complex web, in which each element reacted with every other.

In this book my emphasis upon the everyday life of the local community implies a rejection of the idea of "culture" as existing only in the sense of romantic- or high-culture. Paradoxically, Ireland long has had a large number of scholars and enthusiasts who have appreciated the value of folklore and of the ancient mythological remnants that sometimes are embedded therein; yet this appreciation has been largely at the expense of the history of the workaday culture of the people. This devaluation of the actual folk culture has occurred because those items that are prized most by folklorists and antiquarians have been the cultural museum pieces: legendary links to the Gaelic past, oral poets and vaunted storytellers, great antiquarian burial chambers, and estates with the crumbling Big House. But in reality the nineteenth century Irishman, like the man of any other time, lived in the prosaic present—and for him the present had more to do with earning a living, looking after his family, and exchanging gossip with his neighbours than it did with an ancient past. Thus, to understand a nineteenth century parish on its own terms, one would do well to view culture as the community's entire network of customs and practices, whether they are of ancient or contemporary origin, and whether or not they have any artistic or literary merit.

Inevitably, a book of this sort has a constituency

problem, at least if one does not wish it to become a merely academic exercise. Certainly I wish my fellow academics to find it useful, but equally I want the Islanders to find it interesting. Thus, on certain topics a compromise has been dictated. For example, the chapter on domestic architecture does not deal with the myriad complexities of cottage construction (which would take an entire volume) but with the architectural rudiments, and more important, with how this aspect of physical culture fits into the larger social and cultural context.

The academic reader may find two characteristics of this study vexing, but for neither of them do I apologize. The first is that in discussing various customs (agricultural, magical, religious, or whatever) I do not compare or contrast them to customs elsewhere in Ireland. Fascinating as it might be to point out instances of commonality and of contrast, it would lead the exposition too far afield. I am interested in how the various customs operated in a single community, Islandmagee. Second, I firmly refuse to make any scholarly judgement about whether Islandmagee was typical of small Irish communities, or was unique. My guess—it would be hazardous of me even to speculate—is that it was representative in attitudes and structure of those Ulster communities in which the people were of predominantly English and Scots descent.

In part, the determination to treat Islandmagee on its own terms, without comparative references to customs elsewhere in Ireland, is a product of my resolution to avoid becoming involved in the methodological fray concerning the definition of "culture" that so distracts anthropologists and sociologists. To some, Islandmagee would qualify as a culture in its own right; others would maintain that it should be denominated a "sub-culture." The former term has been used in this book, but those social scientists with strong convictions that sub-culture would be more appropriate, can mentally substitute that hyphenated semantic hermaphrodite without changing the nature of the discussion: this book is an historical discussion of a clearly delimited community, the description of which will stand intact whatever may be its relation to ever-changing social scientific vocabulary.

But why study a community in Northern Ireland? Chiefly because I have become disenchanted with the scores of books and articles that simple-mindedly depict Ulster society as pathological, dysfunctional, and irrational. Human societies do not hold together if they are that sick; the remarkable thing about life in the small communities in Ulster is that they seem to have cohered and to have functioned with a degree of efficiency not markedly less than their counterparts elsewhere in Ireland. Also, a northern community is a logical starting place because Ulster has been better served in regional and local history than the other Irish regions.* In the economic sphere, one can only be grateful for E.R.R. Green's *The Lagan Valley 1800-50. A Local History of the Industrial Revolution* (London: Faber and Faber, 1949) and for W.A. Maguire's *The Downshire Estates in Ireland 1801-1845* (Oxford: Clarendon Press, 1972). Two social anthropologists have produced unusually sensitive studies with important historical implications: John W. Mogey, *Rural Life in Northern Ireland. Five Regional Studies* (London: Oxford University Press, 1947) and Rosemary Harris, *Prejudice and Tolerance in Ulster: A study of Neighbours and "Strangers" in a Border Community* (Manchester: Manchester University Press, 1972). The Public Record Office of Northern Ireland has published a considerable amount of documentary material on various local communities. Particularly valuable as a research aid is Brian Trainor's discussion of the Ordnance Survey Parish Memoirs in his introduction to the *Ordnance Survey Memoir for the Parish of Antrim* (Belfast: Public Record Office of Northern Ireland, 1969). Also helpful as an indication of the range of material available is the record

---

*A notable exception to the dominance of Ulster as a topic of study is James Donnelly's excellent *The Land and People of Nineteenth-Century Cork: The Rural Economy and the Land Question* (London & Boston: Routledge & Kegan Paul, 1975).

office's publication, *Ballymoney. Sources for Local History* (1975).

So many people have helped me, both in Islandmagee and elsewhere, that it would be invidious to name them individually. I hope this book gives them a tithe of the pleasure that their company gave me. The brief archival essay that follows is intended as an abbreviated Baedecker for anyone who is interested in doing a similar project.

* * *

Historians trained in English history and accustomed to the richness of local records in that country are apt to be shocked to find that documents which any English local historian can take for granted rarely exist in Ireland. Whereas many English parishes have extensive registers of births, deaths, and marriages running back to early Reformation times, such records are not found with any degree of comprehensiveness in Ireland. The individual census sheets upon which a demographic parish survey would have to be based were destroyed for the years prior to 1901, and those for the years after 1911 are permanently sealed! Thus, except for the years 1901 and 1911 family reconstitution is impossible. Of course one collects what parish registers one can (and the clergy and vestries of Islandmagee were very generous to me in this regard) but it is a rare Irish parish that has complete records before the last quarter of the nineteenth century.

Fortunately, there is one resource that greatly offsets the fundamental difficulties of doing parish and regional history in Ireland: the Public Record Office of Northern Ireland. Its material is extremely wide-ranging and much of it is of use to a scholar studying a southern Irish parish as well as to anyone interested in the north. Particularly important for the social study of any area are the tithe applotment books for the 1820's and 30's, the records of the first valuation of Ireland (1830's) and the second valuation (late 1850's), as well as edited transcriptions of the ordnance survey memoirs of the 1830's (the original memoirs are in the Royal Irish Academy, Dublin). In addition, the record office holds masses of estate and governmental papers, most of which are thoroughly calendared.

In praising the northern record office, I do not wish to slight the Public Record Office, Dublin. Its staff is unfailingly helpful, but until recently that office has been severely handicapped by governmental parsimony. Most immediately valuable are their holdings of the Irish censuses of 1901 and 1911, which (in admirable contrast to the English 100-year rule) are open to researchers. Although in my own work the materials in the Valuation Office, Belfast, and the Registry of Deeds, Dublin, were not of direct use, these should be examined in any local study.

The Ulster Folk and Transport Museum at Cultra is one of the most useful—and enjoyable—places a social historian can visit. Its archivists have compiled a unique collection of ethnographic material dealing with dialect patterns, social, economic, and cultural practices, as well as an extraordinary collection of physical artifacts used in everyday life in the last century. The Museum's collection of photographs, stretching back well into the century, is fascinating. Even when the artifacts, photographs, and archival material do not bear directly on the parish under study they can point to aspects of nineteenth century Irish folk life that one might otherwise ignore.

The Geological Survey of Northern Ireland generously provides access to data on the physical environment which are fundamental to an understanding of any area's social and economic life. And one could hardly begin a satisfactory local study without obtaining the detailed maps available from the Ordnance Survey.

As for conventional printed material, the Antrim county library system has produced a list of books and articles containing information on the county. The Linen Hall Library, Belfast, has an unequalled collection of Belfast-printed books. The National Library, Dublin, is rather weak in these items, but is of course rich in cognate materials

Preface 7

which would be used by a historian studying life in the other three provinces. Surprisingly, the British Library, London, also is weak in items bearing on Irish local history and one would do well to consult its printed catalogue before planning a special visit.

In contrast to its printed-book holdings on Irish local topics, the British Library (Colindale branch) has a very fine collection of Irish local newspapers. This collection can conveniently be used to fill in gaps in the local newspaper holdings that one finds in most county libraries.

One of the most enjoyable aspects of doing a local or regional study is having the opportunity to meet, and sometimes become close friends with, local residents. Nevertheless, the reader will notice that only rarely—and then when I have special reason to be sure of the accuracy of the story—have I used oral evidence. The reason is simple: I am very suspicious of the historical value of most oral testimony. Time and time again I have checked a piece of oral recollection against contemporary records and found the recollection to be inaccurate. I realize that this scepticism about unstructured oral evidence flies against the conventional wisdom about the ability of the Irish peasant to preserve integrally information about the distant past, but in my experience, the Irish propensity to ramble on about the past is equalled only by their inability to get it right. (Indeed, one is reminded of the malapropism of the late Sam Goldwyn: "oral agreements aren't worth the paper they're written on.")*

Does this mean that personal recollections are of no value? Decidedly not. In contrast to the unstructured reminiscences usually collected by folklorists, the recollections elicited by well-structured questionnaires, of the sort utilized by the staff of the Ulster Folk Museum, are

---

*The Irish Folklore Commission has no material on Islandmagee, so I am here referring only to material I gathered myself. If one is working on an area for which the Commission has transcriptions, one would do well first to read the succinct comment in John C. Messenger, *Inis Beag. Isle of Ireland* (New York: Holt, Rinehart and Winston, 1969), p. 7.

generally reliable, and because the same questions are asked of a large number of individuals, both verification and comparison are possible.

But gossip—as distinct from self-important and uncritical "collecting" of folk material—is often very useful. Over a cup of tea with an elderly lady one can find out whose attic has a nineteenth century diary, where there is a trove of antiquated farm implements, and whose family solicitor has a stash of old documents that he might let one examine.

And yet I suppose the most rewarding thing about doing a local study is that it gives one an excuse to talk to some people who have lived a long time and have thought about it a bit.

1 May 1977

Donald H. Akenson
"Langdale"
Middle Road
Islandmagee

Chapter One.
Revolution: One Try Was Enough

(1)

William McClelland, twenty-two years old, spent the morning of 7 June 1798 marshalling at Knowehead Brae a group of Islandmagee men. Simultaneously, another group assembled on the south part of the Island. Both lots were armed in a primitive way: most of the fifty to sixty men in the Knowehead company had spent the preceding night at the forge of Jamie Adams helping to make pikes, swords, and various improvised weapons. The Knowehead band was well organized (at least for arms manufacture: their military discipline was soon to prove weak).

Throughout the night sentries had watched the roads to the Island and relays of messengers stood ready to pass the word of any approaching military patrol. While some men fabricated weapons, others carried fuel for the fire, worked the bellows, or brought drink from a neighbouring dram house. The manufacturers arranged themselves into work teams so that relief crews could step in when the pace of work lagged. By morning McClelland's men were armed and most were ready to move off: except for some exhausted from their night's work and a few too drunk to be of much use. Finally, the two separate groups of Island men received word that they were to assemble at Redhall, across Larne Lough in the neighbouring parish of Broadisland. The two Island companies met near the causeway (then near Ballykeel Point) transversing the lough, and went on the muster with their cohorts from Ballycarry.¹ Their immediate military goal was the capture of Antrim town. Their ultimate political objective was the overthrow of the government of Ireland.

Doubtless the Islandmagee men shared with other northern rebels many of the experiences that goaded Ulstermen into the '98 rising (although in the present state of Irish historiography it is impossible to speak with full confidence about the cause of the rising). As Presbyterians they knew that for most of the preceding century their religion—like that of the despised Papishes—had been legally penalized by the enactments of a parliament dominated by members of the Established Church. And if these penal acts, in contrast to the laws affecting the Roman Catholics, had been enforced only rarely, their indignity still galled. More tangible and more irritating was the annual tithe that the entire population had to pay for the support of the clergy of the Established Church. Further, because of heavy Ulster emigration to America, people in the north of Ireland were well informed about the American experiment in political democracy. They were especially fascinated by the directness and apparent equality of American social relations. Subsequently, during the 1790's, French revolutionary radicalism took root in many areas, and as the work of the Ballycarry poet James Orr indicates, strongly tinctured the political sensibilities of the region surrounding Islandmagee.²

But there also were specific local stimuli to rebellion. Early in 1770 the leaseholder of the Island, Viscount Dungannon (the non-resident landlord), had thrown open almost the entire Island for leasing through secret bidding. He was interested in amalgamating holdings as well as raising rents, and he allowed any farm under twenty acres to be treated for along with any other near which it was conveniently located.³ In the actual course of events, the leases of most tenants appear to have been renewed, but that is not the point. The point is that this unsettling experience for the Islandmagee tenants coincided with widespread agrarian unrest throughout Ireland. Goaded by rising rents, Established Church tithes—and in some religiously mixed areas by sectarian hatred—agrarian bands formed and struck at land agents, tithe proctors, and other small farmers who dispossessed sitting tenants. These groups, some of which antedated the 'seventies, took names such as the "Whiteboys" (the most important southern Irish confederation) and the "Steelboys" (the leading northern body). In parts of County Antrim the exactions of Lord Donegall aroused considerable resistance among the Steelboys. Comprised mostly of Presbyterians, the Steelboys maimed cattle, burned houses, and practised extortion. They were sufficiently strong to be able to muster several thousand adherents, who on one occasion marched upon Belfast and forced the surrender of one of their members who had been held in custody. The Carrickfergus district was particularly disturbed and the government found that they could not obtain convictions against Steelboys from the Carrick juries.[4]

None of these nearby events was lost on the Islanders. But they were shrewd. Having already been through a renegotiation of leases with their immediate landlord, Viscount Dungannon, they had no intention of suffering any of the punishments that inevitably would be meted out to their neighbours, the contumacious tenants of Lord Donegall. Thus, on 1 April 1772, the Islanders joined with the inhabitants of the nearby parishes of Larne, Kilwaughter, and Raloo in an address to the Lord Lieutenant stating that "... as our present Laws oblige us to pay for all damages done, in our Baronies and Parishes, by the disturbers of the public peace unless we apprehend and convict the Perpetrators thereof ... we shall therefore for the future exert all our power to discover, apprehend and prosecute every person who disturbs the peace of our County...."[5] This was followed by a similar petition, subscribed at the Presbyterian meeting house, Islandmagee, on 12 April 1772. One hundred and fifty-nine

Island men averred their "utter abhorrence and detestation of the many instances of barbarity and cruelty, which for some time past have been practised in this Country, by a set of disorderly licentious people who call themselves 'Hearts of Steel.' " The Islandmen claimed to have formed themselves into an association to defend against violence and to restore tranquility.[6]

Eventually, in 1773-74, the violence in Ulster subsided, and largely because of governmental pressure the most militant agitators emigrated to America.[7] As far as Islandmagee was concerned, the sum of events was this: within a short period, 1770-72, the people of the Island had undergone a renegotiation of tenancies that momentarily threatened the livelihood of almost every member of the society, and then had been forced to prostrate themselves before the coercive power of the central government as it moved against civil disorder elsewhere in County Antrim.

The quashing of the Ulster agitation of the early 1770's led to a threefold irony. The first was that the American excitement resulted in many Ulstermen in the home country acquiring para-military experience in bodies which were formed to protect the country but gave precisely the kind of experience that in other times could be turned against the government. In 1760, during the Seven Years War, a local militia had been formed after a French squadron entered Carrickfergus Bay and landed an attacking party at Kilroot Point. This militia, under the control of local gentry, included a company from Islandmagee.[8] Now, in 1778, another para-military force, the Volunteers, was established in fear of a French invasion. This group grew to be of national political importance, but that is not here germane. What is important is that within Ulster generally, the Volunteer movement gave the Presbyterian middle class para-military training that many of them used against the government in the 1798 rising.[9]

Second, although the more obstreperous agitators fled to America, their unsettling influence upon the British empire actually increased: in particular, the former tenants of Lord

Donegall formed a significant part of the American revolutionary army.[10] Third, these departed Ulster Scots radicals, through communication with their families and friends left at home, continued to inject radical ideas into the north of Ireland, long after their specific actions in the home country had lost direct significance.[11]

The Ulster fascination with America is exemplified by the encapsulation in local folk song of the narrative of the actions of the American privateer, John Paul Jones. On the evening of 20 April 1778, Jones' ship, the *Ranger*, appeared at the entrance of Carrickfergus harbour and attempted to anchor upwind of a British ship, a manoeuvre which failed due to Jones' quartermaster being the worse for drink. Bad weather forced Jones out of Belfast Lough, and he used the opportunity to cross the North Channel and raid Whitehaven and St. Mary's Isle. He returned on the 24th of April and stood off Kilroot Point, from whence he was able to mount a surprise attack. The Islanders were awakened by the reports of heavy guns, and those on the southeast end of the Island witnessed a battle that they soon turned into a ballad. The fight concluded as follows:

> Like two game cocks the vessels fought,
>   The fight was fast and furious, O!
> And broadsides thundered o'er the bay,
>   'Rose smoke and flames like fury, O!
>
> The Drake soon crippled helpless lay,
>   At mercy of the Ranger, O!
> But Jones was kind as he was brave,
>   And he forbade to sink her, O!
>
> Brave Burden at his post did fall,
>   He fought in vain for glory, O!
> Likewise his second in command:
>   They both did die for England, O!
>
> The Yankee ran 'longside the Drake,
>   And asked her to surrender, O!
> Out-matched, out-manned, that good ship struck
>   Her colours to the Ranger, O!

Revolution: One Try Was Enough

> Now while we cheer our own brave crew
> We'll give one for the Yankee, O!
> In honour bright both ships did fight
> That day off Carrickfergus, O!

This ballad (apparently only one among several composed at the time) was made soon after the events and is revealing for its catholicity of enthusiasm. Although the crew of the home-side, the British *Drake,* receives its expected degree of admiration, that for the *Ranger* and its bold, anarchic, American captain is open and undisguised[12]

Enthusiasm for the example of the American democracy, cognizance of the coercive force of the civic powers, and resentment of parish cess and tithes, percolated through Presbyterian Ulster during the 1780's, never coming to a head, yet never disappearing. All that changed with the formation of the United Irishmen in 1791, for suddenly the ideology of French Jacobinism bound together all these grievances, while providing a coherent programme for their removal: revolution. The interaction of United Irish ideology with Irish social grievances was extremely complicated, the more so because the foretold rising was a gospel that was all things to all men. To the Catholic peasantry of Munster it was the lever to remove the rack-renting Protestant gentry, and it was the holy sword that would revenge the Catholic people for the eighteenth century's iniquitous persecution of the faith. In Leinster, priests could help lead a rebellion of which the ideological base was areligious and in its extreme form unabashedly atheistic. To the weavers of north Armagh, the United Irishmen's creed meant something very different. They were independent tenants holding directly from landlords farms averaging five acres or thereabouts and thus had agricultural resources as well as their textile income. They were highly sensitive to taxes, especially unproductive ones such as tithes and cess. In contrast, in the Presbyterian parts of Antrim, medium-sized tenant farmers were dominant. Weavers were settled only as dependent cottiers and were thus less well off than the weavers of North Armagh. The powerful medium-sized tenant farmers had their own grievances, however, and these included not only tithes and cess, but the special rights and arbitrary prerogatives of the landlords. Obviously, in prosecuting their own self-interest, they would be well advised to enlist the support of their "proletarian" dependents, such as the small weavers and other cottiers.[13]

Nowhere in County Antrim was the leadership that the Presbyterian middle class gave to the rising more apparent than in Islandmagee, where the striking figure of William McClelland held centre stage. McClelland was the son of prosperous farmers: his family is listed in the 1770 letting-list as having fifty-eight acres in Portmuck. As a young man he took an interest in the Volunteer movement. In 1784 the movement split; one part became more conservative, the other more radical. The latter gave birth to the Society of United Irishmen in 1791.[14] For young McClelland (he was only twenty-two in 1798), it was a natural transition from the Volunteers to the United Irishmen, as he became convinced that the grievances of Irish society could be redressed only by revolution. Under the aegis of the northern branch of the United Irishmen, he was commissioned to raise a rebel corps in Islandmagee.[15]

So on the seventh of June 1798, it was well-heeled William McClelland (together with a William Curry of Ballycronan of whom little is known) who marshalled the men at Knowehead Brae and marched them, with their counterparts from elsewhere on the Island, to the general muster before Redhall near Ballycarry in neighbouring Broadisland. Similar scenes were enacted that day in many parts of Antrim and Down. The men of Broadisland were enthusiastic for the rising, and according to the investigations of the Ordnance Survey team of the 1830's, "to a man took a more or less active part in it."[16] As recorded by the Ballycarry (parish of Broadisland) poet, James Orr, the Broadisland men had completed their preparations early that morning:[17]

Revolution: One Try Was Enough   17

> While close-leagu'd crappies rais'd the hoards
> o'pikes, pike-shafts, forks, firelocks,
> Some melted lead — some saw'd deal-boards —

(And, to give an honest picture, the cowardice that was to plague the Antrim rising already was in evidence: "Some hade, like hens in byre-neuks.") The Islandmagee and Broadisland men who assembled in front of Red Hall knew that the owner, R. G. Ker, Esq., had a supply of firearms. Ker himself had fled, leaving his butler in charge. The rebels forced their way into the house, but when they reached the gunroom found that Ker had removed the firing devices from the arms. Nevertheless, caught up in the martial spirit, many of the rebels shouldered the worthless guns, and these, together with pikes, scythes, pitchforks, makeshift swords, and a few firearms in working order, made up their arsenal. They marched off towards Antrim town in fine spirits, because shortly before leaving they had heard the (false) news that Carrickfergus had fallen to their compatriots.[18]

Actually, the first serious rebel activity in the area had occurred not at Redhall, but in Larne, and it was with the Larne contingent that the Islandmagee-Ballycarry lads merged, in Glynn, on their way to Antrim. The Larne "battle" had begun somewhat after three o'clock in the morning and the rebels had killed three soldiers, seriously wounded two others and laid siege to the remainder. Most of the rebel force moved off during the morning to rendezvous with others heading for Antrim. Nevertheless, some were left behind, in particular a party of about sixty Islandmagee men stationed on the Island hills opposite Larne. According to one frightened loyalist witness, "we thought our situation desperate in the extreme, the savage disposition of these people being particularly dreaded."[19]

Savage? Hardly. In the Larne affray a pattern surfaced which was to run through the entire affair as it involved local rebels—both on their trek from Redhall to Antrim and on their scurry homeward: when, during the afternoon,

Captain Ellis and part of his troop appeared at Larne, the Islandmagee rebels immediately dispersed.[20]

This pattern—the propensity for prudential disappearance by large numbers of allegedly stalwart rebels—bedeviled the leaders of the main force as it pressed for Antrim. Desertion took many forms. Some rebels stopped by the wayside ostensibly to rest from their night's labours, others went behind a hedge to answer a call of nature, while still others stopped for provisions—but whatever their methods, by the time the force reached Ballyclare, en route to Antrim, a large number already had deserted.[21] Bitterly, Ballycarry's James Orr (himself one of the Presbyterian small farmer-weavers who followed their betters and were let down by them), later described the scene as leaders and followers matched each other's shamming:[22]

> Now *Leaders,* laith to lea the rigs
> Whase leash they fear'd was broken,
> An' *Privates,* cursin' purse-proud prigs,
> Wha brought 'em balls to sloken;
> Repentant Painites at their pray'rs,
> An dastards crousely craikin',
> Move on, heroic, to the wars
> They mean na to partake in,
>   By night, or day.
>
> Some fastin' yet, now strave to eat
> The piece, that butter yellow'd;
> An' some, in flocks, drank out cream crocks,
> That wives but little valu'd:
> Some lettin' on their burn to mak',
> The rear-guard, goadin' hasten'd;
> Some hunk'rin' at a lee dyke back,
> Boost houghel on, ere fasten'd
>   Their breeks, that day.

Not surprisingly, the Islandmagee-Ballycarry-Larne contingent arrived too late for the battle.[23] It already had been lost.[24] With a few exceptions (notably the Islandmagee leader, McClelland, who stayed on helping others to escape), the rebel forces scattered.[25] In Orr's vitriolic phrase:[26]

> An' rush! the pale-fac'd randies
> Took leg, that day.

Yet, although the Islanders certainly were not military victors, neither were they losers. What happened to the Islandmagee rebels? Sensibly, the military authorities under General Nugent pardoned all those who surrendered their arms, with the exception of the leaders. This meant that all the Islandmagee rebels—save William McClelland and William Curry who were among those for whom rewards of fifty guineas were offered[27]—escaped unscathed.

Curry's fate is uncertain (I suspect that he emigrated to America), but that of McClelland was remarkable. After the battle of Antrim he hid from searchers in a cave amidst the cliffs of Portmuck Isle (a small island that was part of his family's farm). After the search had abated somewhat, his family and friends noised it about that he had escaped to America. Actually, it appears that he became involved in an extensive smuggling operation centring on the Low Countries. Finally, the country having been calmed and pardons granted, he returned to the family farm at Portmuck. In the same way that many United Irishmen throughout Ulster became Orangemen to demonstrate their recently reacquired loyalty, McClelland joined the Islandmagee Yeomanry. Moreover, he became a lieutenant and is reported to have been an efficient and worthy officer! As a farmer he was a great success. The 1834 title applotment lists his holdings at fifty-nine acres. He was a noted modernising farmer, introducing machinery and building kilns to produce lime for fertilizer. So well did he consolidate his social position that it was chiefly through his efforts that the Irish Fisheries Board agreed in 1829 to construct Portmuck pier and harbour. He died in 1859, well into his ninth decade, his funeral cortege being attended by an "immense concourse" of his neighbours and friends. In his youth William McClelland had been a rebel and had thought thereby to do good. In later life he became a conservative and, instead, did very *very* well.[28]

(2)

At most, 180 Islandmen took part in the abortive 1798 attempt to overthrow the government.[29] During World War I over two hundred voluntarily served in support of the established constitution. At least sixteen died in this service.[30]

And when, in the years 1918-21, there came a call to national revolution in Ireland, the Islanders heard it—and recoiled.

(3)

This then is the question: why were these people so keen for revolution in 1798 and so loath one hundred and twenty years later? Although this book has very little directly to do with political history, implicitly it focuses on this political-constitutional question, for an answer to the question encompasses the entire economic and cultural history of Islandmagee in the nineteenth century.

In much of Irish national historiography, the apparent conversion of the Ulster Scots from revolutionaries to loyalists is treated as a retrograde aberration. At best, their apparent conservatism in the nineteenth and twentieth centuries is seen as a matter of social pathology over which they had no control and for which therefore they are not to blame, the poor creatures; at worst, it is seen as evidence of a deep moral flaw.

That is naive. The Ulster Scots went out in '98 because to do so made sense. As the discussion of the Islandmagee turn-out indicates, the rebellion was a logical outgrowth of the economic experience, social attitudes, and ideological instincts of the people. The reason that later Islanders did not join the twentieth century Irish revolution was that in the context of their lives that revolution made no sense at all. Whereas revolution is the instinct of an unsuccessful society, affirmation of the status quo is that of a successful one. During the nineteenth century much of Ireland was an unhappy country (although less pervasively unhappy than is usually believed). In many places, economic life was painful, the social fabric was deteriorating (especially after the Great Famine) and the political system was perceived as unjust. Revolution, therefore, was a natural response. But Islandmagee was not part of that Ireland. As a society, Islandmagee was successful. Not that it was paradise—far from it—but in no sector of local life were conditions unbearable: the landlords were not loved, but the tenants had substantial holdings on secure leases; the sea provided alternative sources of income; socially the population was remarkably democratic, distance between rich and poor being much less than elsewhere in Ireland. Religiously, the population was homogeneous; the informal system of social control worked well; civic government was not perceived as oppressive; and even the Famine did not undermine the stability of society.

Of course Islandmagee was part of Ireland, and that is just the point. Ireland in the nineteenth century was not *a* country but an aggregation of small regional societies. Some of these were unhappy, and by force of circumstances rather than through fault of the inhabitants, were unsuccessful. But by emphasizing the pain and the dysfunctional nature of much of Irish life, historians too often have obscured the fact that many of these small worlds ran very happily. Understandably, the inhabitants of the successful communities such as Islandmagee were pleased with their spot on earth.

Chapter Two. The Physical Framework

Had an Islandmagee farmer of the 1920's been able to walk over the Island as it existed in 1798, he would have met no major surprises, only changes in detail. The basic field pattern—consisting of two to five acre enclosed patches, irregularly fitted together like the compartments of a battered chocolate-box—had been set in the eighteenth century. The land had been cleared of trees and brush for several centuries and was intensely cultivated. The vista, therefore, was at once open and unobstructed, yet full and peopled, a land turned completely to use. Most of the parish of Islandmagee was a peninsula seven and a half miles long and from one and one-quarter to two miles wide, crooking from south south-east to north north-west into the sea. Islandmagee's eastern coast was outlined in dark blue by the cold, deep (up to nineteen fathoms) waters of the North Channel of the Irish Sea. The intense blue sea was separated from the equally intense green of the land by a black line of basaltic cliffs. These eastern cliffs, ranging from ninety to 290 feet above the sea, were backed by a series of four hills, varying from 306 to 470 feet. As one crossed to the western side of the Island, the slope became more gradual, and the declivities gentle and undulating, until the shore of Larne Lough was reached.[1]

An Islander of the nineteenth century would have taken

for granted a characteristic of his parish that actually was singular: "There is neither town, village, nor Gentleman's seat in the parish of Islandmagee."[2] Instead, as the Ordnance Survey observed in the 1830's, "the snug houses of the farmers and cottages of the peasantry run from one extremity of the parish to another, disposed so as to occupy its more sheltered and sunny slopes, and present in their whitened fronts and thatched roofs an unusual appearance of cleanliness and comfort. The general aspect of the parish then is sufficient to convey the idea of a population at once industrious and comfortable in their circumstances."[3] Strikingly, so intensive was the land-use, that not only were there no woods, but few hedge rows.[4] The Island comprised 7,036 acres,[5] nearly all of which was arable.[6]

Such intensive land usage was made possible by a fundamentally amiable geology and by a tolerable climate.[7] Most of the Island's surface is covered by boulder clay, a deposit from relatively recent geological times which, when transformed into soil either naturally or by human agency, is arable. In the present century the land has been classified by soil scientists as "B_2" and "B_3", which is to say medium quality agricultural land. Most of the Island is "B_2", meaning that it is of good medium quality, but with a heavy clay texture or with a high water table. On the east coast a wedge of land abutting the high basaltic cliffs is "B_3", that is of medium quality, but affected in places by various adverse factors, such as poor drainage, and uneven soil quality.[8] Intermittently, the boulder clay is interrupted by thrusts of lower basalt, chalk, Keuper Marl, and alluvium.[9]

The climate, although far from gentle, was not implacably hostile. The key problem was the winds, for Islandmagee had no woods or shelter belts, and was open to the full force of easterly gales from the sea. The Ordnance Survey of the late 1830's indicated that the spring winds came chiefly from the east and north-east and frequently blew for several weeks at a time, especially during March and April. In summer the prevailing winds were from the south, and the winter winds were mostly from the south

south-west and north-west. At their worst the strong winds made everyday activity unpleasant and difficult, but on the other hand they considerably reduced the rain and mist to which the area was liable, and the sea breezes kept the Island relatively free from frost.[10]

A modern study of annual average rainfall (for the years 1916-50) showed that Islandmagee had an average of approximately thirty-five inches per year.[11] This is not only considerably less than the average for all of Ireland—43.3 inches—but actually less than that for the British Isles as a whole, which is about forty-one inches.[12] But if the rainfall was not excessive, it was nearly constant: According to studies made in the present century, the Islandmagee area has roughly 225 raindays a year.[13]

The real climatological problem was not the amount of rain (the physical contours of the Island provided natural drainage for all but the most excessive rainfalls), but the scarcity of bright sunshine during most seasons. Throughout Northern Ireland the average amount of sunshine experienced daily throughout the year is only three to three-and-a-half hours.[14] Granted, Islandmagee has more sunshine than most of Ulster, which even in the month of June averages only six to six-and-a-half sun hours daily,[15] but even so the Island is hardly tropical, for in Northern Ireland in July, the average maximum temperature is about sixty-eight degrees fahrenheit, the average minimum a bit more than fifty-eight. At the other extreme, in winter the mean diurnal temperature rarely falls below the freezing point.[16] Thus, the Island experienced a growing season that though temperate was limited in the warm, sunny days necessary for many grains. Oats, therefore, were preferred to wheat, and beans to other legumes.[17]

In describing the geography of his parish a nineteenth century Islander would no more have used the language of geology than he would have employed the terminology of meterology to describe its climate. To the Islandmagee man his peninsula was divided into "townlands," divisions

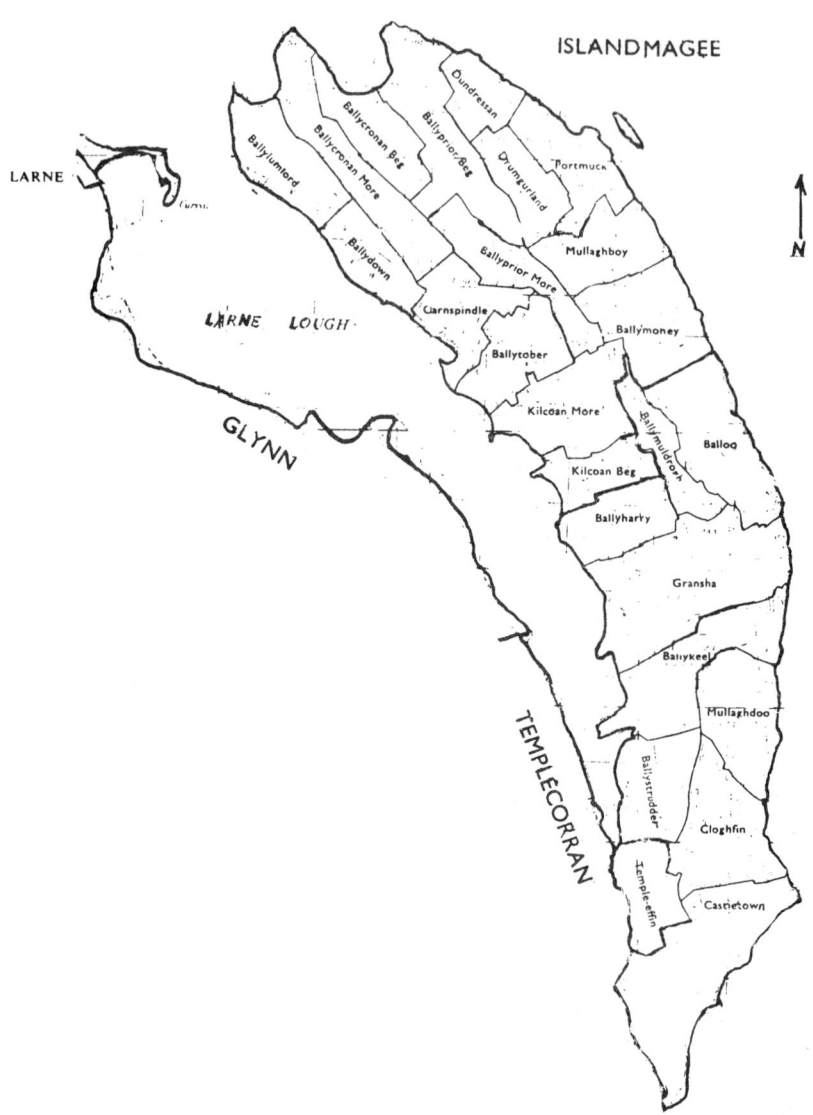

usually of approximately 200 to 350 acres determined in most cases by natural features, such as rock formations and streams. The origin of the townland "system," as well as the individual names, lay well beyond living or recorded memory, and most of the names stemmed from Irish roots far antedating the settlement by Scots and English in the seventeenth century.[18] The townlands are indicated on the accompanying map. Far from being an antiquarian notation, the townlands are important, for how else does one denote location in a parish that has neither village nor Big House?

When not using townland names or obvious physical features to describe location, the nineteenth century Islander was apt to use certain ancient monuments as geographic touchstones: an impressive megalith, called the "druid's altar" (Ballylumford); a tumulus, comprising either an Anglo-Norman motte or a prehistoric burial mound (Ballydown); a conspicuous cairn (in Gransha and Ballymuldrogh); two ruined castles, one at Portmuck, the other, denominated "Castle Chichester," at the foot of the Island (Castletown); a derelict lighthouse (Castletown); several sites of ancient churches (the most notable, in the townland of Ballykeel, having belonged to the Knights of St. John of Jerusalem); and numerous graveyards, some attached to the old church sites, others independent. Many of the ancient monuments, unfortunately, have since been destroyed.[19]

To talk too much about the features of the land would be to distort the geographic template that the nineteenth century Islander carried with him, for the coastline and the sea were as much a part of his mental topography as were the soil, the townlands, and the ancient monuments. The sea coast was not merely a boundary to the Island's arable land, it was a permeable barrier through which the Islander passed not only into another physical environment, but into an entirely different mode of making a living. The Islanders were not solely farmers; they were also fishermen, and in the second-half of the nineteenth century and

The Physical Framework 27

TOPOGRAPHY

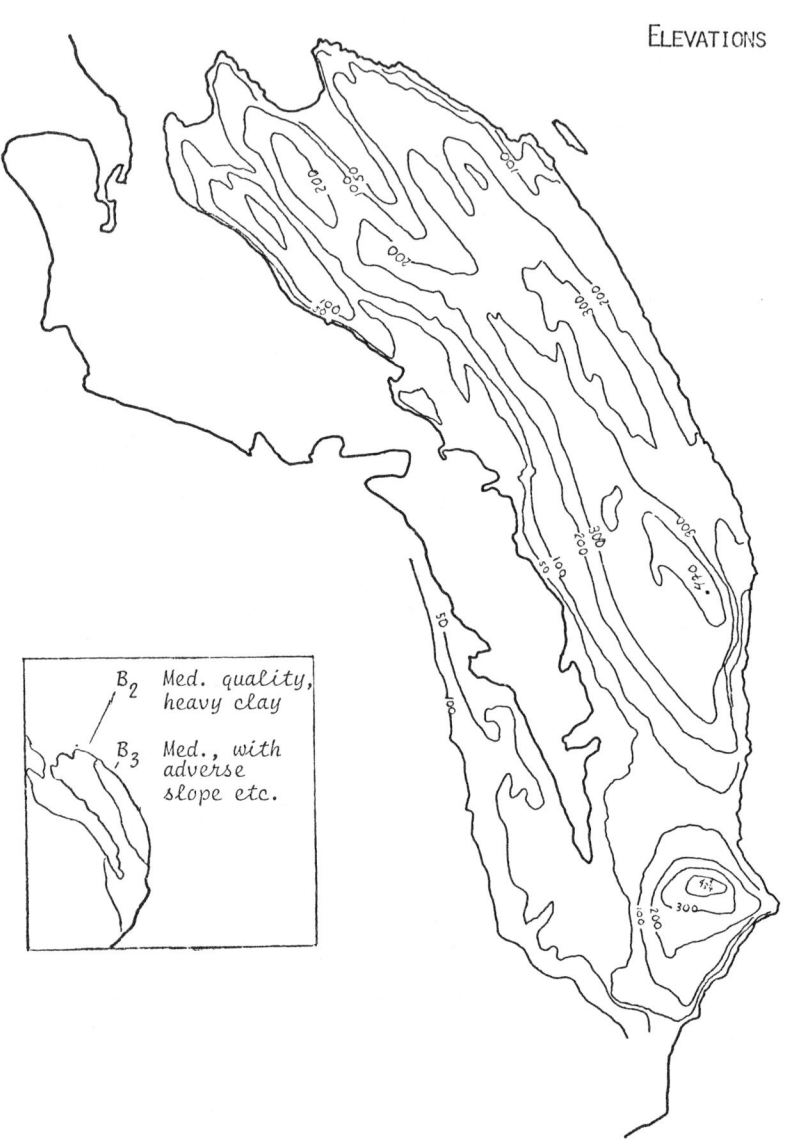

ELEVATIONS

B₂ Med. quality, heavy clay
B₃ Med., with adverse slope etc.

the early twentieth century, the Island became famous in maritime circles as the home of a large number of ocean-going sea captains. According to the original Ordnance Survey, Islandmagee had eighteen and three-quarters miles of coastline. If one started at the south-western side of the peninsula and circumnavigated the Island, the progression was almost continual, beginning in gentle flats and rising to awkward, forbidding basaltic cliffs. The west side of the peninsula fronts on Larne Lough, a shallow salt water body, less than seven miles long. In the 1830's it was about thirty feet deep at its mouth and gradually became shallower, so that the first three miles of its length were navigable by boats drawing up to nine feet, but further up it was accessible only to shallow draft vessels. A natural harbour was formed at Carnspindle Bay (usually known as Mill Bay), where a pier had been erected in 1839 for fishing vessels. Around the tip of the Island, a lighthouse was located on Ferris point, the most westerly point of the Island, just opposite Larne Harbour on the mainland. As one travelled further around the Island, one passed through the fine sandy beach of Brown's Bay. Thereafter, the coastline became more rugged, until at Portmuck Bay on the east coast one was at the edge of the craigy wall of basaltic cliffs. Portmuck harbour held a small fishing pier erected in 1829 and also a jetty for the loading of limestone, constructed in 1827 by William McClelland, of '98 fame. Thereafter, the 200 foot cliffs ranged southward for two miles, broken only by short, narrow, shingle beaches and by several sea caves (used at one time for smuggling by the Islanders). After passing a massive formation known as the "Gobbins," the sea edge became once again more gentle, only to rise in another mile-and-a-half into "Black Head," a formation exceeding two hundred feet, and then, finally, declined into a low shingly beach near Castle Chichester at Islandmagee's far south-eastern extremity.

To the Islander, the sea was as much a means of communication as were the paths and roadways found on land. With this in mind, one needs only a brief glance at a map of the British Isles to see a point central to the cultural and social history of the parish: Islandmagee was much closer to Scotland than it was to Dublin, the administrative heart of Ireland. The maintenance of trade and social relations with lowland Scotland was much easier than with most of the rest of Ireland. And although it was undeniably part of the Irish cultural and economic nexus, Islandmagee simultaneously was part of that distinctive maritime culture shared by the several coastal peoples who lived along the harsh strands where the cold North Atlantic breaks upon the British Isles.[21]

Chapter Three.
A Reasonable Livelihood

(1)

Irish historiography has almost as many myths as Irish literature, and one of the most long-lived is that absentee landlordism in Ireland led to the abuse of the tenantry, to a chronic shortage of capital investment, and perforce to primitive and inefficient agricultural practices. Granted, a large proportion of Irish landowners were absentees—in 1870 approximately one-third of those holding Irish estates did not live in the country,[1] and only about forty-five per cent of all owners, gentry and aristocracy, of estates over one hundred acres lived on or near their property for a significant part of each year[2]—but the accuracy of that observation does not guarantee the validity of the usual conclusions. Certainly the case of Islandmagee indicates that there was no necessary connection between absenteeism and agricultural primitivism or tenant-abuse.

Indeed, Islandmagee "suffered" from a double absenteeism. The primary owners of the freehold were the Chichester family. Until 1891, however, when they resumed the direct landlordship, their contact with the Island was minor: the Chichesters leased all of Islandmagee to the Dungannon branch of the Hill family and the Chichester attachment was limited to the holding of a manorial court until that was abolished in 1867. The Hill family, in their turn, had little to do with the Island, and never were resident.

The Chichester connection began in 1601 when Sir Arthur Chichester, then the regimental commander and military governor of Carrickfergus, wrote to Queen Elizabeth's advisor, Sir Robert Cecil, asking for a grant of a twenty-one year lease on Islandmagee.[3] Previously, Islandmagee had been granted to Walter Devereaux, first Earl of Essex, by a patent of 9 May 1576. In his original optimistic plans to conquer Ulster, Essex had intended that Islandmagee would be set aside for the Queen, but when baulked in his military efforts he tried to salvage for himself as much as he could: he petitioned for the barony of Farney in what is now County Monaghan, and for Islandmagee. These, along with the Earl Marshalship of Ireland, were granted. His son, the second Earl, inherited Islandmagee late in 1576 and held it until his execution for treason in 1601, when it was confiscated by the Crown.[4]

In seeking to acquire the recently escheated lands, Sir Arthur Chichester was following the established tradition of soldiers of fortune and was also seeking a permanent purchase in the country that once had been his refuge: in his youth he had assaulted a royal purveyor and had withdrawn to Ireland until pardon was granted. Thereafter Chichester had served under Drake, had fought against the Spanish Armada, and had commanded troops in various continental countries. He had been colonel of a regiment stationed at Drogheda before becoming commander of Carrickfergus. In 1604 as a reward for his service, he was appointed Lord Deputy of Ireland, and he held that post until 1614. Having been knighted in 1597, he was created Baron Chichester in 1613.[5] But land, as much as honours, was the grail of soldiers of fortune, so the grant of Islandmagee to Chichester by King James I, sometime before 1607, was the impress of professional success.[6] In addition, the family acquired an Irish viscountcy in 1625, the Earldom of Donegall in 1647 and, in 1791, advancement to the Marquisate of Donegall.[7] The Donegall family retained absolute title to Islandmagee until the 1920's, but they were resolutely non-resident. In a letter written in

1607, Sir Arthur expressed his hope of residing on the Island, but that is the closest any of the family ever came.[8]

Unlike much of Ulster at the time Chichester took title, Islandmagee was not depopulated or wasted. Instead, according to an inquisition of 1605, it was in a prosperous state, and peopled largely by relatives and followers of the English soldier-adventurer Sir Moyses Hill, some Scottish settlers, and "loyal" Irish natives.[9]

Mention of the native population leads to one of the most vexing questions about Islandmagee: when and how were the original inhabitants displaced, and who were they? In the sixteenth century Islandmagee came to be dominated by the family of Magee, who came originally from Islay in Scotland and were retainers and relatives of the MacDonald Lords of the Isles. Precisely whom they displaced is uncertain, although the dating of the Magee influx to the years 1550-70 can be postulated with a reasonable degree of probability. To compound the historical uncertainty, these Hiberno-Scottish Magees were themselves displaced by British Protestants in a series of transactions that are largely unrecorded. My own speculation is that the displacement of the Magees began with the Essex patent of 1576 and that it gained momentum with the introduction of the English relatives of Sir Moyses Hill in the late sixteenth and early seventeenth centuries. That the displacement of the Catholic Magees soon was recognized as inevitable and irreversible is indicated by the fact that in July 1620 the Catholic first Earl of Antrim granted lands of 280 acres at Murloch Bay on the north Antrim coast to Alexander Magee. Then, during the Irish civil wars of the 1640s, a considerable number of the remaining Catholics were killed (see pp. 139-40). The evidence of family names makes it clear, however, that a significant minority of the earlier population remained and that this minority converted to Protestantism and adopted the cultural norms of the dominant group.[10]

In any case, in 1592 Sir Moyses Hill had acquired a twenty-one year grant from the Crown of lands around

A Reasonable Livelihood 33

Larne[11] and also had leased (at an unspecified date, but probably during the lifetime of the second Earl of Essex) all of Islandmagee.[12] From this beginning, the Hill family prospered extraordinarily, acquiring an array of titles capped by the Irish Marquisate of Downshire in 1789. By 1801 they held some 100,000 statute acres of land.[13]

Significantly, Sir Arthur Chichester and his descendants leased Islandmagee to Sir Moyses Hill and his descendants, from the early seventeenth century to the last decade of the nineteenth.[14] During the eighteenth century the Islandmagee leasehold passed into the Hill-Trevor branch of the family, usually known as the Viscounts Dungannon. For our purposes, the crucial lease is that of 1769, wherein the Earl of Donegall granted a ninety-nine year lease on Islandmagee to the Viscount Dungannon for the consideration of £18,500 and an annual rental of £200.[15] This was an extraordinary document, for Lord Dungannon and his heirs received an almost unbelievable bargain: in the early nineteenth century Islandmagee was yielding over £3,000 annually in gross revenues, and later considerably more as rents were raised.[16]

What could induce Lord Donegall to give Lord Dungannon and his heirs such a bargain? The basic reason was the Chichester family's lack of fiduciary astuteness or financial restraint. Generation after generation, family members took all they could in immediate revenues irrespective of the long-range interest of the estate. Apparently the family practice of beggaring the future to gratify the present began in 1666, when the then Earl of Donegall sold a sixty-one year extension to the original grant of Islandmagee that was scheduled to expire in 1717. Once the practice was established of taking as much as possible out of the estate in renewal fines, while accepting low rents, it could be broken only by a strong-willed and self-denying tenant-for-life. In fact, the later Chichesters were the opposite in character and outlook.[17] So it was that in the early 1820's Viscount Dungannon was able to secure from the Donegall estate an extension of the leasehold into the 1880's,[18] and in 1841 a further extension until 1890 was obtained.[19]

As for the successive Viscounts Dungannon, although they were considerably more astute in managing their family estates than were the Chichesters, they were not improving landlords. Aside from practicing some minor acts of charity, such as subscriptions to local churches,[20] an attempt to limit the drink trade on Islandmagee, and the introduction of the use of lime as a fertilizer,[21] they collected their rents and stayed away. Nevertheless, the family became embroiled in a complex dispute about the Islandmagee leasehold.

In summary, this is what happened. Arthur Hill, first Viscount Dungannon (of the second creation), made a will in 1770 assigning to his grandson, among other lands, the long-leasehold of Islandmagee, with the provision that thereafter the leasehold should pass down through the male heirs of the grandson. The first Viscount died on 30 January 1771, leaving his wife (who was barred by her marriage settlement from any personal interest in the estate), two daughters, Anne, Countess of Mornington, and Penelope Prudence Leslie, and his grandson. The Dungannon title passed to the grandson with no controversy, as did the estates. The second Viscount made a will in 1829 passing his fee simple estates and his leaseholds to his own son—the great-grandson of the first Viscount. When he died in 1837 the son became the third Viscount Dungannon, although various legal complications prevented his obtaining full control of the Dungannon estate until June 1841. Then, in December 1841, the heirs of the daughters of the first Viscount, Lady Anne Caroline Smith (heir of Anne, the Countess of Mornington), and Christiana Powell Leslie (daughter-in-law of Penelope Prudence Leslie), filed a bill in the Court of Chancery in Ireland to void the bequest of the Islandmagee leasehold. They charged that in so far as leaseholds were concerned, the will of the first Viscount Dungannon was void for remoteness,

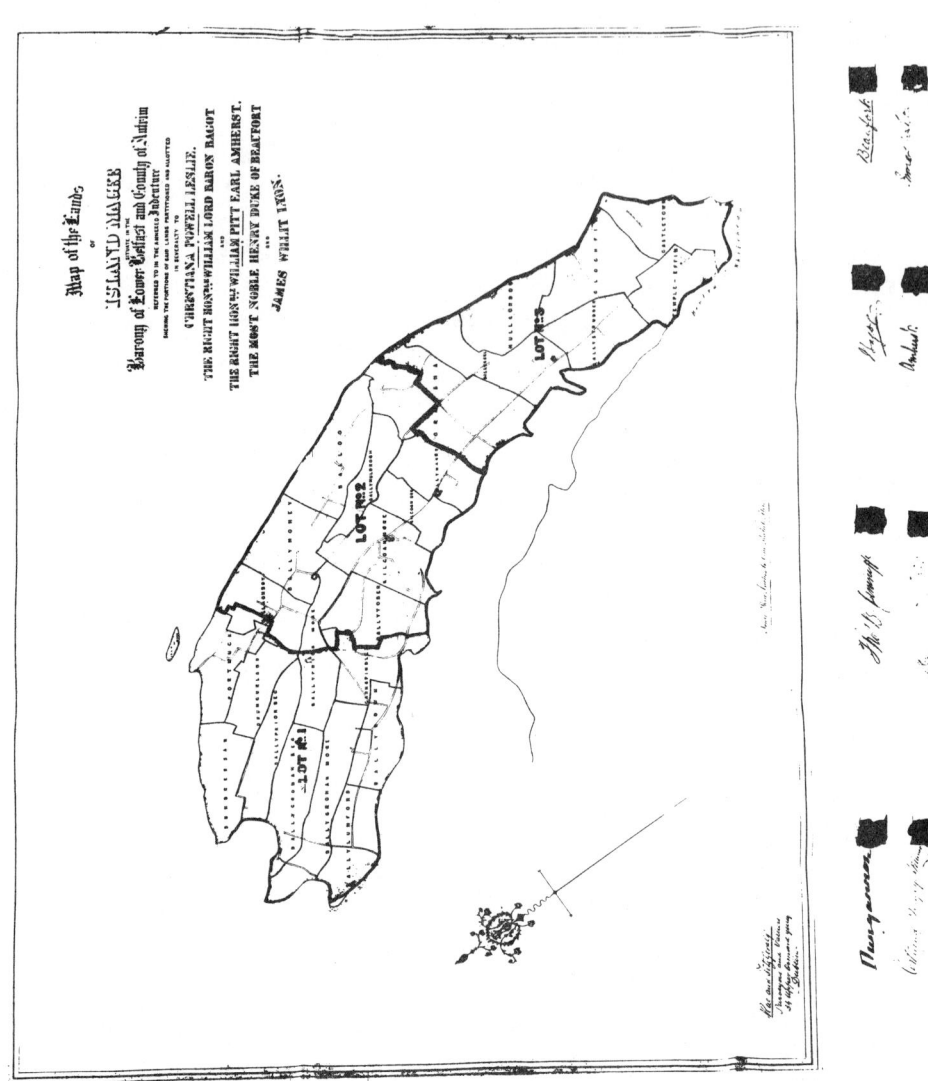

because leasehold property could be devised only for lives in being, plus twenty-one years. Specifically, they demanded that Islandmagee be trisected, one-third to the third Viscount, and one-third each to the other claimants.[22]

The legal battle dragged on until 1846 and can scarcely have been a stimulus to investment in the estate. Then, in a judgement of the House of Lords, the plaintiffs won.[23] The entire Island had to be put in trust, surveyed, and parcelled out. This process took more than a decade and it was not until 1859 that the leasehold was formally trisected.[24] To complicate things further, the Dungannon section was to be held in trust by William Pitt, Earl of Amherst, and by the Lord Baron Bagot; the Smith section went to the executors of William Smith (who had died in the 1850's), namely the Duke of Beaufort and James W. Lyon.[25] Upon the death of the third Viscount Dungannon, his one-third of Islandmagee passed to Lord Arthur Hill-Trevor, a descendant of the third Marquis of Downshire.[26] This tripartite arrangement appears to have continued, at least in modified form, until 1890, when the Chichesters resumed direct control of Islandmagee.[27]

Behind all this confusion lies the simple point that from the beginning of litigation in 1841 until the trisection of 1859 even the most improving landlord (and the Island's leasors never were that) would have been discouraged by the uncertain situation from putting an extra penny into improvements. Once the leasehold litigation was settled, there were less than thirty years to run on the Island's lease, too short a time to encourage large scale capital investment.[28]

In 1853 the hard-pressed fourth Marquis of Donegall broke the entail on the Chichester estate. In so doing he came under the provisions of the Encumbered Estates Act of 1849 and eventually he became merely life-tenant on all the family estates save Islandmagee and Carrickfergus. The bulk of the estates passed to the Countess of Shaftesbury, daughter and sole surviving child of the third Marquis, and henceforth the Donegall family was excluded from its

A Reasonable Livelihood 37

heritable interest in the once-massive estates. Thus, the fourth Marquis, who survived until 1883, was a phantom magnate. According to de Burgh's *Landowners of Ireland* (1878) he held 162,961 acres worth £41,649 annually.[29] Actually, he owned in perpetuity only Islandmagee and Carrickfergus, was life-tenant on the rest of the family lands, and was in debt far beyond his ability to pay. His successor, the fifth Marquis, assumed the title in 1883, with even fewer resources than his predecessor. Not only did the bulk of the family estates pass to the Shaftesburys, but he could not realize the rentals of his largest remaining piece of land, Islandmagee, until the Dungannon leasehold lapsed in 1890. Even then, he needed for his own use every penny he could acquire from the Island and could not put anything back into it. According to one observer, "he had even more creditors than credit and so mortgagees and insurance companies and numerous other claimants sought the rental payable by the sturdy occupiers and tillers of the soil."[30]

In the face of such odds one can only admire the fifth Marquis' domestic vigour. Born in 1822, he was just past eighty when in December 1902, he married a Nova Scotian, Violet Gertrude Twining. Not that he was any stranger to marriage—this was his third—but he had yet to have heirs. His first marriage was contracted in 1859 and annulled four years later, under circumstances that never were fully explained (in 1898 a miserable old woman, wearing a dilapidated dressing gown and carrying a Bible, asked for admittance at Highgate Workhouse; she described herself as the Marchioness of Donegall and eventually substantiated the claim; what happened to her thereafter is unknown). In 1865, the Marquis married again, and this second Marchioness died in 1901. The third Marchioness was said to have travelled a great deal in Russia and South Africa and seems to have been a person of sturdy character, which was a necessity given the Donegalls' situation. In any case, the 23 December 1902 wedding was followed by the birth on 7 October 1903 of a male heir. The fifth Marquis survived his final marriage a scarce seventeen months, and the infant sixth Marquis assumed the title in May 1904.[31] Necessarily, the Islandmagee estate now was administered for a minor child, who would not come of age until 1924. This minority managership, when combined with the impoverishment of the Donegall family, meant that nothing was available for agricultural improvements. Further, although the sixth Marquis claimed "Isle of Magee, Co. Antrim" as his "seat", there was no family dwelling there and no indication that he, or any of his forebears, ever spent so much as a night on the Island, much less resided.[32] Indeed, his agent did not deign to come to Islandmagee to collect rents, but had the tenants call upon him at a hotel in Larne.[33]

Thus, during the years under study, 1798-1920, Islandmagee was controlled by absentee landlords, who took the rents but invested little or nothing in the estate. According to the standard interpretation of Irish agricultural history, this was a certain prescription for agricultural inefficiency and tenant distress.

(2)

In fact, Islandmagee prospered. To understand why this was so, we must look first at land-holding procedures, and then at farming practices. Initially, it is important to establish that despite alternative sources of income (discussed in section five), agriculture was the Island's primary economic sector. The earliest comprehensive figures for Islandmagee, compiled for 1831, indicate that of the 502 families on the Island, 262 were employed directly in agriculture.[34] The proportion of Islandmagee families engaged in agriculture (fifty-two percent in 1831) was almost identical to the proportion for Ireland as a whole (fifty-four percent in 1841).[35] In Islandmagee, nothing happened during the course of the nineteenth and early-twentieth centuries to disturb the reliance on agriculture.

Where Islandmagee was atypical of Irish agriculture was

This Indenture Made the seventeenth day of June in the Year of our Lord One Thousand Eight Hundred and twenty four, BETWEEN the Honourable ARTHUR LORD VISCOUNT DUNGANNON of the one part, and Andrew Brown of the Townland of Ballykeel and County of Antrim farmer of the other part.

WITNESSETH, that the said LORD VISCOUNT DUNGANNON hath demised, granted, released and confirmed, and by these Presents doth demise, grant, release and confirm, unto the said Andrew Brown in his actual possession now being, by virtue of a bargain and sale to him thereof made by the said Viscount, by Indenture bearing date the day next before the day of the date of these Presents, for one whole year from thence next coming, in consideration of Five Shillings sterling, and by force of the Statute for transferring of Uses into Possession, ALL THAT AND THOSE the Farm, Tenement, and Parcel of Land, containing by Survey, fourteen acres three roods and twenty perches Plantation measure or thereabouts and now or late in the tenure, possession or occupation of the said Andrew Brown his undertenants or assigns

with all the Rights, Members, and Appurtenances thereunto belonging, in any wise appertaining; situate, lying, and being in the Townland of Ballykeel and County of Antrim (excepting and always reserving out of this demise, all Mines, Minerals, Quarries, Timber, Trees, growing or to grow, Underwoods, Turbary, Mosses, Roads, made and to be made, Ways, Paths, Passages, Water, Water-courses, Mill-Seats, and all other Royalties whatsoever, with free ingress, egress, and regress, to and for the said Viscount, his Heirs and Assigns, his and their servants, to cut and dig up the said Mines, Quarries, Timber, and Moss, and to carry away the same, on rendering to the Tenant a reasonable recompence for the damage thereby done to the soil; also, free warren and chace.) TO HAVE AND TO HOLD all and singular the said demised Premises, with their Rights, Members, and Appurtenances (except as before excepted) unto the said Andrew Brown his Heirs, Executors, Administrators and Assigns, for and during the full term and time of thirty one years commencing from the First of November, One Thousand Eight Hundred and twenty three from thenceforth fully to be complete and ended; he the said Andrew Brown his Heirs, Executors, Administrators and Assigns, YIELDING AND PAYING therefore and thereout, Yearly and every Year, during this Demise, unto the said Viscount, his Heirs and Assigns, the clear yearly Rent or Sum of fifteen pounds sterling, together with One Shilling for each Pound of Rent, as Agent's Fees, and One Shilling yearly for Acquittances, and Two Days Work for a Man and Horse yearly if required, or Three Shillings Sterling in lieu thereof as Duties at the Election of the said Viscount, his Heirs and Assigns, over and above all Taxes, Subsidies and Impositions whatsoever, imposed or to be imposed, (Quit, Crown, and Chief Rents, only excepted.) The said yearly Rent and Fees to be paid Half-yearly, by two equal Portions, on every first day of May, and every first day of November, yearly and every year during this Demise. AND if it shall happen, that the said Yearly Rent and Fees, or any Part thereof, shall be behind or unpaid by the space of Twenty One Days next after any of the said Days of Payment, wherefore the same ought to be paid as aforesaid, that then, and in every such case, it shall and may be lawful to and for the said Viscount, his Heirs and Assigns, into the said Demised Premises, or any part thereof, to enter and distrain for said Rent and Fees so behind or unpaid, and the Distress or Distresses there found, to lead, drive, and carry away, and the same to dispose of according to Law, until such Rent and Fees, or arrears thereof, be fully satisfied and paid, together with such reasonable charges as the said Viscount, his Heirs or Assigns, shall be at or put to on account of his and their distraining as aforesaid. AND in case no distress can be had or found on the Premises, sufficient to answer such arrear of Rent and Fees as may happen at any time or times during this demise to be behind or unpaid as aforesaid, that then it shall and may be lawful to and for the said Viscount, his Heirs and Assigns, into the said demised Premises, or any part thereof, in the name of the whole to re-enter, and the same to have again, re-possess and enjoy, as in his and their former Estate, any thing herein before contained to the contrary thereof in any wise notwithstanding. AND the said Andrew Brown his Heirs, Executors, Administrators, and Assigns, doth covenant, promise, grant and agree to and with the said Viscount, his Heirs and Assigns, by these presents, that the said Andrew Brown his Heirs, Executors, Administrators and Assigns, shall and will, during this present demise, well and truly pay or cause to be paid, unto the said Viscount, his Heirs and Assigns, the said yearly Rent and Fees, on the days and times, and in the manner and form above mentioned for payment thereof, according to the reservations above mentioned, and the true intent and meaning of these presents: AND that the said Andrew Brown his Heirs, Executors, Administrators, and Assigns, shall and will at all times during this demise, grind all his and their Corn and Grain that shall be expended on the Premises, and that shall grow thereon, and be ground for Sale, at the Mill of Island Magee and pay the usual Toll or Multure for grinding the same at said Mill; or in default thereof, pay unto the said Viscount, his Heirs and Assigns, the sum of Five Shillings sterling, for every barrel of the said Corn or Grain, ground at any other Mill or Mills: AND that the said Andrew Brown his Heirs, Executors, Administrators and Assigns, shall and will, as often as he or they shall be legally summoned, do Suit and Service at Courts Leet and Courts Baron of the Manor of Castle Chichester and shall and will pay, at the same, the usual Fees of Leet-Money or Head-Silver; AND that the said Andrew Brown his Heirs, Executors, Administrators, and Assigns, shall and will preserve and keep up all Houses, Gardens, Orchards, Fences, and other Improvements now made, or that shall hereafter be made on the said Demised Premises during this demise, in good sufficient staunch and tenantable order and repair; and the same shall yield up and deliver in the like good order and repair unto the said Viscount, his Heirs and Assigns, at the end or expiration of the said term, or other sooner determination of this demise. PROVIDED ALWAYS, and it is also hereby further agreed by the said Parties, that the said Andrew Brown or his or their Heirs, Executors, Administrators, and Assigns, shall not let, set, sell, alien, exchange, or dispose of his or their Interest in the within demised Premises, or any parcel thereof, without the full power, license, absolute authority and consent of the within named LORD VISCOUNT DUNGANNON, or his Agent for the time being, or his or their Heirs or Successors, first had and obtained in writing. AND the said LORD VISCOUNT DUNGANNON, for himself, his Heirs and Assigns, doth covenant and agree to and with the said Andrew Brown his Hairs, Executors, Administrators, and Assigns, That he the said Andrew Brown his Heirs, Executors, Administrators, and Assigns, paying the Rent and Fees, and performing the Covenants herein expressed, which on his or their part ought to be paid and performed, shall and may quietly and peaceably have, hold, possess and enjoy the said demised premises, with the appurtenances, (except as before excepted) during this demise, without the let, suit, molestation or disturbance of the said Viscount, his Heirs or Assigns, or of any other person or persons lawfully claiming, or to claim the same, by, from, or under him, them, or any of them. IN WITNESS whereof, the said Parties have hereunto set their hands and seals, the day and year first above written.

Signed, Sealed, and Delivered by Lord Viscount Dungannon in the Presence of

Rob: Jebb

Signed, Sealed and Delivered by the said Andrew Brown in the Presence of

Jn. Pynatt

40 Between Two Revolutions

in land-holding practices. A survey conducted in 1870 revealed that seventy-seven percent of the occupiers of farms in Ireland held land under oral agreements which were terminable upon six months' notice at the end of any given year.[36] In contrast, almost every farmer on Islandmagee held land under a long lease. Fortunately for the historian, the leases for the Island came due in the 1820's and nearly all are preserved in the Public Record Office of Northern Ireland. (An example, signed in the year 1824, is shown on page 40.) Precisely what the length of previous leases had been is unknown, but it well may have been the lease for three lives which was the most popular leasehold in Ulster until the agricultural slump at the end of the Napoleonic wars made both sides wary of such long agreements.[37]

In any case, the Islandmagee tenants received leases of thirty-one years, which provided them with security of tenure into the 1850's.[38] What happened thereafter I have been unable directly to determine, because of the litigation surrounding the leaseholds and because of the absence of a full set of rent rolls for the entire Island. Nevertheless, the indirect evidence is compelling: the rent rolls of the Dungannon family and heirs for the years 1828-29, 1846-47, and 1878-79 indicate that the incidence of changes in the 1846-79 period was only slightly greater than between 1828 and 1847. From this one can infer either that long leases were continued or that shorter renewals were given to tenants with such regularity as to serve effectively as long leases.[39] The lands act of 1870 and of 1881 reinforced the security of the Islandmagee tenants by giving them a perpetual right to occupancy provided they paid their rents and did not sub-let without the landlords' permission.[40] Thus, throughout the nineteenth century, and thereafter, the tenant farmers of Islandmagee had secure long-term attachments to their lands. This was the cornerstone of their prosperity.

Further, unlike much of Ireland, Islandmagee had few agricultural middlemen. All of the major farm tenancies were held directly by the farmers from the estate landlord (the Dungannons and heirs until 1890 and the Donegalls thereafter). Middlemen, as distinct from agents employed directly by the landlords, were especially deleterious to the Irish agricultural system, for having no permanent interest in the land, they sublet it with only immediate profit in view.[41] The standard leases to the Islandmagee agricultural tenancies in the 1820's prohibited letting without the landlord's permission (see the sample lease on page 40). Permission was rarely given. The rent receipts issued by Lord Arthur Hill-Trevor in the 1860's stated that tenants were "not allowed to alter their farms or part with possession..." without the agent's consent.[42] It is not surprising that the valuation surveyor for Islandmagee reported in 1836 that he could find only one instance of agricultural sub-letting.[43] The re-valuation work of the 1860's revealed only four tenants of one statute acre or more who held by sub-letting rather than directly from the Dungannon heirs.[44] And because the low judicial rents fixed under the 1881 act applied only to agricultural tenancies existing at the time of the act's passage, this act added a further effective bar to subdivision.

As for farm size, at mid-century (1849 in this case), the holdings in Islandmagee were distributed as follows:[45]

	Number	Percentage
under one acre	1	.3
above one and not exceeding five	27	8.4
above five and not exceeding fifteen	134	41.6
above fifteen and not exceeding thirty	96	29.8
above thirty	64	19.9
total	322	100.0

In comparison with the national pattern, the Islandmagee tenancies tended to bunch in the five to thirty acre range, with proportionately few very small and few very large tenancies. The national distribution (as of 1851) was as follows:

	Number	Percentage
above one and not exceeding five acres	88,083	15.4
above five and not exceeding fifteen	191,854	33.7
above fifteen and not exceeding thirty	141,311	24.8
above thirty	149,090	26.1
total	570,338	100.0

From the fact that the landlords of Islandmagee did not allow the sub-letting of agricultural tenancies, one should not conclude that there was not a cottager class on the Island. There was, but it was of a particular sort. Its members were not farmers in any real sense,[46] although they may have had a small garden plot. They were labourers, fishermen, and tradesmen.

(The reader probably will have noticed that I have not discussed the pattern of inheritance of land. Obviously, the landlord's prevention of subdivision meant that in most families some conscious choice of an heir to the land had to be made. But the paucity of documentary material prevents any firm conclusions being drawn. For a discussion of the available data, see note to this paragraph.)[47]

But if the successive landlords of Islandmagee did not allow sub-division, how were these cottagers provided for? The answer is that although the landlords did not permit agricultural sub-letting, neither did they wish to bother with the letting of small cottage lands themselves.[48] So they allowed the agricultural tenants to let small house-and-garden plots to cottagers, provided sub-division of agricultural land was not involved. Thus, in the 1860's, for every twenty leases of agricultural land of one acre or more granted by the main landlord to an agricultural tenant, there were eleven lettings of small house-and-garden plots of less than an acre, by the agricultural tenants to the cottagers.[49]

As for the tenant farmers, their relations with the landlord were quite simple. The entire rent calculation was done in money, not in kind.[50] The leases of the 1820's specified payment in sterling, but even before this, British

A Reasonable Livelihood 43

rather than Irish currency probably was employed: in Ulster, as early as 1803, the use of Scottish and English currency was general.[51] In addition to the specific annual rental, the tenant paid five percent agent's fees, plus one shilling annually for "acquittances,"[52] and three shillings a year for "feudal" services (or two days' work for a man and his horse if the Viscount so chose—which he did not). These moneys were to be paid in moieties, twice yearly, on 1 May and 1 November.[53] In addition, the agricultural tenants gave the landlord a monopoly of their corn-milling and also recognized their obligation to the local manorial court, which was essentially a court of small claims.

How much rent were the Islanders paying? The following table indicates annual rents paid per statute acre.[54]

1818-19	8s 8d
1828-29	11s 9d
1838-39	12s 4d
1847-48	19s 6d
1858-59	18s 4d
1868-69	18s 4d
1878-79	18s 4d
1888-89	17s 7d
Late 1890's-1921 (under land acts)	12s 4d

Comparison with rents elsewhere in Ireland indicates that the Islandmagee tenants were giving somewhat above the average. For instance, in the 1840's direct tenants on the massive Downshire estate of 115,000 acres were paying an average of 12s 6d per acre, and those on the 80,000 acre Fitzwilliam estate in County Wicklow averaged less than ten shillings.[55]

Yet, though paying more than other direct tenants in Ireland, the Islandmagee farmers were certainly not being beggared by their landlords. One indication is that they were able to buy and sell leases among themselves at considerable sums. As the sample lease on page 40 makes clear, the long agricultural leaseholds were heritable; that is to say, they passed from one generation to another without difficulty. The lease, however, stated that the tenant and his heir, "shall not let, set, sell, alien, exchange, or dispose of" his interest without the consent of Viscount Dungannon, his heirs, or agent. The rent receipts of Lord Arthur E. Hill-Trevor repeated this prohibition.[56] But unlike agricultural sub-letting, on which Lord Dungannon and his heirs were adamant, permission seems to have been easily obtained by a tenant who wished to sell the "good-will" in his holding to another tenant. (The 1870 land act guaranteed in statute law this tenant right which previously had been based on regional custom.) Thus, the estate managers implicitly followed a policy of allowing the tenants to buy and sell leases, so long as sub-division did not occur. Outside observers were surprised by how much the Islandmagee peasantry were willing and able to pay for the "good-will" value of a lease. "The price at which they buy land from one another ... is enormous," noted the authors of a perceptive Irish travellers' book, published in 1843.[57] The amount paid for the transfer of a few acres under landlord leases was frequently more than twenty pounds per acre and seldom less.[58] The property valuers of the 1830's gave examples of two sales: in one the tenant's interest was purchased for twenty-one pounds an acre, in the other for sixteen pounds an acre.[59] Precise national comparison figures are not available, but it appears that the amount paid in Islandmagee was at least twice as much as the prevailing rate in the south and west of Ireland,[60] although well within the usual range for Ulster tenant-right holdings.[61] Emphatically, one should not follow the usual practice among Irish historians and automatically indicate that the tenants were being impoverished. Quite the opposite was true. The large sums paid by one tenant to another indicate, in the first place, that the tenants had a good deal of capital at their disposal. This becomes clear when one recalls that the average size of an Islandmagee agricultural tenancy was ten to fifteen acres. If this sold for twenty pounds an acre, the tenant, through whatever means, obviously had to have access to a capital sum of

£200 to £300.⁶² Second, the high amount paid for entry into a tenancy is an index of how highly desirable the tenancies were. The landlords' policy of prohibiting subdivision meant that the tenancies did not shrink beyond a viable minimum size, and the tenants' security of tenure meant that so long as they behaved as responsible tenants they held a property for their own lifetime and could pass it on to their children. As Sean O'Faolain noted, "the thirst for security is, above all things, the great obsession of the peasant mind."⁶³

Yet, the Islanders' desire for security was not obsessive or short-sighted, but rather was flint-eyed and realistic. They wanted the substance of security and never mind the ornaments. I think this explains why the Islandmagee tenants did not choose to buy from the Donegalls under the various land acts.⁶⁴ Not until the late 1920's was the Donegall family bought out.⁶⁵ Clearly, the idea of tenant-purchase of land was no burning issue to the Islanders; nor should it have been, for the land act of 1870 had made their security almost perfect and that of 1881 had reduced their rents. That the Lords Donegall possessed the pieces of parchment giving them the freehold of Islandmagee mattered very little, for the Islanders, not the Donegalls, possessed the Island.

(3)

All the talk about rents and the sale of good will is apt to be ethereal, unless we have some idea of what the annual balance sheet of a typical Islandmagee farmer looked like. Granted, in the nineteenth century farmers did not keep accounts in the same fashion as do modern farmers, but we can reconstruct an accurate representative annual accounting with the information we have at hand. Let us assume that we are dealing with an Islandmagee farmer at approximately mid-century, say 1851, and that he holds fifteen statute acres from the Dungannon estate. Further, let us construct this hypothetical annual balance sheet on fairly conservative lines. That is, if we are to err, let it be in the direction of overestimating costs to the farmer and underestimating his income.[66]

His statement of annual expenses would read as follows:

Rent of fifteen acres at one pound per acre	£15	--
Seed for fourteen acres at ten shillings per acre[67] (assume one acre taken by homesites)	7	--
Cess at six shillings per acre[68]	4	10s
Tithe at one shilling per acre[69]	--	15
Tools and capital costs[70]	3	--
One hired labourer[71]	7	--
Work animal and miscellaneous costs[72]	1	--
	£38	5s

Let us assume that fourteen of the farmer's fifteen acres were planted in cash crops. Of course this is a convenient fiction, because a proportion of the land (probably eight to nine acres) would have been in grass that became a cash crop only indirectly, through cattle. Also, some of the grain, instead of being sold directly, would have gone into animal feed, only later to be realized as cash. And, of course, the farmers themselves would have consumed some of the produce and livestock. But the value of agricultural production would have been the same.

Following the Islandmagee pattern, for tillage among farmers of five to fifteen acres, our farmer would have planted his fourteen tillable statute acres in the following way:[73]

wheat	1½ acres
oats	8 acres
beans	2 acres
potatoes	2½ acres

If the average rates of production for County Antrim prevailed in Islandmagee the farmer would have produced:[74]

wheat	2,394 lbs
oats	12,073.6 lbs
beans	3,348 lbs
potatoes	29,820 lbs

These quantities would have fetched the following amounts at market:[75]

wheat	£8 11s 0d
oats	£25 6s 5d
beans	£10 9s 0d
potatoes	£48 10s 8d

This provided a total direct agricultural remuneration of £92 17s 1d. In addition, the typical farmer of this size would have been renting a cottage-and-garden plot on his land, bringing in a small sum, perhaps ten shillings annually,[76] for a total income of £93 7s 1d.

Granted, this accounting is purely notional, because no farmer would sell all his produce and thus force himself to buy his daily food on the open market. It is useful, however, because it makes explicit items of agricultural income that normally are only implicit. The point it makes is that after paying his annual outgoings, our representative fifteen-acre farmer would have produce or cash to the value of about £55 a year plus his housing (included in his agricultural rent). This was not a menial sum: in 1867 clerical workers, living in the much more expensive confines of Belfast, and having to rent accommodation, worked a twelve hour day for £60 a year.[77] Clearly, besides having almost perfect security on his rented land, the Islandmagee tenant farmer was able to earn a satisfactory and reasonable livelihood.

(4)

Throughout the nineteenth century, the Islandmagee farmers practiced a reasonably efficient form of agriculture, involving mixed farming and crop rotation. At mid-century

Islandmagee had the highest proportion of cropped land in south-east Antrim.[78] A visitor of 1809 noted that "the land is mostly arable and well cultivated, producing abundance of wheat, corn, bean, etc., which generally meet a preference in market. There are, however, some fields

"With blossom'd furze,
unprofitably gay."[79]

In the late 'eighties an observer noted, "the land of Island Magee is very good, and it is highly cultivated. Beans, wheat, oats, and potatoes are the principal crops."[80] Fortunately, for the year 1847 and a decade thereafter (but, alas, only for those years), the United Kingdom parliament demanded agricultural returns for Ireland that specified output in parish and poor law units. Taking the year 1849, for example, we can produce a very precise picture of what was being grown on the Island and how the production varied according to farm size. That information is found in the Table on the following page.[81] Exact figures are lacking for later in the century, but in all probability the Islandmagee land followed the national pattern in replacing tillage with pasturage after 1861: in that year the amount of plowed land was at its maximum; by the 1920's it had been reduced almost by half.[82]

John Dubourdieu wrote in his 1812 study of the County Antrim that in the county, "the general course is—1st potatoes, 2ᵈ wheat, 3ᵈ barley ... or oats, fourth clover; after the clover oats are generally sown as they are found to be more certain than wheat. Then the potato is again resorted to."[83] Islandmagee farmers were unusual in Ulster in giving a significant proportion of their lands to beans,[84] so the early nineteenth century Islandmagee rotation might well be altered to read: potatoes, wheat or beans, oats, clover, oats, potatoes. This is only an approximation, and individual farmers must have greatly varied the course.

The yearly calendar for the main tillage crops of oats, wheat, beans, and potatoes in the 1830's was as follows:[85]

November: After the potatoes are raised, sow most of the wheat
Early March: Sow remainder of the wheat

A Reasonable Livelihood 49

Tillage Output of Islandmagee, 1849, in Statute Acres

	Wheat	Oats	Barley	Beans & Peas	Potatoes	Turnips	Meadow & Clover	Other	Total
Holding under 1 acre								1	1
Holdings 1 acre to five acres	1	21		5	10	1	3		41
Holdings above five acres to fifteen acres	49	239	4	60	69	19	54		494
Holdings above fifteen acres to thirty acres	91	389	2	68	83	40	111	2	786
Holdings above thirty acres	289	610	4	181	117	109	223	4	1537
Total acreage	430	1259	10	314	279	169	391	7	2859

Total area of Islandmagee 7037 Statute Acres

March: Sow beans
Late March and early April: Sow oats
April to mid-May: Plant potatoes
Mid-August to mid-September: Reap wheat
September: Harvest oats
October: Pull beans
November: Raise potatoes

The middle months of the year, from mid-May through mid-August, were filled with the tasks of grassland farming, especially hay production. Weather permitting, empty time from November to March was spent in winter plowing.

Despite different planting and maturation dates, the cereals, wheat and oats, may be seen as similar in production. In County Antrim, plowing by horses was the usual practice, a two-horse team being sufficient where the land had been previously in cultivation. In the eighteenth century it had been usual to have not only a plowman, but a plow-boy as well. The boy, or "driver," took charge of the horse and gave the ploughman's commands to the animal. Early in the nineteenth century the single-man arrangement was introduced and quickly gained ground. Where wheat or oats followed a potato course, a simple seed furrow had to be plowed. Even when following a grass fallow, oats were planted after only one plowing. Five bushels of wheat and seven bushels of oat seed per acre were the recommended amounts.[86]

The farmers of Islandmagee were noted for a system of agricultural co-operation known as "neighbouring," which according to one Irish travel book "is carried to a much greater extent there than in any other place."[87] Farmers of large holdings, together with their servants, worked on the farms of those with less land, on one occasion plowing, on another planting, in return for labour from the others, most frequently at harvest time. The grain harvest was especially demanding of co-operative labour. In Ulster, prior to mid-century, the grain was cut by the hand sickle, a device of back-breaking simplicity. After mid-century, the scythe became dominant, and in the last part of the nineteenth century horse-drawn reapers were introduced. In any case, until the advent of horse-drawn reapers with automatic binders, the sheaves had to be hand-made preparatory to collecting for threshing (the first self-binding reaper, or reaper-and-binder, was introduced in Islandmagee in 1891; in the following year several more were added and their use became general).[88]

From the labour-intensive character of the harvest grew a rich variety of social customs, the most interesting concerning the "last sheaf." In Islandmagee the last sheaf on a field was known as the *granny* or *churn* (var. *chirn*). Throughout Ulster a ceremony was attached to its cutting, ranging from a simple shout or cheer to elaborate ritual braiding of the sheaf, to a festival harvest meal. Which practice prevailed in Islandmagee is not recorded, but the use of special terminology for the sheaf points to the existence of some such tradition.[89]

After reaping, the grain had to be threshed. This could be done by hand flail, but from as early as 1806, when Malcolm MacNeill introduced a threshing machine, other means were available. In the 1830's there were twenty threshing machines on Islandmagee. One was water powered, while the other nineteen were propelled by from two to four horses.[90] Thus, there were four-fifths as many machines as townlands, and anyone who threshed his grain by hand probably did so by choice.

The method of growing potatoes—by making a lazy bed with a spade—was almost universally practiced in Ireland and is too well known to require comment. Interestingly, however, some farmers in County Antrim greatly increased the amount of ground they were able to cultivate by substituting the plow for the spade in much of the work.[91]

As already mentioned, Islandmagee was known for producing beans, an unusual crop in Ireland. In the early part of the nineteenth century these were sown broadcast, even though drilling would greatly have improved yields.[92] Being a legume, beans were especially valuable in that they served the purpose of refreshing the soil without involving a nearly-profitless fallowing period. Little material is available about the harvesting and processing of the beans, although when self-binders were introduced in the 1890's they were able to reap beans as well as grain.[93]

In many ways the most interesting part of the agricultural cycle was hay-making, for it possessed a rich and very well documented technology and terminology. Marked variations occurred from region to region in Ulster, and these have been studied by Dr. G.B. Adams of the Ulster Folk Museum.[94] Here is a description of procedures in Islandmagee in the late nineteenth and the early twentieth century, collected from the late Captain Forsythe of Cloghfin, Islandmagee:[95]

> Hay meadow or lea was cut by scythe. Consequently [it] lay in clumps which prevented drying. These had to be spread (*tedding*), when dry, turned with hand rakes and, depending on weather, perhaps turned twice.... It was then *lapped* into lumps about one-half stone made up to turn rain, an air hole being in centre. When dry, these were put into large lumps about one cwt. called *Poor Jones* or *Shake Coles*. When dry these were built into ricks (locally called *rucks*) from 5-10 cwt.

Then, if the ruck was on a slope, "a chain was placed around the bottom of the rucks and the horse *sliped* it home." Otherwise, a cart was used. An intermediate stack was called a *pike,* and finally a large *birt* was built. It had a stone base called the *birt bottom,* and was built near the byre or stable door. Its shape was oblong, with a tapered top to shed water. Putting it together was very hard work, and according to Captain Forsythe, there was always a bottle of whiskey when "putting by the Birt." The Islanders called the winter storage location of the hay the *stack-garden*.[96] Interestingly, given the complexity of this hay-making process, it was not universal throughout Islandmagee. Forsythe described a five-stage process (laps-shake coles, rucks-pikes-birts) but other Island respondents recalled a simpler three and four stage operation.[97] Whatever the method, ropes were needed to transport the hay and to bind the final birt, and here a fine rural art was involved: the making of ropes by hand from oat straw. This was done by the use of *thrawnheuk,* or straw-twister. One man smoothly fed bunches of oat straw to the twister, who by using his hands and a simple hooked device, produced rope able to stand several hundred pounds of strain.

As for livestock, until selective breeding became widespread after World War I, livestock farming was largely a hit-and-miss sideline, useful for raising the odd bit of cash, but not intensively pursued by the Islanders. At mid-century, typical Islandmagee farmers would have had the following upon their farms:[98]

> farmer of 1-5 acres: one head of cattle, two chickens, and perhaps a sheep, pig, or goat, but not a horse, mule or donkey.
> farmer of 5 to 15 acres: two to three head of cattle, one or two sheep, two to three chickens, ducks or geese, and probably a horse, mule, or donkey.
> farmer of 15-30 acres: a horse, five head of cattle, one or two sheep, a pig, and five poultry.
> farmer of above thirty acres: two horses, ten head of cattle, six sheep, one or two pigs, and seven or eight ducks, geese, and chickens.

These are averages, and individual farmers doubtless specialized somewhat, but the conclusion is clear: that specialized livestock production was a long way in the future. Granted, the richer farmers had access to registered stud services for their draught mares,[99] and granted too that as early as 1812 Malcolm McNeill, one of Islandmagee's largest farmers, imported Dutch kine as dairy cattle,[100] but these were exceptions. Indeed, the first important local initiative in livestock improvement came from neighbouring Ballycarry, where just prior to the First World War William Calwell introduced and distributed purebred Friesian stock.[101]

Still, the Islandmagee livestock efforts had points of interest, especially the dairying practices. Because of the unpredictable nature of the activity, the Islandmagee farmers, like farmers throughout Ireland, were especially superstitious or ritualistic about their dairying habits. Some milked cows only from the left side, others only from the right. It was general custom, however, to put a silver coin for luck into the bottom of the milking pail of a newly-calved or first-milked cow. One Islandmagee respondent reported that a visitor was expected to wish someone who was churning butter the "luck of your cow", or otherwise a half-crown had to be dropped into the churn. Cross-eyed people, the respondent added, were thought to bring ill-luck to the dairying process.[102]

Apparently, milk was used only domestically, but butter was a cash crop, sold to neighbours and to near-by shops. The "plunge churn" was the most popular and it took almost an hour of steady hand work to make a quantity of butter. Some farmers used a mechanical device called a "barrel churn" which was mounted on tressels and turned slowly by hand, and a few had churns operated by horses and ponies. Usually a carrot was grated into the butter to give colour. Cheese occasionally was made at home, as were curds and whey, but these seem to have been a domestic, not a cash, product.

Although most of the agricultural economy of Islandmagee was carried on within the confines of the parish, individual farmers often wanted to buy and sell items or quantities not convenient on the Island. Grain could be sold in large quantities to buyers from Belfast who travelled to the countryside,[103] but livestock and other crops had to be taken to market. During the 1820's there was a small weekly market in nearby Ballycarry,[104] but more important were the Ballycarry fairs, held four times yearly in the 1830's[105] and three times yearly from the 1850's onwards.[106] They continued until 1937.[107] I suspect that the Ballycarry fair gradually diminished in importance not because such local trading institutions were as a group diminishing in importance—quite the opposite was happening generally, as tillage was reduced and cattle rearing spread during the second half of the nineteenth century[108]—but that as communications improved, the fairs held every Wednesday in Larne, and every Saturday in Carrickfergus,[109] gradually upstaged the smaller Ballycarry meetings.

Certain fairs served as "hiring fairs" for farm servants, who in County Antrim were engaged for six month periods. These hiring fairs took place in May and November, at Larne, Ballyclare, and Ballymena.[110] By local tradition the people being hired carried an ash plant, and when they had struck an agreement with a farmer, were given half a crown and said to be *earled.* (The similarity to "taking the shilling" from a British recruiting sergeant is obvious.) The fairs were as much social as economic occasions. Again, the articulate Captain Forsythe has left a vivid description of the local fair, usually held at Fair Hill, Larne:[111]

> I think some of the fair girls did find their husbands at the fair. It was the heyday of the Merry-go-Rounds, servant boys and girls engaged themselves to the fill on this, plenty of stalls, dried dulse and wet. Likewise whelks... heavy drill shirts (worn about 6 months) hob nailed boots..., with strong leather whangs, worn daily for more than six months.
>
> The farmer and his wife left home on the horse and cart 9 A.M. [and] returned about milking time about 7 P.M. with the new servant. Having given him or her their dinner in an eating house. Each had a big bowl of good broth and one or two penny baps, and the farmer usually found that this new servant man could handle Grays old swing plough as good as himself.

(5)

Islandmagee was doubly fortunate economically, for not only was its agricultural base profitable, but there were ancillary ways for the Islanders to earn or augment their livelihood. The most important was seafaring in its various forms. Fishing was a common way for farmers to increase their incomes. In the 1830's there were sixty-eight fishing boats on Islandmagee, fifty of them working off the east coast. Altogether they were manned by about 280 hands. The boats were quite small, between fourteen to eighteen feet along the keel and four feet to six feet, six inches in the beam, and were propelled by oars. Most were built in Larne, but a few were constructed on Islandmagee. They were said to handle indifferently. The Ordnance Survey of the 1830's reported that the Islandmagee fishermen were neither expert nor intrepid. This well may have been true, given that fishing was mainly a late spring and summer occupation and that the Islandmen did not take to the high seas. Mostly they caught herrings, cod, pollock, turbot, glashan, lyth, gurnet, and whiting. Lobsters and crabs were taken off the eastern coast. Usually, the catch was sold locally, though the better fish sometimes were sent to the Carrickfergus and Belfast markets. Locally, in 1839, herrings were selling at three shillings per 120 and cod at five to six shillings a dozen.

Fishing was open to great fluctuations, more from bureaucratic than from natural causes. In 1810 the Irish administration began paying a grant to the Islandmagee fishermen as part of a programme of stimulating local fisheries. This grant was paid to the fisherman for outfitting his boat, and was given according to the size and quality of his catch. The Islanders took to the system with such enthusiasm that between 1810 and 1824 they qualified for nearly £5,000 in grants, an extraordinary sum when one considers that in the 1820's the rental Lord Dungannon received annually for the entire Island was only about £4,100. In 1824 the government withdrew the grant (although the fisheries commission did contribute £290 in 1829 towards a fishing quay in Portmuck Bay), and henceforth the number of fishermen dropped.[112] Government again intervened later in the century: in 1854 because of the depleting of the fish in Belfast Lough, the then-commissioners of fishing prohibited trawling in the Lough from Kilroot Point (slightly south of Islandmagee) to Grey Point in the County Down. Successive revisions, however, weakened this regulation until it was repealed in 1869. Subsequent investigation indicated that the supply of fish in the Lough was seriously depleted.[113] About the turn of the century, the fishing pier at Portmuck was wrecked by storm, and successive efforts to gain aid from the Irish government for its rebuilding failed.[114] (In the actual event it was not rebuilt until 1929, and then by the government of Northern Ireland.) All this government ineptitude helps to explain why fishing, though a valuable tertiary aspect of the Islandmagee economy, did not become a primary sector.

The Islandmagee people harvested the sea, not merely through fishing but by becoming professional seamen. This was largely a phenomenon of the second half of the nineteenth and of the twentieth centuries, consequent upon Belfast's development into a maritime centre. In 1906 a pamphlet written by a well-informed local clergyman estimated that in every third or fourth house in Islandmagee one could find one or more of the family engaged in the merchant marine service.[115] The standard of seamanship among these merchant seamen from the Island was internationally famous, and deservedly so. The number of Islandmen who became ships' masters was extraordinarily high in relation to Islandmagee population: even though the Island's participation in the maritime industry had declined (as the shipping trade declined) from the 1930's onward, there were still twenty retired sea captains in Islandmagee in the late 1950s.[116] What these men brought home in forms of culture is discussed in Chapter Nine. The point of the moment is that the seamen maintained their homes and families in Islandmagee and regularly brought back considerable sums of money. Thus, the economy was able to support more individuals at a high level of comfort than would otherwise have been possible.

The sea rewarded those who were opportunistic. A good example of this was John Mawhinney of Islandmagee who became master in 1879 of a ten-year-old Greenock-registered sailing ship of ninety-three tons, the *Volante*. Working for the owner on a "share" basis, Mawhinney followed the coasting trade, calling at Glasgow, Kinvarna, Newport, Galway, Londonderry, and similar ports, employing a crew of four to six, almost all usually Islandmagee men. By 1883 Mawhinney was no longer just the ship's master, but its owner as well, and by 1887 he had made a further transition: now he was the owner, but he employed another Islandmagee man, Robert Ross, as master. Finally, in 1890, Mawhinney sold the sailing ship to another

Islander, Robert McCalmont, who became master as well as owner.[117]

Maritime opportunism could take other forms, of course. Dulse collecting in the shallows during the summer provided income for the poorer people, who sold it at fairs and public gatherings.[118] Shipwrecks off the coast were tragedies, but often they were a boon to the Islanders. From Admiralty reports, it appears that during the mid-nineteenth century at least one wreck a year took place on or near Islandmagee, and although improvements in navigational aids reduced this figure, the scavenging of wrecks has been known in the twentieth century. At one time the Islanders carried on an extensive smuggling trade, but this declined precipitously in the nineteenth century after the introduction of coastguards. The Island was well ringed by these watchers, there being in the 1830's a main station at Portmuck Bay and three substations (Castleton, Ballycroanan-beg, and Mill Bay). That the smuggling trade once was a major operation is indicated by the coastguard's seizure at the mouth of Larne Lough in 1835 of a sloop full of tobacco and brandy. At about the same time, two caves beautifully excavated for the reception of stolen goods were discovered.[119]

Some employment in the community was produced by the construction in the years 1835-39 by the Ballast Board (that is, the Belfast Harbour Commissioners) of a lighthouse on Ferris Point. A full time keeper was employed.[120] A second lighthouse, at Blackhead, was erected in 1903.

During the first one-third of the nineteenth century, the sea provided an outlet for a potentially prosperous limestone industry. Islandmagee contains a good deal of easily worked limestone, and shortly before the end of the eighteenth century, Lord Dungannon erected a lime kiln. Quickly it became apparent what a field dressing of lime would do: the yield of grain and beans doubled on Islandmagee plots that received lime. Soon several individuals erected kilns, and a large export trade to Scotland and County Down developed: in the mid-1830's, twenty

A Reasonable Livelihood 59

lime kilns were operating, some of them of very large size, and most erected near the coast for shipping convenience. Three special piers were constructed at private expense to facilitate the lime export (one was built by the redoubtable William McClelland, for £400, at Portmuck). But trouble struck. In 1812, the Marquis of Donegall had granted a lease of the Parish of Glynn, neighbouring Islandmagee, to a Mr. Farrell. That parish included the Ballylig Lime Works, which exported up to 10,000 tons of limestone and lime each year. Farrell's original interest passed into the possession of John Irving, one of the M.P.s for County Antrim. Irving sought an injunction against the four largest lime burners and exporters on Islandmagee, on the grounds that he owned the mineral rights. An expensive chancery suit (the cost to the defendants was £750) succeeded, and in 1837 the Ballylig Lime Works was confirmed in a monopoly of the home and export lime trade. Islandmagee labourers, investors, and boat owners, all were hurt.[121] The trade never recovered, although limestone quarrying on a reduced basis was resumed sometime during the nineteenth century.[122]

A spectacular, if not very important, source of income for a few hearty souls was the capture of young gos-hawks (known locally as the Gobbin Hawks) from their nests on the Gobbins cliffs. To capture the young birds a person had to be let down over the brow of the two hundred foot cliff to the face of the precipice where the mature hawks nested. Then, clutching the lowering-rope with one hand, the collector had to put the young into a basket and ascend.[123] This practice seems to have died out, as it is not reliably reported after 1815; presumably it declined because the hawks, not the collectors, became scarce.

Had it continued into the late nineteenth century, the performance would have been an excellent tourist draw, but as it was, the Gobbins cliffs became a tourist attraction on their own merits. In 1862 the railway line, the Belfast and Northern Counties Company, was extended to Larne.[124] In the summer, excursionists from Belfast took the train to Larne, and from Larne Harbour used the short ferry crossing to the north end of Islandmagee.[125] In 1892 Berkeley Dean Wise, the celebrated chief engineer of the Belfast and NCC railroad, began a cliff walk stretching from Blackhead, in the southeast corner of Islandmagee, around to the Gobbins cliffs.[126] The wall skirted the towering rock face and included tunnels cut through the rock and metal bridges leading to surf-circled rock outcroppings.[127]

The walk had its gentler aspects as well. A woman who grew up near the Gobbins early in the twentieth century describes the scene:[128]

> The night was calm and the murmur of the sea was pleasant as it gently ebbed over the stones and shingle. There was a nip in the air with a hint of frost, but it was pleasant for walking. The night was studded with stars and the flashing rays from Blackhead lighthouse shone on our path frequently. Mother walked on a little ahead of me for the path was narrow by the low shore.... It stretched for miles past Blackhead and terminated at Whitehead. Many visitors came by train to Whitehead then came by this walk to the Gobbins. Blackhead had its own singular beauty, its caves, and a few bridges and the lovely walk up to the lighthouse. The Cove came next... Here was a formation of rock and grassy slopes; and a spring board out to sea for the benefit of swimmers. It was a favourite spot in summer; here the annual Regatta was held. There were various sports during the summer, greasy poles, boat rowing and fancy dress parades and of course a popular band provided the music. The fifty-two steps a little further on was a delight especially to us children. We would race up and down these wooden steps like young hares. The path occasionally would leave the water's edge and wind inland a bit over soft green grass as soft as velvet. The hills up above were lovely especially in Autumn with blackberries, hips and haws and the black sloe trees. A few more ditches and styles to go over and then round the bend the breath-taking sight of the Gobbins cliffs.

At the height of Islandmagee's popularity touring parties came in great number, some from as far as London:[129] in 1905 the local paper carried Islandmagee property advertisements with the statement that "the district is rapidly increasing in popularity amongst summer visitors and houses are most difficult to obtain during the summer

A Reasonable Livelihood

months."[130] This tourist boom gradually abated, but even at the present time temporary residents are an important part of the summer population.

(6)

A Canadian social scientist who has done a thorough study of the relationship between landlords and tenants in the west of Ireland in the nineteenth century has noted three crucial points. First, that by the third decade of the nineteenth century the landlord-tenant relationship had degenerated into a fierce and vicious conflict. Second, that there existed a religious cleavage between Protestant landlord and Catholic occupier which made worse the inherent conflict between landlord and tenant. And third, that there was an inherent cleavage in Irish society between town and country. But when, in the years 1850-80, this latter cleavage was bridged, the discontents of rural and of urban Ireland became one; and publicans and shopkeepers backed the tenants in their fight against the landlords.[131]

This is a succinct, perceptive analysis of the discontents of much of Ireland. Notice, however, that it is not applicable to Islandmagee. The Islanders were not at loggerheads with their landlords; they were of the same religious persuasion as the landlords; and the Island continued to be completely rural, so no league of rural and urban discontent could be formed (and Whitehead, the new community formed at the foot of Islandmagee, was a semi-exclusive community of professional persons and civil servants).

In relation to the question posed in Chapter One — why the Islanders became so apparently conservative politically during the course of the nineteenth and early twentieth centuries — the answer in large part is that their economic system worked. Despite the mythology about absentee landlordism being a vice, the absentee system worked very well in Islandmagee, in part because the landlords granted long leases and in part because the Islanders used the land intelligently. Ancillary resources—especially the sea—helped, but it was their success as farmers that more than anything else made the Islanders suspicious of wrenching, radical changes in their way of life.

An agricultural tradition: the Ulster gatepost

The old methods—haycocks, Middle Road, 1974.

A small farmstead, c. 1900.

Gobbins head.

Eastern coastline.

Blackhead.

"Sailing Ships off Blackhead, Co. Antrim," by J.W. Carey, 1912.

Brown's Bay, c. 1900

East coast cottage, c. 1900

Coast guard row Portmuck

Nineteenth century labourer's cottage (modernized).

The Manse, Low Road, of First Islandmagee Presbyterian Church.

"Langdale," Middle Road. Originally a two-storey cottage, expanded c. 1900.

Orthodox Presbyterian. First Islandmagee Presbyterian Church (replaced 1900).

Seccessionist Presbyterian. Second Islandmagee Presbyterian Church.

Methodist Chapel.

St. John's (Anglican) Church.

First Islandmagee Presbyterian Church. (opened 1900)

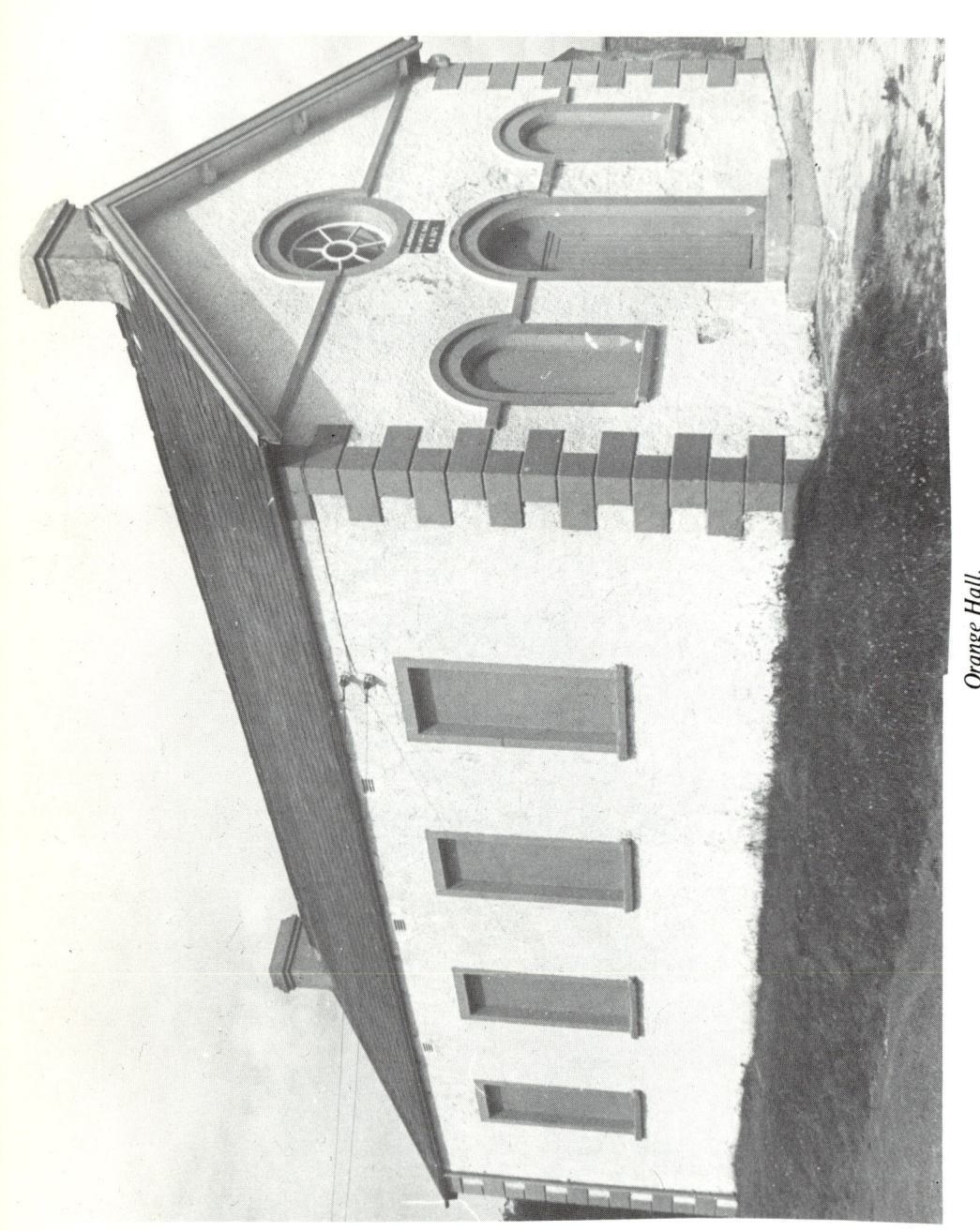

Orange Hall.

Tourism: visitors, c. 1907

Tourism: Gobbins Cafe, c. 1900

Tourism: Gobbins hotel, c. 1905

The Gobbins cliff path, tubular bridge, c. 1910.

SUSPENSION BRIDGE, GOBBINS PATH, ISLANDMAGEE.

Top left. Rev. David Steen.

Top right. Rev. R.H. Shaw

Lower left. Rev. William Campbell.

Lower right. Dixon Donaldson.

Chapter Four. Population: A Non-Existent Problem

During the first half of the nineteenth century, population, not politics, was *the* Irish question. During the eighteenth century and the first half of the nineteenth, the country's populace burgeoned to the absolute limit of agricultural resources. Then, during the Great Famine of the 1840's, population declined precipitously. After the Famine the decline continued, albeit more slowly and now chiefly due to the reorganization of the Irish family. Before the Famine mere subsistence was a problem, during it starvation was a fact, and after it rural depopulation and decline were a reality.

At first glance, it appears that the population pattern of Islandmagee was simply the national trend writ small. This (in rounded figures) was the national pattern before the Famine:[1]

1687	2,167,000
1712	2,791,000
1772	3,584,000
1791	4,753,000
1821	6,802,000
1831	7,767,000
1841	8,175,000

And this was the pre-famine Islandmagee pattern: It went from an estimated 990 in 1669[2] to 2,299 in 1821,[3] to 2,610 in 1831 (the first figures that have any degree of real accuracy, and even they are slightly suspect),[4] and to 2,782 in 1841.[5] Thus, during the eighteenth century Islandmagee's total population grew slightly more slowly than did the national population, but in the last full census decade before the Famine (1831-41) it was growing slightly faster than the national population (6.6 per cent versus 5.3 per cent).

The most widely accepted explanation for the Irish population explosion posits that it was caused chiefly by (1) rising marital fertility that (2) itself was a function of a sharply dropping marriage age, which was declining because (3) the widespread adoption of the potato as the main agricultural crop allowed more people to be fed on the limited amount of agricultural land; (4) to some extent also, the potato, because of its superior nutritive qualities, may have lowered the death rate.[6] Behind this explanation—and behind that of any reasonable alternative explanation—is a crucial observation about the interaction of the Irish population with its physical environment: that, in classically Malthusian fashion, the population inexorably exhausted its environment by reproducing right up to the margin of what the land could support. The Irish strained their national agricultural resources to the limit, and thereby forced a large portion of the populace into a subsistence existence. The lives of millions were constantly at risk because of the ever-present danger of crop failure and famine.

To apply this explanation to Islandmagee would be folly—quite apart from any flaws in the hypothesis as it relates to the entire country.[7] Indeed, because of the vexing absence of pre-Famine manuscript census and individual birth and mortality records, it is impossible to comment decisively about the possibility of either a rising birth rate or dropping death rate in Islandmagee. Inferentially, however, one can reject the notion that Islandmagee shared the national pattern of early marriage and of almost everyone marrying. Statistical analysis has shown that the chief influence on regional variations in reproduction rates in pre-Famine Ireland was the proportion of women who married. Significantly, as shown in the 1841 census, County Antrim had one of the highest proportions of single females in any Irish county. Admittedly, a higher proportion of women aged seventeen to twenty-five were married in Antrim than were married nationally (twenty-one percent as compared to eighteen percent), but this was a sub-pattern followed only by a minority of the County Antrim population. Only sixty-five percent of County Antrim women aged twenty-six to thirty-five (the chief child-bearing age) were married, compared to seventy-two percent nationally; and in the thirty-six to forty-five year old age group, eighty-one per cent were married, as against eighty-five per cent nationally.[8] What this means is that the County Antrim population was acting bimodally: a statistical sub-group was marrying very early, and presumably exhibiting high marital fertility, but a larger statistical sub-group was either marrying late or remaining celibate, thus practising a form of population limitation. Taking both together, it is clear that there existed brakes on population growth not operative elsewhere in Ireland.

Of course, it is possible that the family practices that prevailed generally in County Antrim before the Famine may not have prevailed in Islandmagee. But I suspect that any deviation from the county-wide pattern was in the direction of later marriage and increased spinsterhood. The only professional observer to discuss marriage patterns in Islandmagee—the Ordnance Survey officer of the late 1830's—reported:[9]

> Instances of extreme early marriages have been very unusual in this Parish— *chiefly owing to the obstruction to subletting* (italics mine) and the unwillingness of the Farmers to dispense with the assistance of their sons.

The surveyor noted that those women who married did so usually between the ages of nineteen and twenty-four. "Men seldom marry before 27 or 28 years of age."[10] Indirect confirmation of these observations is found in the

1839 report of the Ordnance Surveyors for Islandmagee's neighbouring parish of Templecorran (or, as it was generally known, "Broadisland"). Like Islandmagee, this parish was overwhelmingly Presbyterian in religious origin, and definitely was not part of the potato culture. "There have not within memory, been nor are there at present, any instances of very early marriages," the surveyor reported. "Men particularly of the better class usually attain the age of 28 or 30 before they encumber themselves and women rarely marry before 19."[11] Thus, at minimum one can accept for Islandmagee the general picture for County Antrim—an overall pattern entailing considerable population limitation—and posit that the Island people probably were even more given to late marriage or to spinsterhood-bachelorhood than was the general population of the county.

In the absence of data, not even an informed guess can be made about whether or not the marriage age and celibacy rates were dropping in Islandmagee in the nineteenth century. But there are two signal and incontrovertible points. The first is, that as established in Chapter Three, the Islandmagee economy was not dependent upon the potato. Oats, beans, and pasturage dominated. Therefore, the potato thesis is inapplicable. Second, unlike the people of Ireland as a whole, the Islanders were not reproducing right up to the margin of subsistence. Their pattern of family formation was considerably different from the national pattern. Implicitly, they were practicing a form of population limitation.[12]

The Irish population declined by 19.5 per cent between 1841 and 1851:[13]

        1841   8,175,124
        1851   6,552,392

In contrast, the population of Islandmagee dropped by only 2.8 per cent:[14]

1841	2,782
1851	2,704

In other words, in Islandmagee the Famine did not take place. If one puts aside for a moment the simplistic notion that the Great Famine was caused by the potato blight— immediately it was, but ultimately it stemmed from the failure of the Irish to limit the size of their families—then one realizes that although the growth curves of Islandmagee and of the nation were similar in the pre-Famine years, they meant something entirely different. In the context of the life-support systems in which the people lived (meaning chiefly, but not entirely, the agricultural domain), it is apparent that whereas in Ireland generally the population had been outbreeding the environment's ability to support life, in Islandmagee the systems of human breeding and of life-support were in harmony. Thus, qualitatively, there is a sharp distinction between the two growth curves.

Ample confirmation of this point is found in the post-Famine census figures which show that the Island's population remained remarkably constant:[15]

1851	2,704
1861	2,786
1871	2,721
1881	2,644

In other words, the people of Islandmagee had *not* been taught by the Famine that their population had exceeded safe limits. Contrast this to the national pattern:[16]

1851	6,552,392
1861	5,798,564
1871	5,412,377
1881	5,174,836

The bulk of the Irish nation had experienced a severe trauma, one that forced a striking and drastic alteration in

Population: A Non-Existent Problem

familial and reproductive patterns, a dislocation not shared by the Islanders.

After 1881, however, once again Islandmagee's total population trend approximated the national pattern. Witness the following table:[17]

	All Ireland	Islandmagee
1881	5,174,836	2,644
1891	4,704,750	2,369
1901	4,458,775	2,281
1911	4,390,219	2,085
1926	4,228,553	2,034

But something was different. In the decades after the Famine the nation as a whole dramatically overcompensated for its pre-Famine failure to keep population within safe environmental limits. To some extent the Irish "exported" their surplus population through emigration, but there was more to the change than that: a complete reorganization of the society occurred. Agricultural practices were radically altered: pasture and cereal tillage replaced potatoes as the dominant element. Landholding practices changed: no longer did small farmers fragment their holdings among their male children. Now they held the land intact and it passed on to one son. Whenever possible, holdings were amalgamated. Because marriage could take place only when an adequate agricultural holding was available, and because the number of holdings was constant or declining (through amalgamations), it followed that the possibility of marriage declined. This decline brought the society's procreative activities into line with its available resources.[18]

Inevitably, many people were *forced* to remain single for life and the average age of those who did marry was high. Of all women marrying in Ireland in 1864, eighteen percent were under twenty-one. By 1911 the figure had dropped to five percent. Similarly, in 1864 seventy-one percent of women entering first marriage were under twenty-five, but by 1911 the figure was down to fifty-one percent.[19] The duration of this pattern was amazing: as late as 1945-46 the average marriage age of men in Northern Ireland was 30.4, of women 26.8 years. In the Republic it was 33.1 and 28.0 years for men and women respectively. Moreover, the two parts of Ireland had the highest celibacy rates in the world. In 1937, 24.3 percent of Northern Irish males aged 40-49 were still unmarried, as were 26.2 percent of females; in the Irish Republic the figures were an astounding 34.0 percent for men and 26.5 percent for women.[20] Of course these limits on population growth would not have worked if there had been any significant degree of non-marital heterosexual activity in the society. In most of the country, the Roman Catholic Church was able to suppress such behaviour with a rigor unmatched elsewhere in the world.[21] The extent of the Catholic Church's power is indicated in the fact that in the 1890's the Irish illegitimacy rate was 2.6 percent of total births and for the area which eventually became the Irish Republic (which is to say the almost-entirely Roman Catholic portions of the country), the rate was as low as 1.63 per cent in 1871-80. This compares with 4.1 per cent in England and Wales in the 1890's, or, to take the international extreme of Catholic Portugal, with 12.1 per cent in the 1890's.[22]

None of these pressures appertained to Islandmagee. Agricultural practices did not change radically after the Famine. The Island had not been dominated by potato-agriculture, and so there was now no need to abandon it. Since holdings always had been relatively large and had been passed on intact (see Chapter Three), landholding practices were not changed. The Islanders had successfully practiced population limitation long before the Famine, so they did not have to undergo the trauma of adopting a new and severely restrictive code of family formation. They had never been noted for being sexually inhibited. In 1840 the Ordnance Survey reported:

> Conjugal fidelity is among all classes a virtue but little practised on the part of either husband or wife, and still less so by the latter than by the former. It more frequently than otherwise

happens that a girl has become a mother or is pregnant at the period of her marriage, but this is so common that it is not noticed.[23]

And there is no evidence of a new Puritanism arising after the Famine,[24] certainly not of the oppressive and health-endangering sort that came to dominate most rural Roman Catholic areas.[25]

What was happening on Islandmagee was not part of the Irish reaction to the horror of the Great Famine with its severe inhibitions on family formation, but instead was part of the British phenomenon of rural depopulation stemming from quite different causes. The so-called "drift from the land" characterized Great Britain from the mid-nineteenth century onwards, and it was to the technologically advanced British economy that the Belfast region (including Islandmagee) belonged, not the agrarian economy of the rest of Ireland. In that context, several pressures tended to reduce population. First, this was the era of Belfast's great industrial expansion and attractive employment opportunities drew population from the surrounding countryside.[26] Second, the latter half of the nineteenth century and the pre-war period of the twentieth was the great era of maritime opportunity for Northern Irishmen. This was related in large part to the flourishing of the Belfast shipbuilding industry. The opportunities were especially relevant to the Islanders, who long had had a tradition of small-boat seafaring. Now they made their considerable reputation as masters and mates of large vessels on international runs, and it is in this period that the Island became well known as the home of master mariners. Third, a revision of agricultural rents under the land acts of 1881 tended to reduce population. This occurred because the reduction of the rent that had to be paid to the landlord made the tenants' interest in his holding (under the Ulster custom) more valuable since he could make more profits. Thus, the capital value of a tenancy increased, making a "settlement" harder for young couples to acquire. Fourth, as discussed in Chapter Three, from 1861 onwards pasturage tended to replace tillage throughout Ulster. The switch from arable to pasture agriculture substituted land for labour and so reduced employment opportunities in the countryside. Fifth, from the 1890's onward rudimentary mechanisation (again, see Chapter Three), tended to limit population. It did so by reducing the amount of farm labour required and also by making farming an increasingly capital-intensive operation and therefore one more difficult for young people to enter. Taken together, after 1881 these five pressures produced a population decline of which the contours approximated those of the entire Irish nation, but the causes of which were radically dissimilar.[27]

Given that excessive population was the great Irish problem of the first half of the nineteenth century, the Islandmagee people were extremely fortunate. Unlike the Irish nation as a whole, they limited their numbers and out of their issue came no unhappy affliction.

Chapter Five.
The Famine That Did Not Happen

Modern Irish social history pivots about the Great Famine. This series of catastrophes in 1845-49 burned a path across the nation, irrevocably separating what came before from everything that occurred thereafter. The Famine forced a radical reorientation in Irish family and agricultural patterns and scored into the folk-mind the belief that Englishmen had stood idly by while Irishmen starved. But the Famine—as distinct from a potato failure—was not universal in Ireland. Obviously, those areas which escaped the Famine must have been very different in their social and agricultural patterns from those which were hit. Less obvious, but equally important, the areas which did not undergo the trauma of the Famine would remain for generations different in social practices and political attitudes from the parts of the country that suffered.

By juxtaposing the material in Chapters Three and Four, it is clear why Islandmagee was destined to escape the Famine: its people were engaged in a balanced agricultural system, well above the subsistence line, and they practiced a form of population limitation. In contrast, Ireland as a whole lived on the edge of disaster, depending too heavily on a single nutritional source, the potato, and procreating to the point of overpopulation. Crises of mortality were a common Irish phenomenon: one authority lists thirty periods of potato failure and subsequent scarcity or starvation between 1724 and 1842.[1] The Great Famine began with the potato failure of 1845, and did not conclude until the termination of a second peak of mortality in 1849.[2]

County Antrim, like the rest of Ireland, lost most of its potato crop during the Famine years—in 1846 failure was reported as being nearly total in Antrim—but the amount of destitution caused by the Famine was slight. Despite the loss of the crop, the relief inspectors noted that there was no scarcity of food and that County Antrim was largely independent of relief. This is not to say that the loss of the potato crop was not painful, for surely it was. And this is not to say that social arrangements were not influenced by the crop's failure: in the areas hardest hit, there was a population shift, from rural to urban, as labourers left the land to seek employment in the towns. But these consequences were minor when compared with those in the nation as a whole. In part, the greater prominence of grain products (especially oatmeal) in the diet explained why Antrim was relatively unscathed; in part, the existence of various domestic industries was responsible.[3] Islandmagee, as typical of the county, was affected by the potato failure. As indicated in Chapter Three, the potato was an important crop to the Island farmers, even after the Famine: in 1849, approximately four per cent of the land was still given over to potato culture. The loss of this source of food obviously had severe implications for the daily life of the Islandmagee people.

Nevertheless, when we examine every major index of social trauma, it becomes clear that for the Islanders the Famine was a major inconvenience, not a societal disaster. First, on the major axis of population, recall the material in Chapter Four concerning population patterns: whereas the national population dropped by 19.5 per cent between 1841 and 1851, that of Islandmagee declined by only 2.8 per cent. A second, related index of Famine trauma is rural depopulation. Here, Islandmagee suffered even less than the East Antrim region as a whole, for the 2.8 per cent loss in Islandmagee (an entirely rural parish) compares with a 9.9 per cent rural depopulation rate in the entire East Antrim region.[4] Third, although we do not have direct emigration figures for Islandmagee, they must have been very low compared with the rest of the nation, for Antrim was one of only seven counties that had an emigration rate (expressed as a percentage of the population in 1841) of under 7.5 per cent between 1846 and 1851.[5] Since Islandmagee's rural depopulation rate was much lower than the regional rate, in all probability its emigration rate too was lower than that of the county as a whole. Fourth, unlike the situation prevailing in most of Ireland, rents did not drop because of the Famine. The average rent stayed effectively stable, at an average 19s 7d per statute acre in 1846-47 and 19s 6d in 1847-48.[6] Fifth, Islandmagee was part of a strip along the Antrim and Down coast where destitution, as measured in terms of the incidence of pauperism, was negligible: in none of the years 1847, '48, '49, was as much as five per cent of the population in this area on poor relief. This stands in contrast to the national situation. In most of the country at least one fifth of the population was pauperized in at least one of those years.[7] The Larne Poor Law Union, of which Islandmagee was a part, had a fiscal balance on hand in 1847, and reported that it "supports its own poor," a capacity shown by only four of the 130 poor law unions in Ireland.[8] Even in mid-1847, the local authorities did not find it necessary to provide outdoor relief in the form of food. Nor did they need to seek any of the special loans available from the Dublin administration.[9] Indeed, in the fall of 1848, the Larne workhouse and fever ward had a total accommodation of 980, but only 653 occupants.[10]

Obviously, after mid-century, the view of the world held by inhabitants of parishes that had experienced the Great Famine would differ radically from that in places like Islandmagee, where the people underwent only a shortage of potatoes.

Chapter Six. Domestic Architecture: The Hearthside Order

"The tenantry are all of one class, no gentry holding any of the land or residing in the place," reported Mr. and Mrs. S. C. Hall, referring to Islandmagee in their remarkable three volume travellers' description of Ireland, published in 1843. "There is no glebe or house for the clergyman, or fixed or suitable dwelling for the Presbyterian ministers; although the houses of the tenantry are, in general, commodious and good."[1] The general valuation of Islandmagee of 1859 revealed that there was one large landholder of 505 acres, but he did not reside—he lived in Larne.[2] As discussed in Chapter Four, most farmers were in the five to thirty acre category. There was, of course, a large body of cottagers, who made their living as agricultural labourers, craftsmen, and seafarers, and in service occupations: the 1859 valuation showed 225 separate small plots rented for cottage-and-gardens.[3] Significantly, between the farmers and the cottagers, the social gradation was not steep. For one thing, there was not a male servant class: in 1831 only twenty-two of 585 employed males twenty years or over were servants (there were 129 female servants). Further, the alternative occupations available to the small cottagers (in 1833, 100 men were engaged in handicrafts, plus an undetermined number in seafaring) meant that those cottagers who worked as full-time farm labourers (139 in 1831) were not trapped in a buyers' market as far as their labour services were concerned.[4]

On Islandmagee, then, the usual social pyramid did not exist. Both the top (the aristocracy and gentry) and the bottom (the destitute) were under-represented and the result more resembled a gently tapering column than the standard pyramid. This relative social equality of the Islandmagee people is symbolized by the Ordnance Surveyor's comment that even among those who had servants, only a very few chose to eat separately from the domestics.[5] Although there were gradations of wealth, there was not the chasm between the artifacts of the Big House and those of the peasant hovel, so characteristic of most of Ireland. One can speak with accuracy of the Islanders sharing a single physical culture.

The houses ranged from merely adequate to commodious, very few being either pathetic or impressive. This is a description published in 1812:[6]

> The houses of the farmers, though in general not more than one storey, nor very spacious, are neat and warm, often roughcast and whitened: the windows sashed and with doors painted; covered with a good coat of thatch, and in many instances slated.

The observer added that when circumstances permitted, the farmers added a second storey; and even a casual inventory of Islandmagee's nineteenth century domestic buildings confirms that as the century wore on most inhabitants came to possess two-storey homes.

Fortunately, we have data that allow us to compare the housing provision on Islandmagee with that of the rest of Ireland, as of 1851. The census of that year divided Irish dwellings into four classes. The fourth was made up of cabins having only one room, the third of cottages with windows and two to four rooms, the second of houses with windows and five to nine rooms, and the first class of high standard housing suitable for the upper middle classes:[7]

Class Of Housing—Percentages

	First	Second	Third	Fourth
All-Ireland	4.8	30.5	51.8	12.9
Province of Ulster	3.2	36.6	53.5	6.7
County of Antrim	3.5	37.7	55.2	3.6
Islandmagee	2.3	25.6	68.0	4.1

Examination of this table produces two conclusions. The first is that in comparison to the national and provincial patterns, the Islanders' homes were much more of a single type. They had proportionately fewer hovels and fewer large houses and tended to bunch into the third class, the substantial farmers' and artisans' dwellings. The second conclusion is that the Islanders' standard of housing was only about average for the country, which is rather surprising, given Islandmagee's relative prosperity.

What did the typical Islandmagee house of, say, the era 1850-1900 look like? To begin with, it followed the general pattern common throughout Ireland. This has been defined by one scholar as: (a) a basic rectangular plan, with each room occupying the full width of the house and each room opening on the next without any central hallway; (b) thick walls (in Islandmagee they were of stone); (c) a roof supported by the walls, not by internal pillars; (d) an open hearth at floor level, situated somewhere on the long axis of the house; (e) doors in the side walls; and (f) a steeply-pitched thatch roof.[8] Beyond these common elements, Irish houses of the period tend to fall into two categories: those with a central hearth and those with the hearth in the gable end. Islandmagee houses are in the second category, as are most of the cottages in the north of Ireland.[9]

A floor plan of a typical Islandmagee cottage is given on the following page.[10]

The structure is notable for strength of construction: it was built on a stone foundation, about twenty-seven inches thick, and although it incorporated very little mortar it was remarkably durable. The walls were eighteen inches thick, consisting of two series of courses of nine inches each.

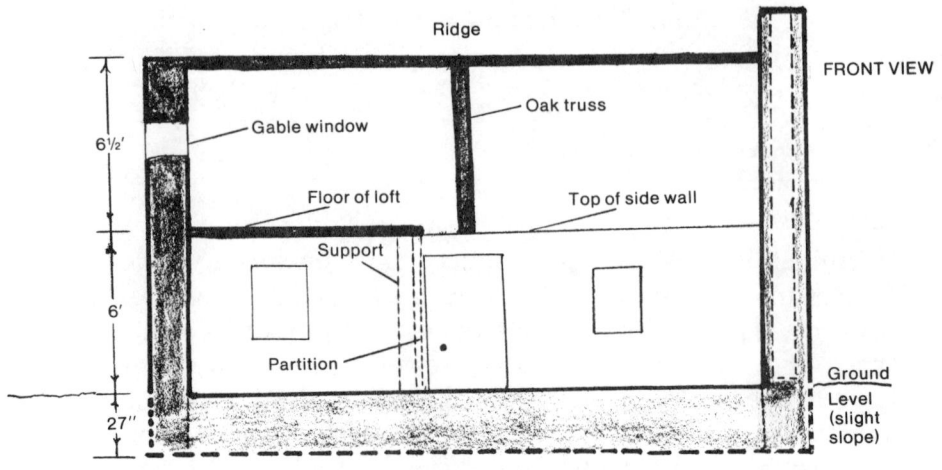
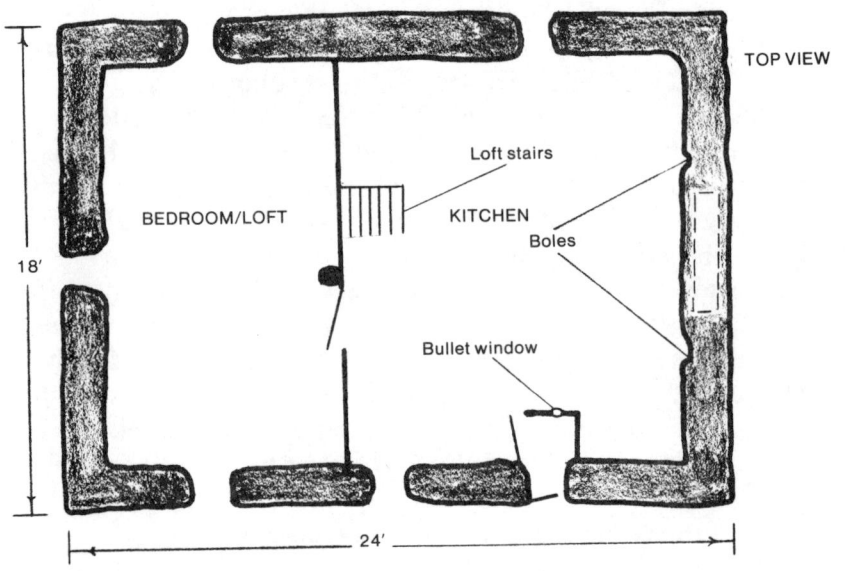

Although mortar was used only across the top of the wall, this was sufficient to join permanently the two courses. The load-bearing abilities of the gables and side walls were prodigious and evenness of weight distribution was helped by having a split oak truss in the middle of the building, thus precluding too much of the weight of the roof from resting on the gable walls. This oak truss was not built into the side wall, but merely sat upon it, a very simple construction technique. Obviously, the building of a stone-walled cottage was very heavy work indeed, and one can understand the custom of putting out a flag or some appropriate substitute, when the chimney-stage has been reached—a hint to the owner that some drink or gratuity would speed up the job's completion.[11]

The two-storey (or more accurately, one and a half-story) farm dwelling was typical, and the resemblance of these buildings to the typical weaver's cottage is obvious. This resemblance can scarcely have been accidental: nearby Ballycarry was a centre of home-weaving and the advantage of the home-and-loft arrangement must have been obvious to farmers as well as weavers.

In Islandmagee, the hearth was screened from the door by a wall running parallel to the side walls. This was fitted with a "bullet" or small spy-hole, enabling those inside to view visitors without themselves being seen.[12] There is also an indication of the former existence in Islandmagee of the sleeping niche, or "bed outshot" (not shown in the illustrated example), which was a small alcove jutting out from the basic rectangle, providing extra sleeping accommodation.[13]

The Islandmagee method of making a roof was to lay fine branches across the ridge pole, and parallel purlins, and the trusswork, forming a network that then was covered with "sweet grass" cut in Larne Lough. This grass was said to be nearly indestructible. Next sods, two inches thick, were put over the entire roof, and finally straw, from one to two feet thick. In Islandmagee *scollop thatch* was employed.[14] This is a method whereby the straw is placed on the roof in

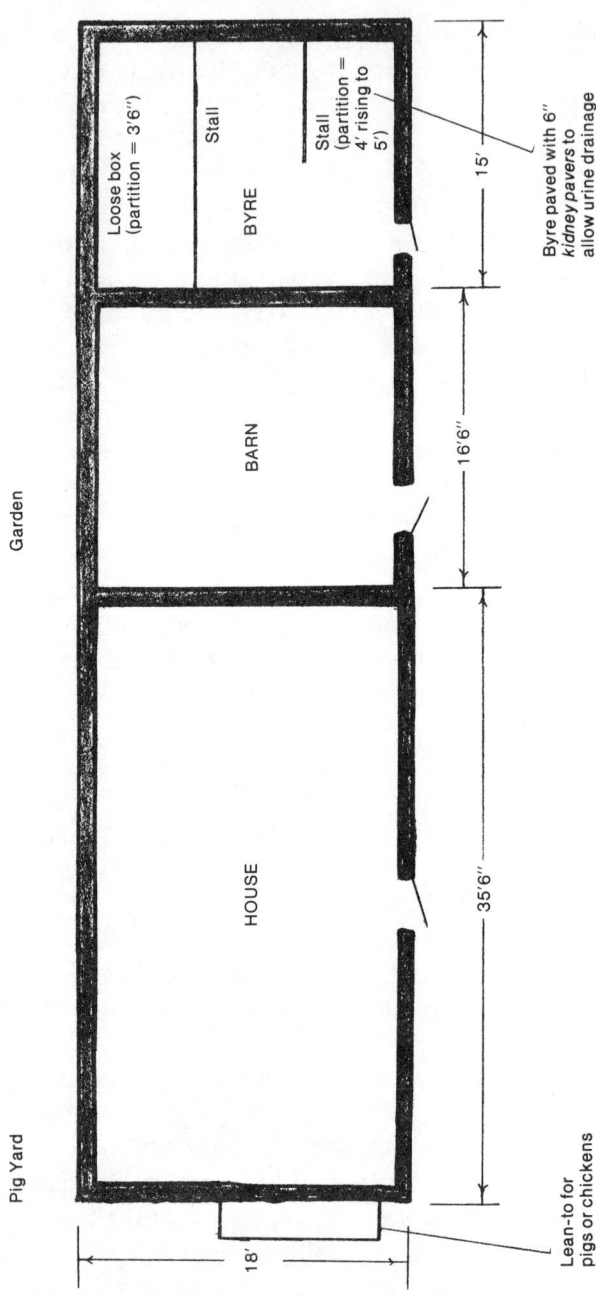

separate bundles, each of which is secured to the roof by thin briar rods, known generally as "scollops" and locally as *scobes*.[15] With the years, subsequent layers of straw would be added, so that the straw on the roof often became well over two feet thick.

"The offices of a farm-house, consist of a stable...a cow-house...and a barn; to these may always be added a house for one or more pigs, a shed for his calves, and in many instances an open house to contain turf, cars, and other farming implements...." So John Dubourdieu wrote about Islandmagee in his 1812 survey of county Antrim.[16] Typically, on Islandmagee the barn and byre were attached to the farm cottage. This arrangement derived from a type of house once common in Western Europe in which the cattle and people lived together, with kitchen, bedroom, and cattle byre being contained in one large rectangular room. In its primitive form, the hearth was at one gable end, and the cows were tethered on the opposite side with their tails towards the hearth. In the course of architectural evolution, the long room eventually was walled to form separate kitchen and sleeping compartments, and the cattle were moved to a compartment on the far side of the gable wall.[17] An example of the arrangement common in Islandmagee in the nineteenth century is given on the preceding page.[18]

Inside, the most important part of the house was the hearth, and around it centred a rich variety of artifacts and customs. On Islandmagee the fire typically was raised above floor level on an iron grate. The large family cooking pot was set on a *crane,* but even at the turn of the century the *pot oven* was sometimes used in Islandmagee. This was a very simple cooking device, consisting of a flat-bottomed cast iron pot, 12-15 inches in diameter and 14-15 inches high, that sat on three legs. Hot embers were packed around it and placed on the lid, thus providing a slow simmering heat. At the side of the fireplace usually were two *boles,* small alcoves where the man of the house's pipe and tobacco were kept, and the woman's delph (crockery).

The best seat by the fire went to the man, although whether this was the right or left side varied by family (in some places, there was an accepted fixed pattern for the entire parish). Crickets were associated with hearths, and a cricket brought good luck to a house. Many Islanders believed that if one killed a cricket in the house, stockings left on the hearth-crane to dry overnight would be riddled with holes in the morning. Not surprisingly, since the hearth was the centre of rural life, and the weather the great imponderable, it was used as an arena for divining weather. For example, a cat arching its back to the fire was recognized as a sure sign of rain, and blue flames coming from the fire were a certain portent of a storm. And the centrality of the hearth to human life was affirmed in the following Islandmagee taboo: if a person died in a room where a fire was burning, the Islanders refused to remove the dead embers until the corpse itself was taken away.[19]

As for the furniture, the chief articles were in the kitchen. (In the bedroom there would be a *tester bed*—a canopy bed—of some sort, and perhaps a small bureau or chest of drawers.) Kitchen furnishings consisted of three central pieces. One of these was the dresser, which on Islandmagee invariably sat against a cross wall, on the opposite side of the kitchen from the hearth. Second, there was always a kitchen table, which, because of the dresser's being on the cross wall, either sat against the long back wall or under the window in the front wall. Tables usually were four-legged and sturdily built, but before the turn of the century the two-legged, *falling table* was known. This was a table hinged to the wall which folded up when not in use. Most farm kitchens possessed at least a third piece of furniture, a bed of some sort. Sometimes this was a pallet, other times a *box bed,* sheeted in timber to a height of about six feet, and sometimes a *settle bed,* that is, a bench that converted into a bed.[20] In addition to these basic items, individual farmers' cottages usually contained various chairs, china shelves, etc., as is indicated in the following description of a turn-of-the-century Islandmagee cottage:

Our home was humble and poor...My home had a living room or kitchen, as it was called in those days, a pantry as you came in the porch to the left. A little end window looked over the meadow to the sea. There was a brown sink with a water tap; the pipe was attached to a rain water barrel outside. We had a working bench with the water buckets and saucepans underneath. On a shelf right round the entire walls were a dozen of tea pots of various sizes, china, delph and enamel.... The kitchen had a big wide fireplace with hobs on either side and a steel fender. A window on either side of the fireplace looked out onto the sea and cliffs. There was a double mantel board stacked with various things, ornaments, photo frames, vases and two old china dogs belonging to my great grandmother. We had two scrubbed tables with a few stools underneath, an old leather couch and father's arm chair. A big cupboard with glass doors held all our china.... The cement floor had many cracks in it, but it was scrubbed clean each day. We had one home made rug at the hearth.[21]

Definitive information on the Islandmagee diet is not available, but one thing is certain: fish played a very large part in it. In the late 1830's the Ordnance Surveyor reported that the farmers of the parish lived frugally and rarely ate meat except on occasions of festivity. Fish, on the other hand, was eaten daily, being caught off Islandmagee's coast and hawked throughout the parish. During the summer the fish were eaten fresh, and immense quantities, especially herrings, were salted away for the winter. Fish, plus salt pork, bacon, eggs, oat bread, and potatoes constituted the farmers' noontime dinner. Tea was always drunk for breakfast and frequently in the evening as well, when it was taken with oat or potato bread. Beef was extremely rare, and, although some cheese was made by the farmers, it was of an inferior quality.[22]

The main item of cottagers' diet at that time consisted almost entirely of fresh fish during the summer and salt herrings in the other seasons, with potatoes and milk. In the late 1830's the cottagers were said not to consume much meal, except when made into bread. They, like the farmers, were very partial to tea, and drank it daily, but without cream or sugar. The diet of domestic servants was somewhat more interesting than the cottagers', consisting of porridge or potatoes and milk for breakfast and supper, and whatever the farmers were having for noon dinner.[23]

One obvious reason for the scarcity of beef in the Islandmagee diet was the abundance of cheap fish. In any case there were no butchers on the Island, so meat could not be obtained in small quantities. Thus, beef was reserved for festive occasions, when large quantities would be consumed, such as at a Christmas feast, or Easter dinner. Although I cannot pinpoint the date when the Islanders came to depend more upon meat than upon fish, it undoubtedly was during the second half of the century. As communications improved, grocers' and butchers' services became available. Indeed, by 1915 home deliveries of such basic items as bread were being made.[24]

To pass abruptly from matters of diet to practices of folk medicine might be seen as a judgement on the Island's culinary practices, but at least one observer made the connection: the Ordnance Surveyor claimed that the cottagers' dependence upon salt fish gave rise to scrofula and to other skin diseases.[25] Be that as it may, whatever ailment the kitchen caused, it was expected to cure, and almost every other ill as well. Often the pot hanging over the fire held some folk medicine being prepared to cure chilbains, the grip, or the ague. The provisions of conventional medical services will be discussed in Chapter Eight, but the point here is that there was a hearthside branch of medicine, one that was just as much a part of the domestic culture as was the preparation of food. The "potato cure" for warts involved cutting a potato into nine pieces, wrapping them in a bundle, and throwing them over the left shoulder. Another Islandmagee method of treating warts was to rub the affliction with a snail, and then to stick the snail onto a thorn. Such cures were known as *charms* and persons who dispensed them were known as *charmers*. As in most societies (including our own), these practitioners engaged in a mixture of sound medicine and faith healing. A sprain, for instance, was treated by wrapping it in a wet cloth (which would reduce swelling), and "words were said over it." The practitioners of hearthside medicine, like those of conventional medicine, kept excuses as well as cures in their bag. For example, an Islandmagee youth was confined to Larne Hospital with kidney trouble and bleeding. His parents sought an old woman and asked her to charm the disease away. She said that she would try, but that she could not guarantee that her methods would work across water—that is, all the way across Larne Lough!![26]

Chapter Seven. Communications

In metaphor, Islandmagee may at times have been at the crossroads (such as during the national crises of 1798 and 1920), but in physical reality, never. The Island is not on the beaten path from anywhere to anywhere (it is, after all, a peninsula), and natural traffic patterns have not served it well. In the first half of the nineteenth century, it was miserably provided with roads, and the only thing that can be said in mitigation is that bad as communications were, they had been much worse earlier.

Roadmaking in Ireland has a flaccid history. From 1613 to 1763 it was almost entirely a matter of local concern. In the former year the Irish parliament passed an act making it the duty of the local parishes of the Established Church to repair the roads in their vicinity. The churchwardens were to meet each Easter and fix a road-repair week wherein each occupier was to contribute work and tools, and six days' labour. Amending acts of 1710 and 1727 recapitulated the six-days' labour principle, despite its being markedly unsatisfactory. In particular, in areas such as Islandmagee in which most people did not belong to the Established Church, having the Anglican vestry in charge of the roads was a poor means of enlisting civic aid (even if, de facto, the vestry in some way took into account the desires of the Island's Presbyterian majority). Because this parish system was insufficient, during the eighteenth century county grand juries became involved in raising funds and supervising the building of important roads. The Grand Jury Act of 1763 formalized this situation and replaced the old vestry system of enforced labour with the "presentment" system. Thereunder, the initiation of a new road construction project became in effect the prerogative of the county gentry. The process was as follows. A substantial citizen would apply for a road. He would have the course measured by two surveyors who would swear to the dimensions and costs before a Justice of the Peace. The certificate of specifications would be presented to the grand jury for the county, which would decide whether or not to grant the presentment. If it was approved, the applicant immediately began to construct the road and did so at his own expense. Meanwhile, the grand jury laid a tax upon the county and from the proceeds reimbursed the road builder. The disadvantages are obvious: one had to be a well-off citizen to propose a road (because one had to expend the money out of one's own pocket before being repaid by the county), and further, the grand jury was dominated by large landowners. This meant that the roads would be built to suit the convenience of the landowners, not to meet the needs of the tenantry. Nevertheless, the road cess was paid by the occupiers. Thus, the system embodied a form of corruption (or at least a form of irresponsible government) as its central principle, since those who paid for the projects were only accidentally and indirectly those who benefited.[1]

The implications of this system for Islandmagee were especially severe, for there was not a resident landlord to further the Island's interest, and yet the Islanders had to share in the County Antrim tax rates, which before the Famine were the second highest in Ireland.[2] Summarizing the situation in the late 1830's, the Ordnance Surveyor stated that the parish of Islandmagee was amply supplied with roads (22 miles in all, counting seven miles of crossroads), but that "in their quality and general construction, they are so very inferior as to afford but little facility in forwarding or promoting agricultural improvement, and are very deficient in the convenience which they should afford to so populous and highly cultivated a district."[3]

Basically, there were two roads running most of the length of Islandmagee. The western one (known as the "Great Road" in the eighteenth century and now called the "Low Road") entered the southern end of the parish and proceeded north to within half a mile of Ferris' point. Near the northern tip of the Island it met a major crossroads at right angles. Within a mile of its southern end, the Great Road branched off to form the "Mill Road" (now known as the "Middle Road"). The Mill Road ran northwards along the spine of Islandmagee, one sub-branch going to Portmuck, another intersecting at Brown's Bay the major crossroad that ran near the top of the Island.

Three things should be noted about this road network. First, as mentioned earlier, it was of remarkably poor quality. Although the average breadth of the fifteen miles of main road was about average for the time (about twenty feet wide), both main roads were steep and full of bends. At one spot in Kilcoanmore the Great Road had an incline of one in eight feet, in another one in nine, and in two others one in eleven.[4] In the era of cart traffic, this was more than an inconvenience, it was an obstacle. Second, the road network left unserved a large portion of the Island, the southeast coast, a situation that was not remedied until the 1920's when the Gobbins Road (still referred to by most Islanders as "the New Road") was constructed. Third, Islandmagee's straggly network of roads came close to a main road—the Carrickfergus road—only at the far southwest corner of the Island. This obviously made it very inconvenient for most farmers to take their produce outside the Island to market, a difficulty made even greater by the fact that the Carrickfergus road itself was an engineer's nightmare, being only twenty feet wide and very hilly.[5]

In 1836, a reforming statute removed most of the corruption from the Irish road-making system by transfer-

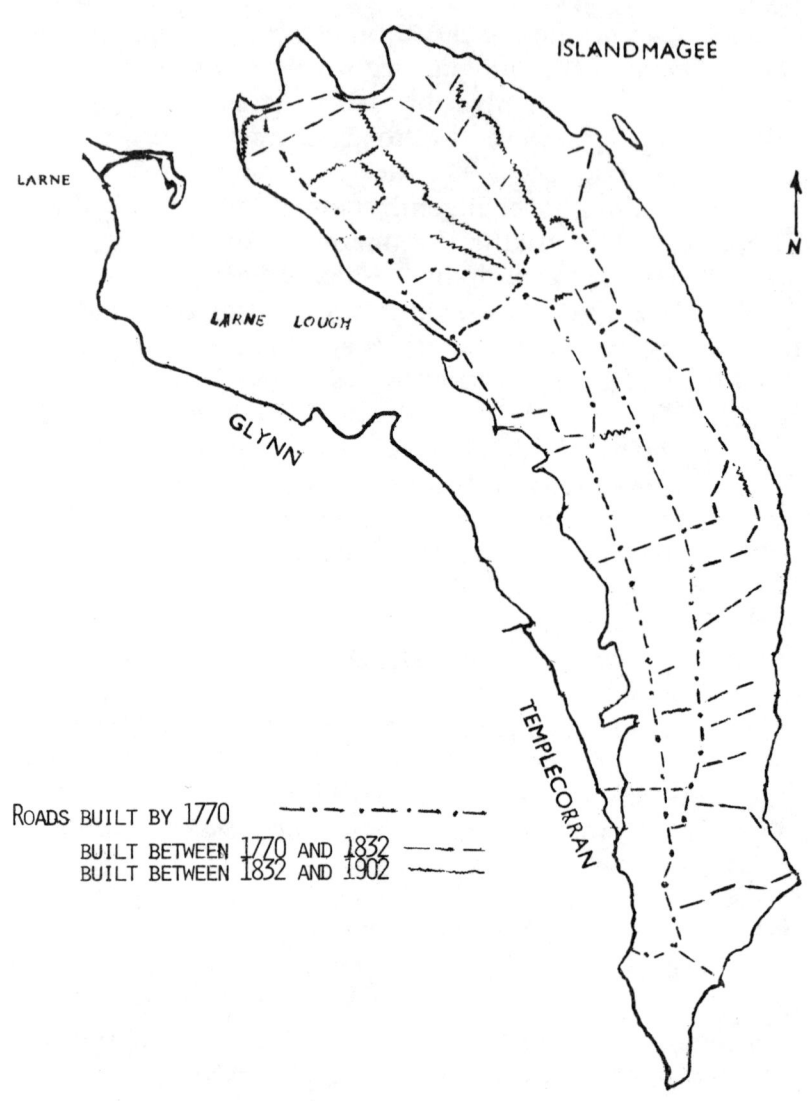

COMMUNICATIONS

ring the supervision of expenditure on road works to county surveyors. This system continued until 1898, when the Local Government Act placed control of roads under rural district and county councils.[6] The act of 1836 made the Irish road construction system less corrupt, and that of 1898 made it more responsive to local needs, but the acts did not greatly alter the pattern of roads for Islandmagee. As the map on page 94 indicates, the road network extant in 1920 was not greatly different from that of 1798.[7] The chief difference was the improvement in quality as the roads were widened, inclines reduced, drainage improved, and metalling increased. Nevertheless, it often remained awkward to get from one side of the Island to the other.

But awkwardness is not the same thing as isolation, and even in the mid-nineteenth century Islandmagee was tied (albeit tenuously) to the provincial communication grid. Although in the 1830s there was no regular heavy transport to Larne, Carrickfergus, or Belfast, two daily passenger coaches running between Larne and Belfast (via Carrickfergus) passed through the southern end of the parish.[8] Further, as the Irish railway system grew in the second half of the nineteenth century, Islandmagee acquired ties to it, and thus access to wider markets. The Belfast and Northern Counties railway was incorporated in 1845 and its first section, from Belfast to Ballymena, opened in 1848.[9] In the same year an extension of the line connected Belfast and Carrickfergus. Five trains a day ran in each direction, and by the mid-1850's, road coach ties were made between Larne and Carrickfergus, so that the Islandmagee people had daily access to Belfast. Then, in 1862, the Carrickfergus and Larne Railway company extended the line, so that one now could go entirely by rail from Larne to Belfast.[10] (The line ran independently until 1890, when it was taken over by the Belfast and Northern Counties Railway,[11] which itself was taken over in 1903 by the Midlands Railway Company of England.)[12] This railway line was accessible to Islanders at four points: Larne Harbour and Larne Town stations (reached by ferry from the north end of Islandmagee), Ballycarry station (which was just across the mouth of Larne Lough), and Whitehead station (just south of Islandmagee).[13] In addition to this standard gauge line, Larne Town and Larne Harbour were served by a narrow gauge system, the Ballymena and Larne Railway, opened in 1874.[14] As a result of these services, in the last third of the nineteenth century the inconvenience previously imposed upon the Islanders by the inadequate network of roads was largely overcome. Islanders now could conveniently travel to Belfast, Carrickfergus, Ballymena, Ballyclare, Ballymoney, and Ballycastle, and heavy goods from those places (especially Belfast) could be shipped within convenient distance. Moreover, Larne could now develop as an important agricultural market town where large numbers of livestock were collected for trans-shipment to population centres. So, paradoxically, Islandmagee in the late nineteenth century was a parish of poor roads, but of efficient communication.

Also, from well before the beginning of the nineteenth century, the Islanders' access to waterways had helped make up for the primitive roads. Especially important were the ferries which ran from the north end of Islandmagee across to Larne. Undoubtedly this ferry run was of venerable origin, and one can admire, if not accept, the Islandmagee tradition that the ferry was blessed by Saint Patrick, whose blessing explains why not a single life had been lost on the short crossing.[15] The Ordnance Survey reported that in the late 1830's two separate services operated, taking passengers across to Larne in a fifteen foot open boat for a penny, or 1½d return. The boats held no more than eight passengers and took seven to ten minutes to make the crossing, depending on wind and tide. Despite being clumsy and leaky, they were safe, and the average number of daily passenger crossings was about 110.[16] Sometime before World War I motor boats were introduced, but they continued to be open boats, just as in the old days.[17] Although these boats were too small to take cattle or produce in significant amounts, the link to Larne was crucial, for Larne was tied by road, railway, and sea to the markets of Belfast, Scotland, and the north of England; which is to say that although it was an overwhelmingly rural community, Islandmagee, unlike similar rural areas in the west and south of Ireland, was in regular, if indirect, contact with the markets and culture of the British industrial revolution.

This is seen clearly in shipping patterns. Although from the early seventeenth century onward, sailings to Scotland from Portmuck and Port Davy on Islandmagee had frequently taken place,[18] and although (as discussed in Chapter Three) a lime-export trade to Scotland and to County Down flourished briefly in the first third of the nineteenth century, Larne Harbour, not the small Islandmagee ports, was the natural focus for regular sea traffic. This traffic was of seven sorts. Some of it was around Belfast Lough: in the days before the railways were fully developed, boat travel being more convenient than coach. From 1861 onwards, various Bangor-based boats served Bangor, Larne, and Belfast, and at their most efficient, in the 1890's, provided two daily round trips from Belfast to Larne Harbour. These services became erratic in the twentieth century, and seem to have degenerated into excursion runs.[19]

Second, for a time Larne Harbour was tied to Liverpool by a service that made regular calls at Larne, a part of a Portrush-Liverpool run. This service operated in the 1830's, but soon lapsed. A similar service was introduced in the 1880's, when Larne was made a stop on the Westport-Liverpool run. This service continued to operate until 1957.[20]

Third, for a time in the 1830's there was a regular route between Glasgow and Larne, a run which was revived in 1879 and continued on a twice weekly schedule until 1917.[21]

A fourth service was from Larne to Ayr in Scotland which began in 1875 and ran three times weekly from 1889 until terminated in 1935.[22]

Fifth, and most important, were the regular Larne-

Stranraer crossings. Using the newly-formed Carrickfergus and Larne Railway as a base, a local group had tried to start a regular service in 1862-63, but this failed. In 1871, however, a successful company, the Larne and Stranraer Steamboat Company, was formed. This group's service connected Larne with Glasgow, through Stranraer-Glasgow rail links; and through further rail connections, with England. In fact, it provided the first fixed-hour sailing service available between England and Ireland. By the 1890's, the Larne-Stranraer run had established itself as not only a successful passenger service but a major element in the cattle and sheep trade. Thus, with a little effort, the larger farmers of Islandmagee could buy and sell livestock not only in Larne and Belfast, but in the major Scottish markets as well. The Stranraer service has continued to the present day.[23]

Further, Larne was tied into the transoceanic passenger traffic in two ways: by cross-channel sailings to Liverpool or Glasgow (from whence travellers or emigrants could board ships to Canada, the United States, or Australia), and by ships on the major runs—especially Glasgow-New York—calling at Larne to pick up passengers for the New World.[24] Finally, there was a vigorous traffic by coasters, travelling from one port on the British coastal basin to another, carrying consignments of raw materials, manufactured goods, and agricultural produce.

Like so much of Islandmagee life, the communications situation was seemingly contradictory and paradoxical. The Island never was in the direct path of the nineteenth century communications revolution, in roads, railways, or water transport; but neither was it ever decisively out of touch. As will be discussed in Chapter Nine, the communications position is a telling analogue to the Island's cultural situation: the society remained intensely parochial and localized, yet simultaneously was remarkably cosmopolitan and regularly in contact with the life of the British economic and cultural empire.

Chapter Eight. Social Control And Social Risks

(1)

"The tempestuous course of Irish history in the nineteenth century often seems to resemble a mountain torrent in flood, where foam and swirling water hide the rocks and boulders."[1] So writes Professor E.R.R. Green, Director of the Institute of Irish Studies, the Queen's University of Belfast. "The excitement of politics," he continues, "is like the rush and roar which so easily hold our attention" when we should be giving more notice to fundamental economic and social structure. Midway between the hypnotic eddies of nationalist-unionist politics and the basic economic channel of Irish society, were the strong, surging, and irregular currents of social disorder and social control. At times of greatest Irish unrest, such as during the land agitation of the last quarter of the nineteenth century, the currents of disorder broke the surface, merging in complex patterns with the new politics of nationalism. At other times, equally strong, but usually silent forces worked against societal agitation. The social order or disorder of any local community is important because it serves as an indication of the economic and social structures underlying the civil order, and simultaneously acts as a causal link in forming the people's political outlook and attitudes towards authority.

The striking thing about Islandmagee, as is true of most

of County Antrim, is that it experienced almost no crime related to dissatisfaction with fundamental economic and social arrangements. In the 1870's, when much of Ireland was "proclaimed" because of land-reform agitation, Antrim was much the most peaceful county: only the parish of Shankill (Belfast) was proclaimed,[2] and that was because of sectarian feelings, not general discontent with the rural economic structure. This is not to say that there were not some crimes stemming from agrarian dissatisfaction, but the proportion was small, and this held throughout the century. For example, in the year 1831 there were disproportionately few instances of damage to property: eight in Antrim, and 657 in the entire country; there were only four attacks on County Antrim houses, but 2,296 nationally; 885 cases of assaults associated with ribbonism (agrarian violence) took place nationally, but only five in County Antrim; although there were 293 cases of houghing (maiming) cattle in all Ireland, there were none in County Antrim; and the homicide level was much lower here, there being only three killings compared to 210 nationally.[3] Much the same conclusion regarding the fundamental peacefulness of the county can be inferred from noting that in the 1840's it was necessary to post only two stipendiary magistrates in County Antrim, as part of a national total of 152 such judicial officers.[4] No policeman was stationed in Islandmagee.

The fact that despite the absence of a formal police organization there were practically no crimes against persons, property, and livestock, indicates that an unspoken, but pervasive system of social control was operative in Islandmagee. It was the entire culture, not any police force, which prevented major thefts and assaults from occurring. The outlines of this invisible system of social control can be traced by indicating what kind of crimes, arguments, or social deviancies were *not* prevented by the Island's social network and therefore had to be referred to formal judicial mechanisms. By-and-large, these were minor matters, one of the most important being litigation between Islanders which could not be resolved informally.

A manor court was held in Islandmagee under the hegemony of the freehold landowner, the Marquess of Donegall (in the 1830's Viscount Dungannon contested the Donegall jurisdiction, and held his own court, but in 1837 conceded to the Donegalls).[5] The court was run by the seneschal of the Marquess of Donegall and held sway not only over Islandmagee but over the Curran of Larne as well. It was limited to the recovery of debts and the adjudication of claims of not more than £20.[6] Effectively, this meant that minor arguments about fences, lost livestock, drainage responsibilities, and accidental damage were its main business. In theory, the court had criminal jurisdiction in that it was supposed to help stamp out smuggling, cockfighting, and illegal drinking, but since it had no legal powers to punish these acts, its responsibility was largely a fiction. Yet, as a court of first instance in local disputes it was useful. Usually trials were held before a jury of locals at a "law day" held once or twice a year. In poor weather a large granary, specially prepared, was used as a courthouse. In fine weather, the court met out-of-doors. Occasionally the seneschal dispensed with the jury and decided cases on his own. In one such instance, he summarily dealt with suits brought by two farmers against each other, the one for trespass by his neighbour's geese, the counter suit for the killing of the geese: the seneschal found in favour of the man who had lost the geese and awarded the injured party, as damage, half an acre of land from the other's farm.[7] Although the one on Islandmagee seems to have given satisfaction, across Ireland manor courts became increasingly unpopular as the century passed, and they were abolished in 1867.

With the manor courts gone, litigious Islanders turned to the petty sessions. At mid-century, there were twenty-one such sessions in County Antrim, each presided over by a Justice of the Peace.[8] Islandmagee litigants could go either to the Larne or to the Carrickfergus session, but most went to Larne. A representative petty session case was Thomas Hill's charging Hugh McGookin, in 1865, with malicious injury to an old fence which passed across a footpath. After listening to the arguments, the bench simply dismissed the case.[9] Less representative in substance, but typical in the pettiness of the issues involved, was the 1867 litigation brought by Robert Tweed against Anne and Samuel Orr (all of Islandmagee) charging the defendents with having scavenged coal from a wreck of which Tweed had bought the salvage rights; the J.P. fined the defendants ten shillings, with one shilling costs.[10]

Matters of greater moment, or appeals from the judgements of individual justices, could be brought before quarter sessions whereon two or more Justices of the Peace acted as a juridical bench. The sites of the quarter sessions varied during the century, but as in most counties, the Antrim quarter sessions were held in four or five towns each year, usually twice in each place. In the 1830's Carrickfergus was the nearest town to Islandmagee in which a quarter session was held,[11] but at the start of the twentieth century half-yearly sessions were being held in Larne.[12] Debts were recoverable in these courts, and so, for example, in 1902 one finds James Aiken, coal merchant of Islandmagee, suing Thomas McIlwaine, Islandmagee, for £2 13s and 9d, allegedly due for coal. After a vitriolic argument about the reliability of the merchant's bookkeeping, judgement was given for 19s and 6d.[13] Occasionally, Islanders brought matters to quarter sessions other than those nearest home, such as the successful claim for £40 brought in 1899 by Samuel Brown against Agnes Brown, administrator of a Brown family estate, at the Lisburn quarter session.[14]

On rare occasions, matters were taken to the high courts in Dublin. The executrix Agnes Brown mentioned above entered a case in Dublin on behalf of the estate she administered (in this instance the case was settled before it came to trial).[15] More contentious was the case brought before the King's Bench, Dublin, by Mary Hawthorne,

Islandmagee, on behalf of her sixteen year old daughter, against John and Sarah Colville, husband and wife, also of Islandmagee. Mrs. Hawthorne charged the Colvilles with slander in that they deliberately and publicly accused the young girl of unchaste behaviour. Despite the plaintiff's claim that the girl was caused "the greatest amount of pain," the Dublin Justice referred the case back to the county courts of Antrim. [16]

In themselves the cases that came before the old manorial courts, the petty and quarter sessions, and the Dublin courts, are of little moment, but taken together they begin to give us an indication of the parameters of Islandmagee's system of informal social control. Cases that went before the courts for adjudication were, by definition, matters which could not be settled within the rubrics of neighbourly compromise or subdued by the pressures of social disapproval. [17]

The Hawthorne slander mentioned above can be considered as an extreme example of a kind of social tension that sometimes could not be contained by the communal control system: attacks upon character. In a tightly-knit society such as Islandmagee, where neighbours not only knew each other well, but each other's business very well, a person's good name was extremely important, and if one could not protect it by informal social pressure, one had to go to law. For example, in 1865 there were two complicated cases in the Larne petty sessions involving charges for use of threatening and abusive language. In one case Mary Anne McKay charged William John Wright with saying that "with her sugar and tay, he would pitch her the gutter among. And he put her in a bodily fright and tried her fair name to disgrace; he gave vent to venomous spite...." (The case was thrown out of court). [18] In another case, a Mary Ann Ellison brought suit against Mary Ellen Bell for calling her "most opproprious names" and throwing a can of water at her. (Bell countersued and the cases were dismissed, and according to the local newspaper, "the parties returned seemingly dissatisfied with the result.") [19]

Social Control And Social Risks 103

Usually, instances of unjust personal vilification were adjusted within the local society, but both of the cases just mentioned involved not only alleged slander but implied physical intimidation as well. Personal violence by one individual against another was rare on Islandmagee—which is to say that the communal culture held it in check—but when it did occur the community could not deal with it by itself, and therefore recourse to the courts was necessary. Note however, that it was *personal* violence which could not be handled within the society, not communal violence. In the early years of the nineteenth century, faction fights between the men of Islandmagee and those of the neighbouring parish were common. These centred on the Ballycarry fair and injured not only the participants, but the fair as well, for the gang fights deterred peaceable citizens from attending. Faction fighting, unlike violence by specific individuals against other individuals within the parish of Islandmagee, was not disruptive of the communal fabric; quite the opposite, for it served to bond Islanders together against outsiders. (The fights had disappeared by the 1830's, for unspecified reasons; I suspect chiefly because of the decline of the importance of the Ballycarry fair).[20]

Personal violence, rare though it was, was quite another matter. One can understand why a woman would bring charges (unsuccessfully as it turned out) against another woman who she believed threw stones at her children,[21] and why a couple would seek damages (in this case successfully) against a man who had knocked the woman about during the course of an argument about a path right of way.[22] But the noteworthy point is that so tightly regulated internally was Islandmagee society that personal violence of a criminal nature (as distinct from that producing mere civil suits) was virtually non-existent.[23]

Similarly, although minor putative violations of property rights were rife (as reflected in litigation about fence lines, drainage rights, etc.), criminal offenses against private property were exceedingly rare. The only major case of alleged criminal damage to property was that brought in 1912 against a well-respected Islandmagee farmer, Luke Jackson, who was arrested on charges of arson to his own barn. After five special sessions held in the Larne court, he was sent for trial at the Belfast assize, where the judge directed an acquittal on all counts.[24]

The only socially dysfunctional activity which was both prevalent and beyond the local society's ability to control, was excessive drinking. If Islandmagee had been overwhelmingly teetotal, social disapproval of alcohol consumption would have made it easy to control abuse. But this was not the case, for on the Island, as in most Irish society, drinking alcohol was an important and generally approved social activity. The Ordnance Surveyer of the late 1830s, a man who admired many of the characteristics of the Islandmagee people, nevertheless reported:[25]

> Their drunkenness and intemperance is everywhere proverbial throughout the surrounding districts, but particularly in the towns of Carrickfergus and Larne.... The women whenever from home or indeed whenever they can procure the means, drink raw spirits in such quantities as would astonish any but a native. The farmers drink on all occasions to excess, whether from home or at home and so habitual has intemperance become that it is now no longer considered discreditable. And on Sunday when coming from "Meeting" drunken farmers will be seen staggering along the road in presence of their clergymen, for whom they seem in this Parish to entertain little respect. A space of half an hour, termed "intermission," elapses between the two services in Presbyterian churches during summer. On retiring for this space, they were in the habit of adjourning to a convenient ale house and there remain during the second service and until they became quite drunk....
>
> The effects of it on the men are perceptible. They are old and stupid looking before their time.... The number of sudden, violent and premature deaths among them solely from the effects of intemperance is appalling. They do not amount to less, on an average, than six yearly. Some have fallen off carts or staggered into a hole on their way home. Others have been smothered. Two have committed suicide. Several have lost their reason.

> There is unfortunately no one in the Parish for whom they entertain any respect, or before whom they fear or are ashamed to be seen while inebriated.

Lord Dungannon tried, in 1839, to reduce drunkenness by having all fourteen of the Island's public houses broken up, but five shebeens immediately sprang up to supply the demand.[26] Significantly, drunkenness was the instance of two important breaches of the Island's social control code, each involving violence against the person: in one, in 1876, an Islandmagee resident was given three years hard labour for physical assault,[27] and in the second, in the 1890's, a rural letter carrier was had up for indecent assault while he was the worse for drink.[28]

Having stated that gross intemperance was a serious problem in the nineteenth century, one must add that by the mid-twentieth century it was not. Precisely when Islandmagee crossed the line into relative sobriety is impossible to ascertain, but I suspect that it was in the early 1920s. In 1921 an act of the new Northern Ireland government put an end to spirit-groceries. Proprietors of these establishments had to choose between operating as a retail grocery or as a public house. After 1921 there was only one public house on the Island, at Millbay, the next closest being opposite the Ballycarry railway station and this latter closed in the 1920s.[29] For serious drinking, therefore, the Islanders either had to drink in Millbay, or travel to Larne, Ballycarry, or Whitehead.

In Chapter Nine the culture of Islandmagee will be discussed in detail. Here the important points are fourfold. The first is that there was no serious dissonance between the local society and the economic framework upon which it rested. Therefore, agrarian agitation, so common elsewhere in Ireland, was absent. Second, the implicit social control mechanism pervading this rural parish effectively prevented malicious destruction of private property and violence against the individual. How this mechanism operated is problematical, but its reality is not. Third, although remarkably resilient, the accepted system of communal values could not contain or adjudicate all matters of conflict between private individuals. Hence, the Islanders' recourse to the lower courts to collect private debts, settle boundary disputes, and protect individual reputations against traducement. Finally, the society was not able—or did not wish—to deal effectively with excessive drinking. This is understandable, for within the culture heavy drinking was not considered a serious vice, so that drunkenness could scarcely be limited. But despite such weaknesses, one has to be impressed with the efficiency with which the Islanders' set of shared cultural conventions kept to a minimum instances of destructive social deviance.

(2)

The inhabitants of Islandmagee, like those of any society, developed ways of protecting and insuring each other against the uncertainties of life, especially sickness, old age, and unavoidable poverty. The Islanders never had to cope with the extreme poverty common elsewhere in Ireland, but in other matters they were just as vulnerable to the quirks of fate. As in most rural societies, the Islanders' mechanisms for meeting the uncertainties of life were chiefly familial. If a wife was struck with an incurable disease, if parents became senile, if a son was lost at sea—in all such cases the immediate family or near kin were expected to help. Community social pressures enforced these expectations, and it was a rare family that shirked its obligations.

This situation presents a problem for the historian: familial social welfare arrangements were almost invisible in the sense that they rarely were recorded, and, unlike anthropologists, historians cannot generate their own data by directly asking questions of members of the community involved. Thus, we must proceed in defining the welfare "system" in much the same way that we dealt with the system of social control: by using the formal mechanisms as a negative that defines for us the areas *not* adequately covered by informal arrangements. Then, by reversing this picture, in much the same way a photographic negative is turned into a positive image, we can define clearly the outline (although not the internal filigree) of the complex network of family and kinship that aided the individual Islander in meeting unkind strokes of Providence.

Before the 1840s, Islandmagee had to rely entirely on familial arrangements and voluntary welfare schemes. In 1834, for example, the married mariners of the parish enrolled as members in the Merchant Seaman's Widows Fund of Belfast. Each man subscribed one shilling annually and each master two shillings. In case of death at sea, the widow of a master was to receive £6 and that of a seaman £4, and each child, of either, £2. This insurance scheme was a sensible arrangement, since between 1815 and 1840, fifty-one men, natives of Islandmagee, were drowned at sea.[30]

Islandmagee had no charity organization of its own. The town of Larne had a large mendicity society which distributed nearly £300 a year in charity, but it limited its work to its immediate vicinity, thus excluding Islandmagee.[31] The local churches, however, acted to some extent as agencies of charity, taking regular collections for those in need.[32]

In fact, the family-based welfare arrangements worked successfully. Testifying before the Irish poor law investigation commission of the 1830s, the Rev. William Campbell of the First Islandmagee Presbyterian Church stated that there was only one deserted child in Islandmagee who had to be supported by the parish. There were, he added, no bastard children above the age of three who were not supported by their reputed fathers. "Very few" widows and their children had no relation who supported them. When asked how many labourers from Islandmagee were in the habit of working in England for part of the year (a practice common in many parishes to augment inadequate wages and insufficient local charity), the Rev. Mr. Campbell answered "scarcely any." As for beggars, there were only three in the parish and to them alms usually were given. Had any one died in Islandmagee from destitution in the last three years? "None."[33]

In 1843 the Larne Poor Law Union Workhouse opened to serve the entire Larne area, including Islandmagee.[34] This was a result of the Irish Poor Law Act of 1838, which set up a national board of poor law commissioners and 130 poor law unions (the number was later increased) covering the entire country.[35] Management of the individual poor law unions was in the hands of locally elected poor law guardians. Twenty-five guardians managed the Larne union, being elected from thirteen separate electoral divisions. Islandmagee constituted a distinct electoral division and chose two guardians.[36] The amount each electoral division paid towards poor relief varied. In 1848 it ranged from 6d to 1s 6d in the pound, rateable valuation. Islandmagee was assessed at only 6d and was responsible for providing £183 towards a union-wide total of £3,255.[37] Originally built to house 400 indigent (at a capital cost to the ratepayers of the Larne union of £7,600),[38] the Larne workhouse rarely was full even in the hard times of the 1840s: in the spring of 1844 the number in residence was 262, in 1846, 313,[39] and in 1849, 302.[40] Yet, for some reason, the workhouse's capacity was expanded to 740 in the early 1850s, at a time when it actually housed about 375 inmates.[41] In the 1870s it still could hold 700 paupers, but then it had only 230.[42]

The indoor relief system covered every group considered vulnerable—the blind, orphaned, aged, and, also, destitute women—but did not provide for men who had become indigent through loss of employment.[43] Unlike their English counterparts, the Irish workhouses were not intended to be markedly more unpleasant than was working class life outside, but certainly few people would have entered them by choice. Until the practice mercifully was dropped near century's end, husbands and wives, even among the aged, were separated. Daily life was run by a rigid schedule, and no tobacco or alcohol was allowed.[44] The able-bodied female inmates of the Larne workhouse spent their days shoemaking, sewing, knitting, and picking oakum. They made all the clothing used in the workhouse and also helped raise the produce consumed.[45] From the ratepayers' point of view this was an admirable arrangement, for it kept costs low: in the mid 1860s the average weekly cost of a healthy inmate was 10½d,[46] and a decade later it had dropped slightly, to 8½d.[47]

Children, either orphans or offspring of mothers who were forced into the workhouse, were in a separate administrative category, and the Larne guardians gave them a good deal more attention than any other group. Children under sixteen years of age made up a considerable proportion of the workhouse population: in the mid 1870s, seventy-one boys and girls were housed, constituting more than one-third of the entire workhouse population;[48] and in the early 1890s, fifty-seven boys and girls under sixteen were in the workhouse, or just under one-third of the population.[49] The guardians took the education of the children seriously. They operated a school that was affiliated with the national system of education.[50] Thus, the pauper children received the same primary education as did most Irish children. The guardians employed full-time both a schoolmaster and a mistress;[51] given that there were about sixty pupils, the pupil-teacher ratio was as good as or better than that existing in most Irish schools today. The only complaint about the workhouse school came on religious, not educational, grounds. Cardinal Cullen complained before the 1861 select committee on the poor in Ireland that though Catholic children constituted one-quarter of the pupils, no member of the workhouse staff or school staff was Catholic.[52] His complaint availed not, and a return of 1879 revealed that one-fifth of the school pupils were Roman Catholic, but that the teachers were all Protestant.[53] Just or unjust, this Catholic grievance was irrelevant to Islandmagee, with its tiny Catholic population.

In addition to their schooling, the boys in the workhouse

were employed growing crops and the girls in learning to knit and sew.[54] In the early days of the Larne workhouse's operation, some attempt was made to teach a few of the boys the trade of shoemaking, and some older boys and girls (aged thirteen and fourteen) were sent out from the workhouse to do domestic service.[55] The flashiest thing that the guardians did with the destitute children was to found the Larne Workhouse Boys' Band. Lord Antrim, president of the board, provided each member with a uniform and the lads were put under regular musical instruction.[56] The band became a regular feature of civic and ceremonial occasions, and although from the perspective of our own times it may seem a bit patronizing to have the pauper children drilled as civic minstrels, for them the business must have been a great deal more interesting than sitting in the workhouse being conventionally and tediously industrious.

Because of the lack of sanitoriums for those suffering from various medical and emotional problems, the Larne workhouse served as a general centre for those who nowadays would receive specialist care. The blind, for example, often were housed in the workhouse.[57] So too were the mentally handicapped. The nearest lunatic asylum was in Belfast,[58] so the Larne area was in effect without facilities. In the mid 1870s, to take a representative time, the Larne workhouse sheltered fifteen idiots and imbeciles and fifteen other "harmless lunatics."[59] The mentally handicapped made up about ten percent of the workhouse population.

Older people, sixty-five years of age and above, constituted one-third or more of the workhouse inmates in normal times.[60]

Thus, in the Larne poor law union, which contained Islandmagee, about one-third of the workhouse inmates were homeless youths, another one-third resourceless old people, and ten to twelve per cent mentally handicapped or blind. This accounted for three-quarters of the inmates, the remaining quarter being mostly young widows who were unable to support their children, or the physically handicapped of either sex.

Under the Dispensaries Act of 1851, the Larne board of poor law guardians divided their area into several districts, each served by a dispensary that provided medical relief for the poor, paid for by the rates. The nearest such dispensary to Islandmagee was quite close, being in the neighbouring parish, at Ballycarry. It opened in February 1852 and provided twice-weekly consulting services.[61]

In addition, under the Poor Law Amendment Act, 1847, the Larne guardians provided "outdoor relief" for the sick, the infirm, and widows with two or more children. Also, the temporarily destitute, meaning chiefly men who had lost employment, could be aided (although until a further amending act was passed in 1862 anyone occupying more than one-quarter acre of land was not eligible for such relief).[62] Potentially, the outdoor relief system could have operated as a proto-unemployment-relief scheme, protecting adults from the worst effects of temporary joblessness; in practice, however, the Larne poor law guardians refused outdoor relief to the able-bodied.[63]

Where, in this Larne-based scheme, did Islandmagee fit? Because the Island was the least accessible part of the Larne union, Islanders constituted a high proportion of those who were given relief in their own homes rather than required to reside in the Larne workhouse. In 1898, for instance, Islanders were twenty-two of the twenty-eight people receiving outdoor relief from the Larne poor law guardians.[64] Conversely, Islanders were sparsely represented inside the workhouse: in spring 1874, for example, of 214 persons in the Larne workhouse, only fourteen were from Islandmagee.[65]

But those are statistics, and one too easily forgets that behind the numbers were human beings facing personal situations with which they could not cope. The registers kept by the poor law guardians are complete from 1862 onwards for those receiving outdoor relief and give brief particulars of each Islander who received aid.[66] Mostly, outdoor relief went to people who were alone. Thirty-four of the 128 names of Islanders found on the outdoor relief rolls between 1862 and 1921 were widows about sixty years of age. Most were in their seventies and eighties when they began receiving poor law aid and they were kept on the rolls until their deaths. Typical cases were those of Eliza F., Temple Effin, who came on the rolls in 1890, aged seventy-two, and stayed on until her death in 1903; and of Margaret M., of Kilcoan, who began to receive outdoor relief in 1895 at the age of eighty-three and continued to receive it until her death in 1899. Equally alone and in need of assistance were single women who were too old to work. (Thirty of the 128 Island names on the outdoor relief rolls were spinsters over sixty.) These usually were women of the working or artisan classes, such as Catherine McB., Ballykeel, a labourer who came on the rolls in 1884 at age seventy, and Catherine M., seamstress, aged eighty when she began to receive aid in 1897. (Insofar as the aged were concerned, the Old Age Pensions Act of 1908 served to reinforce the poor law provisions, but did not replace the earlier act.)

The theme of aloneness runs through most of the poor law rolls. Almost all of the eight single women under sixty years of age who received aid were in their fifties when they began to take outdoor relief and they really were in no different position than the older spinsters. The five children who during the years 1862-1921 were given aid had been deserted or orphaned. And although the eleven Islandmagee widows left with dependent children were not living by themselves—certainly not Mary R., aged forty-two, of Gransha, widowed with six children and receiving aid in 1892, or Mary McK., Drumgurland, widowed with three children and given relief in 1894—they were alone in the world insofar as financial resources were concerned. In all these cases—widowing, spinsterhood, and orphaning—the outdoor relief system was filling gaps which the familial and kinship arrangements did not cover.

Here a question arises, one which is unanswerable

directly but is nevertheless worth posing: did the existence of the poor law system (a) fill in gaps in Islandmagee's familial-kinship network which otherwise would not have been covered? or (b) by its very existence lead the Islanders to reduce their previously-accepted sense of obligation to care for their kin?, or (c) both?

What we *do* know is: (1) that before the poor law system was established, Islandmagee had almost no overt destitution, which means either that the loners and cripples of the society were automatically taken care of, or that they suffered in silence; (2) that the chief impact of the public welfare system as it operated from the mid 1840s onwards was to place upon local government bodies responsibility for the care of those individuals who were in physical or economic distress and who were alone in society; (3) that in addition to the loners (orphans, widows, and aged spinsters) who always had been recognized as needy, the poor law system expanded the general definition of need to include younger married men with dependants (thirteen of the 128 names on the outdoor relief rolls), as well as retired men over sixty, married or unmarried (twenty-two of the 128 Islandmagee names on the outdoor rolls); (4) that— and this is somewhat surprising—the outdoor relief rolls contain a number of names of individuals related, at least distantly, to substantial Islandmagee families. To some extent, it appears that the governmental relief system allowed Islanders to abandon their direct responsibilities for distant relatives, since the public welfare mechanism now took care of them.

So, paradoxically, it seems that during the nineteenth and early twentieth centuries, the social welfare arrangements became simultaneously harsher and gentler. Harsher, because the sense of communal and kinship responsibility for victims of age and ill-health was diminished. Gentler, because the definition of need became broader and because formal governmental means of defending against misfortune—defences such as the poor law system, the medical dispensary units, and old age pensions—became markedly stronger.

A snapshot of the situation during a representative period, say the 1890's, would reveal that only between thirty and forty Islanders were so destitute and alone as to need poor relief; this in a total Islandmagee population of about 2,300, in which, if normal age profiles were operative, one would have found approximately two hundred elderly persons beyond the age of self-support, in addition to all the other categories of persons needing aid. It is clear that the primary responsibility for protecting and caring for the aged, the handicapped, and the orphaned was being borne by the family and kinship system, and that Islandmagee still was a long way from needing the welfare state.

(3)

In the lives of most Islanders, government was peripheral and politics irrelevant. Granted, there was a system of local government, but throughout most of the nineteenth century it was weak. The parish-based system of local government, so successful in England, was impossible in Ireland, because the civil and ecclesiastical parishes were not coterminous. In very few places in Ireland were the majority of the population Anglican, yet it was the parish of the Established Church which was supposed to function as the local government unit. The weaknesses of this system were obvious and (as discussed in Chapter Seven), the most important parochial responsibilities, such as roads and public works, were transferred to the county grand juries in mid-eighteenth century.

In the early nineteenth century the local parish operated on two levels. A "select vestry" composed of rate-paying members of the Church of Ireland (the religious minority on Islandmagee), laid certain small taxes for the physical maintenance of the Established Church and for the payment of minor church officers, such as the sexton. There was also a "general vestry," which after the late-eighteenth century abolition of the penal laws included all ratepayers regardless of religious affiliation. The general vestry could vote taxes, make contributions to road works, pay constables, and aid the poor. The general vestry was not as useful an agency as it could have been, despite its admitting all ratepayers to membership, because by law all officers were required to be members of the Established Church—hardly a recommendation in solidly Presbyterian Islandmagee. In the face of mounting national criticism during the 1820's (mostly from Catholics), the Tory government in 1826 removed the general vestry's right to tax the parish for social welfare measures, such as the support of orphans or the relief of the poor. This was a bizarre bit of reform, for it took away the most acceptable of the parish government's activities (the principle of aiding the poor from local tax revenues was generally acceptable), while leaving the select vestry with the irksome power to levy a general cess for Established Church purposes. This extraordinarily insensitive 1826 act transformed the parish system of government into a general grievance, pure and simple, and, not surprisingly, in 1833, the reforming Whig government abolished altogether the old parish system of local government. [67]

This left the County Antrim Grand Jury, the Larne Poor Law Union (f. 1843), and the Ballycarry Dispensary District Committee (f. 1851), as the only agencies of local government affecting Islandmagee. In 1898 the Local Government Act redefined the county's authority and amalgamated the poor law and dispensary activities under the newly-created Larne Rural District Council. In addition to welfare duties, the new rural council had minor responsibilities in education, public health, and communications.

The new system, while doubtless an improvement, did not loom large to the Islanders. For one thing, its responsibilities were relatively unimportant, being the kind of activity which, at best, rated a short notice in the local weekly newspaper. Second, during the first two decades of the twentieth century, the nearby new town of Whitehead was shouldering aside the surrounding rural areas, such as Islandmagee, as the focus of local government activity.[68] (Eventually, in 1927, Whitehead became a separate Urban Council.)[69]

The distance from the various local government systems evinced throughout the nineteenth and early twentieth centuries by the Islanders does not mean that they were socially fragmented, apathetic, or ademocratic. Quite the contrary was true. As discussed in Chapter Six, the Island's social structure was one of relative equality, in which the inhabitants took their social cues not from the gentry of a Big House, but from each other; as will be discussed in Chapter Nine, the system of church government of the Presbyterian Church, to which most Islanders belonged, gave them experience in a very democratic form of representational self-government; and, as also will be discussed in Chapter Ten, the local society defined its own leaders and its own system of voluntary civic engagement, by criteria and methods indigenous to the Island. In point of fact, the Islandmagee population was functionally self-governing, and the formal agencies of local government were a sometimes useful, but largely redundant overlay.

Chapter Nine. A Cohesive Culture—I. The Island Cosmology

(1)

The culture of Islandmagee as it existed in the years 1798-1920 is best embodied in the concept of community. Community included shared beliefs, attitudes, and superstitions; community embraced the formally-organized enterprises of the society, such as the churches, lodges, and schools; and it comprehended the informal mechanisms, the shared social practices which sprang up with seeming spontaneity and were accepted universally. For the sake of expository convenience, some aspects of community already have been discussed—economic cooperation, social control, and communal welfare measures—and others follow, but the crucial point is that in the Islandmagee community in the nineteenth and early twentieth centuries, everything overlapped, forming a cultural web that was at once comprehensive and cohesive.[1]

The centre of the Island's culture of course was the family. In saying this, alas, one is in danger of uttering a truism, for we know much less than we wish about the Islandmagee family. As discussed in the Preface, Irish parochial records are too thin to permit family reconstruction on a valid scale, and the gathering of "field material" from the present day and projecting it backward into the early nineteenth century is patently invalid.[2] We do know that in contrast to the general Irish practice the Islanders did not marry early before the Famine, and did not seem to be tempted by the national trend to ever-earlier marriage. Most men in the 1830's were reported not to marry before twenty-seven or twenty-eight, and the common age for women was nineteen to twenty-four.[3] Also, as discussed in Chapters Four and Five, family life on Islandmagee, in contrast to that in most of Ireland, was not disoriented as a result of the Great Famine. Inferentially, from population patterns one can conclude that the age of family-formation, as well as its incidence, were much the same in the later nineteenth and early twentieth centuries as they were before the Famine.[4] Thus, unlike the common Irish experience, the basic outlines of family life on Islandmagee were the same from generation to generation throughout the nineteenth and early twentieth centuries.

Another point: the average size of the Islandmagee family remained stable. Indeed, in the first three-quarters of the nineteenth century, it barely changed at all: it was an average of 4.8 persons per family in 1821, 4.7 in 1871 and 4.5 in 1881.[5] The average family size had dropped to 4.1 by the 1911 census,[6] but even that, I think, overstates the degree of change. The introduction of old age pensions, combined with outdoor poor relief, meant that old people who previously had been forced to live with their children in their declining years, now could maintain their own homes longer than had previously been possible. In other words, even the moderate decline in average family size that occurred after 1881 was more apparent than real; in reality the statistics indicated not a true decline in family size, but an improvement in local housing standards. Actually, I doubt if true family size declined at all.

But statistics of family size mask wide ranges of possible variation. Fortunately, the original manuscript census forms for 1901 and 1911 escaped destruction and are preserved in the Public Record Office, Dublin. Family structure and number of children in the family unit are summarized below, from the 1911 data:[7]

	Number of Children								
	0	1	2	3	4	5	6	7 or more	Totals
Couple, both living	29	93	90	51	58	18	15	12	366
Widow	22	12	16	10	6	0	2	0	68
Widower	14	3	4	4	2	1	0	2	30
Bachelor	30	0	0	0	0	0	0	0	30
Spinster	15	0	0	0	0	0	0	0	15
Totals	110	108	110	65	66	19	17	14	509

Clearly, the Islandmagee social norm was familial: only 15.9 per cent of the units were composed of single individuals, and only 21.6 per cent of all units did not have children in the home.

Under what terms were families formed on Islandmagee? We know, first, that in the usual case young people were not permitted to marry until they could support themselves, which in most cases meant until they had inherited a farm. Second, the usual practice was for the groom to be older than the bride, by about ten years. Third, it appears that the individual young people had a great deal more personal choice than usually is imagined. Naturally, in a society wherein the parents controlled inheritance of land, the old people had a considerable influence on courting patterns. But they did not have anything like the control over their children's marriage prospects which rural parents in the south of Ireland exercised after the Famine.[8] Why? Because, as discussed in Chapter Three, the economic base of Islandmagee was not solely agricultural and young Islanders always had the option of getting married and earning a living from the sea, should their farming parents prove completely unreasonable. Significantly, on Islandmagee, one finds no evidence of marriage broking, a practice common in most of Ireland. A system evolved in which the parents could influence the choice of their offspring's spouse and when and under what economic conditions that marriage took place. But ultimately, control was in the children's hands.

The clearest indication of the young people's considerable freedom in family formation is found in reports of the pre-marital sexual practices. In the late 1830's the Ordnance Surveyer reported that "seldom does a marriage take place that has not been preceded by an improper intimacy of greater or less (sic) duration between the parties."[9] He also stated: "It more frequently than otherwise happens, that a girl has become a mother or is pregnant at the period of her marriage. But this is so common that it is not noticed."[10] Even allowing for some overstatement on the part of the Ordnance Surveyer (who did seem to be rather excitable on moral issues), there is no questioning the reality on Islandmagee of widespread pre-marital sexual intercourse and, *mutatis mutandis,* of considerable freedom of choice in marital partners. In this crucial matter, then, the Islanders seem to have been following low-land Scottish rather than general Irish patterns.[11]

Yet, despite the relative sexual freedom of the Islandmagee young people, the illegitimacy rate was very low: the baptismal register of the Second Islandmagee Presbyterian Church records 1,338 baptisms between 1854-1920, inclusive, of which only twenty-one (1.6 per cent) are of illegitimate children.[12] This compares with an all-Ireland rate of 2.5 per cent in 1880, a north-eastern counties rate of 4.9 per cent in the same year,[13] and an England and Wales rate of 4.1 per cent for the 1890's.[14]

Why such a low rate, in view of the apparently common pre-marital sexual relations? In small part, it may be because fewer of the illegitimate children were baptized than of the legitimate, but I suspect that in that tightly-knit rural community, such dropping-from-the faith was relatively rare. No, the real reason for the low illegitimacy rate was that suggested by the Ordnance Surveyer when he observed concerning early pre-marital pregnancy, that it almost never operated to the girl's disadvantage, "for instances of desertion have been very rare."[15] Thus, although we can posit a very low illegitimacy rate, the proportion of women who came to the altar pregnant was quite high: of the 200 women married in the First Presbyterian Church, Islandmagee, from 1845 to 1867 inclusive, twenty-seven bore children before nine months were up.[16] And, if one makes an incremental correction for those girls who were pregnant upon marriage but subsequently had a miscarriage and for those who mistakenly thought they were pregnant but were not, probably twenty per cent of the Islanders being married either "had to" get married, or thought they had to.

What this adds up to is a pattern atypical by post-Famine Irish standards, in which the young people had considerable latitude in the choice of their marriage partners and in which pre-marital sex was not viewed as seriously undermining the stability of the society. Instead it was incorporated as a functional part of family practices. This was possible because, unlike most of Ireland, Islandmagee as a community had enough economic security to permit accidents to happen. Although parents discouraged their sons from getting married until their late twenties, they permitted them to keep company with girls. If one got in the family way, well, the lad would marry her and either take over the father's farm or go to sea. Thus, the Island society combined a considerable degree of pre-marital sexual activity with the maintenance of an extremely stable and strong family life.

When noting the impressive strength of the Islander's family arrangements, it is easy to fall into the mistake of assuming that the society was endogamous, or at least highly inbred. This is a natural error, because the Island was off the beaten track, and one could incorrectly conclude, as did a reporter (almost certainly the renowned antiquarian Samuel McSkimin) in *The Belfast Magazine* in 1809, that "their remote situation obstruct[s] their marriages with the interior."[17] And one could easily enough romanticize the Island's isolation, as did Jack London in *The Strength of the Strong,* in which he claimed that Islandmagee seamen always came back to the Island to find their wives, and that no sailorman ever had brought back a wife from overseas and lived to boast about it, and indeed, that a poor creature of a schoolmaster once married a woman from the far side of Larne Lough and even he lived under a cloud all his days![18] But all that is romantic vapouring. Actually, an examination of church marriage registers reveals that a great deal of intermarriage with outsiders took place: of the 200 marriages that took place in the First Presbyterian Church, Islandmagee, from 1847 to 1867, inclusive, in thirty-seven one of the partners was from the Island, the other from outside;[19] in thirteen of the sixty marriages conducted in St. John's Anglican Church, Islandmagee, from 1845 to 1920 inclusive, Islanders wed outsiders;[20] and so it was in five of the sixteen weddings in the Methodist chapel from 1866 to 1920 inclusive.[21]

As a result of this continuous out-breeding, new families were constantly being introduced to Islandmagee, even as old ones died out. This process went back as far as the seventeenth century. For example, of the 101 family names on the 1669 hearth tax rolls, only eleven were found in letting notices published in 1770.[22] Admittedly, the 1770 list included only the larger tenants (there were sixty-four family names on the list, as compared with 101 on the early tax roll), but even if one doubles the number of continuing names in order to compensate for the thinness of the 1770 roll, one finds a striking degree of change: at most only one-fifth of the families that tenanted the island in 1669 were there a century later. That this high degree of change is a reality, not merely a statistical accident caused by the thinness of the 1770 letting notices, is confirmed by comparing the hearth roll tax list of 1669 with a later tally of comparable completeness, namely the 1834 tithe applotment survey. (Actually, this later survey probably is slightly more complete than the earlier survey, containing as it does 131 family names, compared to 101). Only sixteen of the 101 family names on the 1669 rolls were found on the Island in 1834.[23] Clearly, during the eighteenth century most of the original settler families were replaced by immigrants, and in the early nineteenth century a high proportion of the Islanders were descendants of the later settlers.

This process of replacing old families with new was not disruptive of the Island's social fabric, for two reasons. First, because it occurred gradually, and second, because the mechanism of the replacement process was the marriage of Islanders and outsiders. If widescale emigration had accounted for the disappearance of many families, this would have been disruptive (actually, emigration from the Island seems to have been very light; for example, in 1836-39, the only years for which data are available, a total of only nineteen individuals emigrated from the parish).[24] Or if large numbers of new outside tenants had suddenly been introduced by the landlords, this would have been disruptive. However, the landlords' long-leasing practices precluded this happening. Because by intermarriage old Island families were melded with new ones, the changes in the family names on Islandmagee represent not so much a displacement of old families *by* new, as a transformation of old families *into* new ones. It is the continuation of this gradual process, begun in the seventeenth century, that we are witnessing when we tally the significant proportion of Islandmagee marriages with outsiders recorded in the nineteenth and early twentieth century registers.

So the Island family was strong, and simultaneously flexible. It was strong in the sense that family life was the universally accepted hub of the communal culture. It was this strength that permitted the society to be flexible about family formation: the Islanders were open to frequent intermarriage with outsiders, without any risk to the community's cultural integrity. Similarly, by Irish standards the Islanders were permissive about pre-marital sexual activity and generous in allowing a good deal of choice to the young people in the selection of spouses. Such flexibility in marriage patterns was possible only in a community that was fully confident of the strength of its family system and sure of the local economy's ability to support these arrangements.

(2)

To the Islander of the nineteenth century, the family was not a solitary body travelling through darkened space, but a unit that operated in a rich and vividly populated universe. The Islander's mental geography was complex. The hub was the individual family. Religious beliefs and superstitions, social conventions, and instinctive attitudes, were the laws that related an individual and his family to all others. Taken together, these beliefs, attitudes and conventions formed nothing less than a cosmology; and, in the case of some of the superstitions, a demonology.

(In the discussion that follows, I am not interested in the institutional aspects of the Islanders' belief system—that will come later—but only in the beliefs themselves.)

Religion was central to the Islanders' cosmology, for it provided a set of practical guidelines for everyday behaviour and a conceptual bridge into another, invisible world. But what the Islanders believed cannot be specified precisely. What religion meant to the ministers and what it meant to members of the flock were quite different things. The overwhelming majority (86.4 per cent according to the religion census of 1834) were Presbyterians and most of the rest were Anglican, that is, Established Church (8.6 per cent) or Methodist (3.3 per cent).[25] Each of these Protestant denominations had a fully articulated theology, intellectually demanding and devotionally rigorous, but the theology in its full adumbration was a matter to be comprehended only by the clergy and a few gifted laymen. Looking at religion from the average layman's point of view, what did he experience? Liturgically, he partook of a bare service, which was short on colour and long on solemnity. This held true for the Anglicans and their offshoot the Methodists (Irish Anglicanism was extremely low church without being extremely evangelical), as well as for the Presbyterians. To the extent that theology influenced the pastoral sermons, the layman had his ears filled with an attenuated Calvinism in the Presbyterian churches, and a valitudinarian Puritanism in the Anglican. Still, the churches keyed the Islandmagee layman into an awareness of a permanent celestial order which transcended his immediate life on earth.

Crucially, individual acts committed in this world had consequences in the next (precisely what consequence depended upon the brand of theology involved). The churches, therefore, were important in articulating and reinforcing the community's moral standards. As noted in Chapter Eight, serious crime was virtually non-existent on the Island, and as the Ordnance Surveyer noted in the late 1830's, "the entire population bear a character, to which they are just [sic] entitled—namely of being remarkably honest. They are very punctual in fulfilling their engagements and fair in their dealings and transactions. Theft is virtually unknown among [them] and a dishonest act is held in extreme abhorrence."[26] Granted, to some extent their honesty and lack of social violence may have been taught to the Islanders by their pastors. Perhaps. But I would suggest that in this case there was a congruity between many of the Christian virtues and the social characteristics that made a rural society run smoothly. Thus, rather than introducing a higher morality the clergymen actually were giving religious sanction and reinforcement to a pattern of social morality that would have been practiced even without the invocation of Christian theology.

That this is the case is affirmed by noting those instances in which the demands of Christian morality conflicted with the Islanders' social predisposition. One has been mentioned already: fornication. This is explicitly against the Christian code. Yet, as we have seen, at a conservative estimate one-fifth of the women getting married were pregnant, or believed that they were. The proportion who had had pre-marital sexual relations must have been much higher, perhaps in the forty to sixty per cent range. How did the churches deal with this deviation from Christian norms? By denouncing the practice (sometimes by explicitly naming the offenders before the congregation), and inevitably, by quietly surrendering, baptizing the offspring, and continuing the parents in communion.

Another issue was the Sabbath. Ulster Protestantism always has had a strong sabbatarian streak. It may not have been quite as strong on Islandmagee as in the small towns,[27] but it was strong. Yet, in the late 1830's not only could the Presbyterian clergy not keep the Islanders out of the public houses on Sunday, they could not even prevent them from getting drunk between the twice-Sunday services![28] And in the less rambunctious days of the early twentieth century, the caterers to the rapidly-developing tourist trade closed on Sunday, but opened for "old friends," one rationalization being that "I never have been asked to entertain them on a Sabbath before so this is an exception and I am sure the good Lord understands."[29] Doubtless he did.

In addition to clearly articulating and giving the sanctification of religion to much of the Islandmagee social-moral code, the churches helped to bond together members of the Island community. This was especially true of the Presbyterian churches. Calvinism is a religion of the elect. The Islanders were set apart geographically and were distinct culturally, and the religious cognate of their separateness was a faith that allowed them to think of themselves as elect spiritually. And, in a more general manner, the common Protestantism of the Islanders served both as an expression of their cultural oneness and as a reinforcement of that identity.

From the viewpoint of social status, Presbyterianism was ideally suited to the Islandmagee community. As discussed in earlier chapters on economic and social life, there were no gentry and thus there was no social pyramid. The only exceptions were the Presbyterian clergy, whose education entitled them to a special status.[30] The social equality of the Island society was replicated in the ecclesiastical democracy of the Presbyterian polity: each Presbyterian church was essentially self-governing, with the clergyman being merely the first among equals. As in secular life, so in religious.

The institutional details of Islandmagee religious life will be discussed in Chapter Ten; here the point concerns the contribution to the Islanders' cosmology made by religion, and one can only be impressed by how well the religious system fitted with the realities of their social and economic life. How, indeed, could they *not* be religious when religion worked so well? And since religion reflected so accurately the visible world, it was only sensible to trust its depiction of the invisible.

Important as it was in shaping the Islanders' mental geography, religion was not alone. Formal schooling was important, and obvious as it seems, this is easy to overlook. Whether or not a culture is predominantly literate or illiterate is extremely important in determining the horizons of that culture. The earliest indication of the degree of literacy on the Island is found in the lease renewals which fell due for almost the entire Island in the 1820's. At that time, 35.9 per cent of the signatures on the leases (including those of witnesses) were by mark.[31] The overall illiteracy rate doubtless was higher than this figure, because the leaseholding farmers were more apt to be literate than were the cottagers, and because leases most often were signed by men, who in traditional societies are more likely than women to be literate. A forty to fifty per cent illiteracy rate in the 1820's would be a tolerable supposition. (This agrees reasonably closely with the all-Ulster illiteracy rate of forty-four per cent in 1841; the national rate in that year was fifty-three per cent.)[32]

Historians have made much of the thirst for schooling of the lowland Scots, and one would expect the Antrim Scots to possess the same drive. Given this expectation, the Islandmagee illiteracy rate is surprisingly high. Apparently the Islanders in the first three or four decades of the nineteenth century were at a cultural ebb. Not that they did not have schools: in the 1830's no less than ten schools were in operation, supported entirely by the fees paid by parents. But of the ten schoolmasters, only one was reported capable of teaching English grammar, geography, and mathematics, and he was usually drunk. Of the others, scarcely one could write legibly. They taught the three Rs and nothing else. After collecting information on the state of education in the early days of the Islandmagee settlement, the Ordnance Surveyor concluded that schooling on the Island was as backward in the 1830's as it had been in the late seventeenth century, if not more so.[33]

The corner was turned in 1836, when the Islanders first put a school into connection with the national system of education which had been founded in 1831, and which was administered from Dublin.[34] The result was revolutionary: by 1881 only 4.8 per cent of those five years of age and above were illiterate. This compared to an Ulster figure of twenty per cent and an all-Ireland rate of twenty-five per cent.[35]

Certainly the national schools were significant in teaching elementary literacy and mathematical skills, but their real importance lay not in the functional skills they taught, but elsewhere. The transformation of Islandmagee from a just-barely literate society into one in which all but a tiny minority were literate greatly expanded the Island's cultural perimeters. Now almost every Islander came into contact with the standard West British culture, as defined by the commissioners of national education in Dublin, and with the London-dominated culture that enswirled the local newspapers (for example, a high proportion of the items in the Larne weekly paper came from London sources).

Yet—and this is crucial—the control and curriculum of the schools were arranged so as not to threaten the fundamental values of the local culture. Management of the local schools (including choice of teachers and control over the timetable) was in community hands. The largest schools were under the management of the Presbyterian churches with the individual clergymen as trustees. This meant that the very same people whom the Islanders recognized as their leaders in other fields controlled the local schools.

Further, the curriculum of the national schools, while

neutral as among Christian denominations, prescribed texts that were full of Bible stories and crammed with moral lessons. Children were taught in the *First Book of Lessons* that God is love and sent his Son to save mankind. In the *Second Book* the story of creation was given, and in the *Fourth,* the birth and work of Christ were covered. Thus, the teachers automatically mixed literary and religious instruction. In addition, the national school texts taught basic lessons of social behaviour, such as the virtue of telling the truth, the need for cleanliness, and the desirability of boys and girls being good and kind to their parents. The result was that although the national schools greatly expanded the boundaries of the Island's culture, they did so in a manner that did not undercut the fundamental religious and social patterns of the local society. Great changes were effected on the veneer of society (especially in the regrettable stifling of the Lallans vernacular), but bedrock matters were not touched.[36]

An analogous influence on the Island culture—involving an expansion of cultural parameters without threatening the social cohesion—was the sea trade. The Ordnance Surveyer reported that in the 1830's eighteen to twenty Islanders were either owners or part owners of boats in the coasting trade, and that because of the need to fill crews, almost every Island family sent at least one member to sea.[37] (Presumably the estimate included small fishing boats.) As Belfast evolved into a major shipping port and then into a major shipbuilding centre, the Islandmagee seaman tended to turn to long distance seafaring. In the early twentieth century it was estimated that every third or fourth family (here the meaning clearly was nuclear family) had a member in the merchant marine.[38]

The seamen influenced Islandmagee's culture in three ways. First (albeit least important), they provided figures for enshrinement in Island folklore. In the middle third of the nineteenth century, Islanders still were telling tales about three eighteenth-century Islandmagee men who had become admirals in the Royal Navy. One, Robert Symington, had been sent to sea as punishment for maiming a horse by pulling the hair from its tail, but subsequently had made good; another, Robert Brice, who later changed his name to Kingsmill upon marrying an English fortune, was the great grandson (through an illegitimate line) of Edward Brice, supposedly the first Presbyterian minister in Ireland; the third was Charles Hudson, a farmer's son who was a protege of Admiral Kingsmill (mentioned above) and distinguished himself in fighting against the Americans during their war of independence.[39] Later in the century the name of William Hoy became part of local legend. Hoy was an Island seaman with a good deal of experience on the Great Lakes of North America. In the late spring of 1875 he was on board a White Star Line liner as a passenger (he had decided to emigrate to Canada) when the ship fetched up on a sunken reef off the coast of Nova Scotia. Many passengers were lost, but of those who remained alive, Hoy dominated the scene. An expert swimmer, he contrived to get a rope between the wreck and the great rocks that lay nearby. Then, seeing that most of the remaining passengers were too weak to make the passage to safety unaided, he lay for hours on a rock in the freezing surf and helped them across. When his hands became immobilized with cold, he used his teeth upon their clothing to pull them to safety. Altogether he saved about one hundred lives.[40]

Second, through their correspondence home, the seamen introduced an almost palpable contact with foreign parts. By their nature, these personal items were evanescent, but one set of merchantman's letters, those of Captain Samuel Smiley of Ballypriormore, have survived and are in the Public Record Office of Northern Ireland. Smiley was a ship's master who during the 1850's sailed large vessels from Liverpool to the American cotton ports and to the combat harbours of the Crimean War. The interesting thing is that he wrote to his family (usually his brother) at least fortnightly, telling them of his activities. On some occasions he gave his opinions on various family matters (which implies that he was being kept informed of matters at home) and on others he told of meeting on his travels other Islanders in the merchant service. The orientation of the letters is significant, for although Smiley sailed the world, the centre of his universe clearly was Islandmagee. His letters, therefore, expanded the world view of the people at home, but did not in any way unsettle it.[41]

Third, by their conversation while at home—either between voyages or after retirement—the seamen directly influenced the content of the local culture.[42] The result was an impressive but almost bizarre mixture of parochialism and cosmopolitanism. (This mixture persists to this day: I have heard Islanders in a pub discussing one minute the boundary line between the local townlands of Balloo and Ballymuldrogh, the next arguing about the location of various brothels in Kuala Lumpur, and the next talking about the character of their local clergyman). The seamen helped make the Islanders aware of the configuration of the outside world, but without undercutting the integrity of the local culture.

The tourist trade probably did the same thing. Tourism had begun early on the Island: as early as 1796 one finds an advertisement in the *Northern Star* for a "neat cabin" to be let on Brown's Bay, Islandmagee, during the bathing season.[43] But it was not until the recreational development activities of the Midland Railway (NCC) in the 1890's that tourism became an important part of the local economy and a significant influence on local social life. Large numbers from Belfast came to Islandmagee for day excursions and for longer holidays. Other visitors came from elsewhere in Ireland and from Scotland. Occasionally, trippers came from London.[44] Undeniably, the visitors made the Islanders better acquainted with external cultures that they previously had known only vaguely, and to some extent this was potentially disruptive. But notice the context. Visitors were coming to Islandmagee to share something the Islanders possessed: impressive scenery, a bracing climate, rural peace. In so doing they were affirming to the Islanders that Islandmagee was something special, a place of worth. So, while expanding awareness of the outside world the tourists implicitly were strengthening the Islanders' belief in the value of their own tiny parish.[45]

(3)

Here let me change focus. I began the preceding section by talking about religion, sets of beliefs and attitudes which were related both to the visible world and to the invisible. Now let me discuss superstitions, concepts which also combined observations of the tangible world with beliefs about the intangible. Although for analytic convenience I am discussing them separately, the whole range of beliefs, religious and superstitious, Christian and pagan, concerning the tangible and the intangible, overlapped.

Islandmagee was famous in the eighteenth century as the source of a notorious witch trial. In 1710, the widow of a former Presbyterian minister, living at Knowehead, Islandmagee, began to be pestered by extra-physical occurrences, such as stones thrown at her by an unseen agency, her bedclothes being inexplicably molested, and a strange, "dead" cat that moved about. These and other torments continued for months. A relative of the widow had come to stay with the old lady after her husband's death, and she too was struck by a strange, apparently bewitched, illness. She fell into fits and had visions, in which eventually she named four Islandmagee women as responsible for the unnatural occurrences. In March of 1711 the four women were arrested, sent to Carrickfergus jail, and bound over for trial. The mysterious attacks continued, but now involved other persons, especially those who were prosecuting the alleged witches. The prisoners were not legally represented. The two judges on the case disagreed, one directing acquittal, the other conviction. The jury brought in a verdict of guilty and the women were sentenced to twelve months' imprisonment, plus four appearances in the public pillory.[46]

Precisely how strong the belief in witchcraft was in the nineteenth and twentieth centuries is uncertain, but there is no doubt that many of the Islanders worried about it. The Ordnance Surveyer, writing in the late 1830's, stated:[47]

> In no part of Ireland are the people more generally and inveterately superstitious than here. Most of the better educated class implicitly believe in witchcraft, fairies, brownies and enchantments and there are few who are not perfectly convinced of the guilt of the unfortunate individuals convicted of witchcraft alleged to have been committed here in 1711. The utmost attention is paid to dreams and to omens. Many have seen the Devil in the shape of a pig or a black dog. The house in which the witchcraft alluded to was enacted... is still considered as haunted, and though inhabited, many, even men, will not pass it alone, at night. In a house in Balloo, strange noises have been heard and in several parts of the parish, the Fairies have been seen and their music has been heard. Many old women practice card cutting and cup tossing, telling fortunes and interpreting dreams.

Well into the twentieth century it was common practice for Islanders to place a "witch stone" (also called a "luck stone" or "fairy stone") in the cattle byre. This was usually about the size of a goose egg and was suspended over the cow's head. According to Islanders, its purpose was simple: "It kept the cows from being bewitched"; "Anyone who practiced the black arts had no power...."[48] Perhaps for some, hanging the witch stone was simply a ritual piece of good-luck wishing, like hanging a horse shoe over a door in North America, but for many the fears—of unspecified evil forces, if not witches in particular—must have been real and unsettling.

In Chapter Three I noted that a silver coin had to be put into the pail of a newly freshened cow to guarantee its milking bountifully. Similarly, a person who called in on a neighbour who was churning (making butter) had to wish good-luck to the churner. To some people this must have been merely benign custom, continued into the twentieth century by force of habit. But there is one case from the first quarter of this century in which a woman was convinced that a visitor who had failed to wish her the luck of the churn had taken away her luck. She had recourse to a charm, obtained from her grandmother, which when combined with mystic movements of the branch of a particular tree or shrub broke the evil spell.[49]

The same tension, the same fear of evil, led to other unusual methods of protection. Thus an Islandmagee farm wife was known to protect against evil befalling her cows by ritually strewing the threshold of the byre with marigolds on May eve. In another case, a farmer used ritual purification by fire to deal with the evil spirits which might hover about his newborn calves. He had two helpers swing the calf back and forth over a burning wisp of hay or straw, and then passed a similar fire three times under and over the dam. A crowing hen was looked upon as a particularly evil omen, and trouble could be avoided only by catching the offending bird while it was crowing and twisting off its head. The first two practices mentioned above date from the late nineteenth or early twentieth century, and the third is reported in the 1920's.[50]

Obviously, even in the early twentieth century, the belief in the ability to influence human events by preternatural means remained widespread. Recall at this point the discussion of folk medicine in Chapter Six, which involved a mixture of common-sense remedies with supernatural cures. Note then that even in the 1920's there were at least half a dozen individuals, and probably more, who claimed to be able to cure diseases by charms and incantations.[51] According to an old Islandman, speaking in the 1960's, "Some people said the people who had charms practiced the works of the devil, but this was not true."[52]

To some extent the Islanders' superstitions and their recourse to magic seem fanciful, but in some instances they were not. Within the context of their lives, these beliefs and practices made sense. They recognized that the material world in which they lived could not be controlled by mere mechanical forces, so they turned to preternatural ones. In postulating a world of invisible forces, they were only following the direction (if not the details) of the Christian religion, for Christianity is nothing if not supernatural in character. Reference to the supernatural was intellectually reassuring, if not perhaps completely satisfying, for it provided explanations of occurrences that otherwise were inexplicable. And in performing rituals against evil and ill-fortune, they were at least reducing their anxiety about the unknown future. The magical practices may have been inefficacious, but they were comforting.

The alliance of superstition, Christianity, and practicality was clearly shown in local wake customs. Wakes have since disappeared on Islandmagee, but in the early twentieth century they were still carried on in much the same fashion as in the early nineteenth century.[53] Whenever a person died, the chamber was tidied but the ashes in the grate were left, not to be removed until the corpse was carried from the house (the equation of the hearth fire and life is obvious). The carpenter was sent for, and he measured the body, dressed it, and went off to make the coffin. Blinds were drawn, windows opened slightly, mirrors in the house were shrouded, and the house was quiet all day until the wake began at night. Then friends, relatives, and neighbours called at the house. During the evening the minister invariably called. The wake went on all night (and in some cases two nights). Clay pipes and tobacco were supplied for men and tea for the ladies. There is no indication of music or entertainment, but a good deal of heavy drinking took place. Although strongly denounced by moral reformers, the wakes served the dual purpose of affirming community solidarity in the face of death, and more practically, of tiring the grieving family so they could fall asleep.

Next day, if the graveyard was nearby, the coffin was placed on a bier and carried to the churchyard. Otherwise a horse drawn hearse was used. The funeral procession moved in time-honoured order. Near relations walked directly behind the hearse or bier, then friends and acquaintances. Those following occupied the whole width of the road, moving slowly to one side to enable other traffic to pass. When the graveyard was reached, the coffin was removed from the hearse or bier, placed on the shoulders of chosen pallbearers, and carried to the grave, where the Christian service for the burial of the dead was read.

At the graveside service the minister, and sometimes the doctor and the hearse driver, wore specially-made mourning scarves. These were elaborate talismans tailored especially for each funeral, usually by the draper's shop in nearby Ballycarry. The scarves were made either from a length of black crepe, or of fine white linen about four yards long, pleated, and folded in two lengthwise. At the fold was a complicated rosette of silk. Another bow was sewn about a foot from the bottom. A colour code indicated the status of the deceased: black material with white ribbons for an elderly woman, and black ribbon and black material for an elderly man; white linen with white silk ribbons for a child or young unmarried person, and white linen with black ribbons for young or middle aged married people. Not only did the minister wear one of these scarves (which certainly were not of Christian origin) at the burial service, but the scarf was laid over the side of the pulpit, to the right of the clergyman, at the first Sunday service after the funeral.

After the committal service the grave was filled. Friends left slowly; the family waited until the end and then returned to the bereaved's home for a substantial meal. Usually the minister came too, and in the evening friends quietly dropped in for a short visit.[54] So death was met: with a measure of superstition (not removing the ashes, shrouding the mirrors and wrapping the funerary officers with talismanic scarves), with a Christian service, with some practicality (the bereaved family was carried through the days immediately following death by a pre-determined social and religious ritual), and with an affirmation of community solidarity.

Given the rich array of practices related to the invisible world, it is only natural to expect that the Islanders of the last century had an entire code of beliefs about ghosts, fairies, and spirits, as well as about witches. Doubtless they did, but unfortunately they have left almost no trace. Dixon Donaldson in writing his local history in the 1920's referred to the many accounts of other-worldly visitations he had heard from his grandfather's time, but recorded only one of these, the story of the Castle Chester ghost.[55] Hence, although one can infer the existence of beliefs in spirits, ghosts, and fairies, from the practices used to dispel them, the precise nature of the other-world creatures cannot be determined.

One reason that the details of the Islanders' superstitions do not survive is that they were not embodied in a distinctive folklore. Indeed, in contrast to many parts of Ireland, Islandmagee did not possess a codified folklore, certainly not like the elaborate trains of tales found in the west of Ireland. This is not surprising, because the immigrant culture from which the Islanders stemmed was a dislocated one, being an amalgamation of lowland Scots and English settlers, all of whom had severed their cultural roots to emigrate to Ulster. The Island folklore, then, consisted of randomly collected anecdotes involving Island people, but having no roots in a mythic past.

The most vivid bit of folklore preserved by the Islanders reflects badly upon them. It was a piece of false history, the false history of a non-existent massacre. According to oral tradition, in January 1642 (N.S.), in the midst of the flaring Irish civil war, the Protestant garrison at Carrickfergus butchered the Catholic inhabitants of Islandmagee. Some were supposed to have been killed at a place called Slaughterford (the opportunities for false etymology are obvious) and the rest thrown over the Gobbins cliffs. Claims of the numbers allegedly massacred went as high as three thousand. Such was the Islanders' tradition in the early nineteenth century, when the great antiquarian Samuel McSkimin patiently demolished it. Actually at most fifty Catholics were killed, and none were driven over the cliffs.[56] But the old story lived. It was reported in the late 1830's by the Ordnance Surveyor as being the only remarkable event of which there was either local record or tradition.[57] It continued to be repeated throughout the nineteenth century, and in the 1920's Dixon Donaldson, the local historian, carefully marshalled evidence and tried to banish it once and for all.[58] Yet the story seems indestructible. Reference to it has been incorporated in an Orange folksong ("and the Fenians blood ran down like water, from Belfast Lough, right to the Irish sea."), and as late as the mid-1960's, the usually accurate *Shell Guide* reprinted the tale of the Gobbin cliff massacre as gospel truth.[59] Clearly, the people of Islandmagee kept the story alive because it served some need. In part the false history lived because the inhabitants of any area naturally prize anything that makes their homeland distinctive. In part the massacre story survived because it was memorable: the truth is usually harder to remember than is a vivid story. But something else was also at play, keeping the tale alive. The anti-Catholicism of an impacted Protestant community must have been contributory. And in a more general sense, the instinctive exclusiveness of an isolated parish was involved: the cleansing of the community of alien elements left a pure community. A tiny, rural *herrenvolk* myth had been established.

(4)

Another facet of the Islanders' cosmology involved time. In addition to the agrarian calendar (discussed in Chapter Three) they had a cultural calendar that was a mixture of community social ritual, Christian celebration, and pagan custom. The year can be thought of as beginning a week or two before Christmas. At that time mummers' plays were put on. Although known as "Christmas Rhymers," or Christmas mummers, the players and their plays actually had little to do with the Christian celebration. They were death-and-revival plays which harkened to the aboriginal Indo-European celebration of the winter solstice rather than the Semitic tradition of the Messiah. In any case, these plays were part of a compact regional tradition which prevailed with minor variations in south-east Antrim, including Ballyclare, Larne, Kilwaughter, and Ballycarry, as well as Islandmagee. How long the tradition of winter mumming lasted in Islandmagee is uncertain, but in nearby Ballycarry the rhymes still were being performed (albeit after a hiatus of several years) in the mid-1960's.

A typical play went like this: the presenter of a group of mummers, eight to fourteen in number, knocked at the door of a farmhouse. When granted admission he called in the first two players, Prince George and the Turkey (Turkish) Champion. They were dressed in militaristic gear, with swords in hand. They fought and the Turkey Champion fell slain. Enter the Turkey Champion's Mother. She, like all the characters, was played by a man. She called a Doctor and he raised her son. Thereafter, the play became a dramatic shambles, with an expandable number of costumed characters passing through, saying short pieces— Cromwell, St. Patrick, Jack Straw, and Beelzebub, to name just some. All this was done in rhyme, and the entire performance took only five or ten minutes. At the end the performers usually joined hands, sang a Christmas carol and collected their gratuity.

The form of the play is interesting because, as noted above, its central structure had nothing to do with the Christian celebration of Christmas. The singing of the carol at the end and a casual mention of Christmas by one of the minor characters were merely peripheral additions. It is also interesting because of its origin. Despite the south-east Antrim area's being overwhelmingly Scottish in ethnic origin, it has been decisively argued that the plays were English in origin, probably coming from northern England in the seventeenth century. The rhymes used in the plays took on Lallans vernacular patterns, and peculiarly Irish characters were introduced, but the fundamental structure remained English.[60]

Christmas itself was not celebrated in an unusual fashion and few distinctive local customs were attached to it.

New Year's Day, on the other hand, was a day of omens. The things done on this day influenced, by magical analogy, the events of the coming year. (The following practices and superstititions were alive in the twentieth century, so the variety extant in the nineteenth must have been rich indeed.) In particular, dark forces had to be propitiated or avoided. If the first person to enter a house on New Year's Day was fair, that was bad luck. Entry of a dark person was welcome. It was especially fortunate if the first visitor brought in a black object, and there is a recorded case of an Islandmagee woman who would buy a bag of slack coal to be delivered on New Year's Day, just to guarantee her protection from ill fortune for the coming year. Similarly, men refused to cleanse themselves on New Year's, an abstinence recommended in local rhyme:

> If you wash on New Year's Day
> You are washing a friend away.

Ashes could be removed from the hearth only in the afternoon. One did not work or lend on New Year's Day. And it was especially bad luck to meet a cross-eyed girl or to turn away a beggar. On the morning of the first day of the year, Muldersleigh Hill was visited by fairies.[61]

The next major day on the traditional calendar was Easter, but that, like Christmas, was celebrated in a traditional Christian fashion and, it appears, in quite a restrained way.

May Day was livelier. In part the day was important for economic reasons: the half-year's rent was due, and by local custom cattle were changed from one grazing pasture to another. As for superstitions, they were mostly related to love and marriage, which is not surprising, given the association of springtime and fertility. The Islanders said that the first one in the family at the well would be the luckiest one and that any girl washing her face in the May Morn dew would become beautiful. A rhyme said by young girls encapsulated another belief:

> Ye yarrow, yarrow I pull thee—
> And under my pillow I'll put thee

>And the first young man that speaks to me,
>Will my own true love be.

These fertility-related superstitions were practiced in the twentieth century and were largely free of fears about evil fortune.[62] Not so a century earlier, when May Day was associated with evil spirits. Then it was the Islandmagee practice to strew the March Marigold (known locally as the May-Flower) on the doorsteps and thresholds of farmers' barns and byres to deter ill-intent of fairies and prevent evil spells for the next twelve months.[63]

Through the 1870's and '80's All Hallow's Eve was a well-marked day; thereafter it declined. Some of the celebrating was benign, involving simple games played by young and old. But the Devil was supposed to be abroad that night and it was a half-serious, half-facetious fear of him that prompted some activities: for example it was said that if you ran around a corn stalk a certain number of times while uttering an incantation, you were sure to meet him. Young people worked themselves into a delicious fright tempting the Evil One, and practical jokers costumed themselves satanically to scare the unwary.[64]

(5)

Stepping back now to reflect on the Islanders' culture and their cosmology, one has to be struck with several characteristics: first those of the cosmology which dealt both with the visible and the invisible world. The invisible was filled with both Christian beliefs and superstitions. The visible world was crammed with social customs, and while being intensely parochial was simultaneously expansive, and able to assimilate outside elements. Second, the self-consistency of the culture was remarkable. Almost all the components fitted well with each other. Third, the culture joined smoothly with the economic and social system. Finally, as a result of the preceding three characteristics, the culture was notably self-confident. You could always tell an Islander, but he could tell you a lot and would.

Chapter Ten. A Cohesive Culture—II. Social Life And Institutions

(1)

Much of the informal social culture of Islandmagee was evanescent and left no historical record, but that does not negate its significance. Naturally, in a family-oriented society the evenings sitting in the kitchen were more common and more important than the more spectacular community-wide celebrations. In an agrarian society, many social events took place as footnotes to economic activities such as harvests, markets, and fairs (they are discussed in Chapter Three). And in a society which took drink with such enthusiasm, many evenings were of course spent in public houses.

From the early nineteenth century onwards, the Islanders' social life seems to have become more and more "respectable" if not less lively. The Ordnance Surveyor, writing in the late 1830's, noted that:[1]

> "More time was formerly devoted to, and more money expended in amusement than now. The principal check given to their extreme fondness for recreation, chiefly for dancing and attending fairs, was in the decline of the wages for spinning, consequent on the introduction of mill spun yarn about the year 1832."

Not that things were dull, even then, for the surveyor adumbrated the amusements which survived in the late

1830's, all of which were said to be of a "Scottish character." Dancing was the favourite. "Punch dances" were held in public houses, and dances in farmers' barns still occurred, although not as frequently as in the past. Organized recreational shoots at poultry—chiefly geese and turkeys—were put on at Christmas. Also a form of gambling, involving card-playing for the fowl, took place. At Easter, the Islanders spent a day or two at cockfighting and drinking. "Churns," that is, harvest celebrations, took place in the fall. Quiltings were common, the work beginning at the middle of the day and concluding with dancing that was kept up until an early hour the next morning. A favourite amusement was "sitting up" with a couple who had just had a baby. Invited guests only were welcome and the company sat up all night with the couple, celebrating and amusing themselves. A more general form of evening party was termed a "tea party," which through Islandmagee clanishness usually was limited to members of a single family connection.[2]

As the century progressed, and Islandmagee came increasingly into contact with external cultures, the rough edges were smoothed off the Islanders' social life and they took on some of the trappings of Victorian middle class respectability. Thus, we find in 1870, that a benefit "soiree" was held at the Mullaghdubh national school, with readings, recitations, tea, and some music.[3] And in 1876, we read of James Milliken of Islandmagee giving a recitation "in a tasteful and happy style" at the "soiree and ball" of the Ballycarry young men's dancing class, the event being held at the Ballycarry Agricultural National School.[4] So the soiree and the ball replaced the dance in the Islanders' lexicon, but not all the energy went out of the proceedings. For example in 1893 one finds that when the "Islandmagee quadrille class," a group which for several years met in the Orange Hall, gave its annual meeting, "after tea, dancing commenced and was carried on with vigour until an early hour the following morning."[5] Yet, even granting that the lads danced with enthusiasm and doubtless drank more than tea, one cannot deny that the affairs were becoming increasingly modern in character. The old dances, step dances and hornpipes, were replaced by the new steps imported by the dancing classes, so that at a soiree and ball held in the Islandmagee Orange Hall in 1910, a special feature was the performance of the old dances which "quite charmed the younger generation of the company who are not now so familiar with such dances..."[6]

Similarly, boat racing, originally a rough, spontaneous sport for local fishermen, became a formalized, respectable activity, dominated by recreational sailors. In fact, in the early twentieth century the annual Portmuck regatta was sufficiently prestigious socially to rate the local M.P. as a vice president. The card was dominated by six polite sailing events, one race for motor boats, and only one for rowing boats.[7] An annual Brownsbay regatta also prospered, and for a time regattas were held at Blackhead and at the Cove on the east coast.[8]

This same mixture of vigorous community life with increasingly cloying politeness in form and terminology, is seen in the introduction of "fetes" for school children. In 1908 an annual fete, held during the August holidays, was established at Millbay. The young people, both summer visitors and residents, tumbled over each other fighting for prizes donated by merchants and residents. The usual booths and tea tables that one would find at an English vicarage party were in operation.[9] A similar children's fete was established for the other side of Islandmagee, at Mullaghboy, in 1909. This one took place in the committee rooms of the Portmuck regatta committee, and included music by the Islandmagee flute band and dancing until an advanced hour in the evening.[10]

Thus, by the early twentieth century Islandmagee's social culture had been substantially transformed, even though its energy remained undiminished. When in 1906 the music pupils of the brave Mrs. Gibb gave a concert, it was not a concert of traditional music, but of a miniature symphony, and the instruments were not the traditional ones, but the piano, violin, and (yes) a solitary "cymbal" made from a tea tray![11] Other social events were of an improving or informative character, such as lectures by returned missionaries on the vice, error, and appalling darkness of the Africans, or by returned travellers on the presumably less appalling state of the inhabitants of the United States and Canada.[12]

Responsibility for the modulation in the character of the Island's social life, from almost entirely parochial to a mixture of parochial and international social conventions, in part lies with the educational system. Literacy brought an awareness of extra-parochial norms that previously had been unknown, and the West British attitudes inculcated by the school system fostered a desire to emulate national social conventions.

In part, individual personalities were responsible for bringing about the change. The Rev. R.H. Shaw, minister of the Second Islandmagee Presbyterian Church, was the Island's dominant social personality during the second half of the nineteenth century. During his ministry, which ran the unusual length of thirty-nine years, from 1853 to 1892 inclusive, he was a central figure in many of the Island's voluntary social organizations.

At about the turn of the century, a triumvirate was formed that dominated local social life. It consisted of the leading schoolmaster on the Island, Dixon Donaldson, the more prominent Presbyterian clergyman, the Reverend David Steen, and the Ballycarry dispensary doctor, Charles Dundee. Each of these was a man of education and of strong will. The most important of the three as far as Islandmagee's social life was concerned was Donaldson. He was born in 1866. His father had been the principal of the Kilcoan National School on the Island, and at the age of twelve the younger Donaldson became a monitor in the same school. After his training, he held various posts, becoming principal of Mullaghboy National School at age twenty-four. He succeeded his father as principal of Kilcoan

National School in 1895, and held that post until 1931. Known by the traditional Irish sobriquet as "The Master," he acquired a great influence in the Island's social life through his teaching activities. This influence was considerably augmented by his having inherited his father's mantle, so that he had an imputed power not only over those whom he had taught directly, but also over his father's former pupils. Donaldson's influence, however, stemmed as much from his active intelligence and amazing energy as from his educational position. He knew more about the Island's history than the rest of its inhabitants combined (his history of Islandmagee is a very impressive piece of amateur work), he was an expert on sailing, knew carpentry and joinery, was a guide to the Belfast Naturalists Field Club, and at the drop of a suggestion was willing to organize almost anything.[13]

His friendly rival was the Reverend David Steen of First Islandmagee Presbyterian Church. Steen was slightly older than Donaldson. He had taken a B.A. at Queen's in 1874, had been licensed in the same year by the Belfast presbytery, and was ordained to First Islandmagee in 1877. He was a great figure of a man, with flowing beard and stentorian voice. Islandmagee was the only charge he ever had, for he stayed in the same pulpit until his retirement in 1931.[14] The people accepted him not only as a religious leader, but as a head of voluntary secular causes as well, and one continually finds his name on the organizing committees of civic functions. His devotion to the Islanders matched theirs to him, and is exemplified in a story that began to go the rounds in the early 1920's (the truth of the story is irrelevant to the point at hand, namely his status in the community). About 1920 a red-hot Ulster American evangelist visited Islandmagee. He frightened the people with the emotion of his preaching, but they were buoyed by seeing the Rev. Steen in the congregation. The evangelist got right down among the people and demanded, "Everyone who wants to go to heaven, stand up." No one rose, for the Islandmagee people were not used to this kind of yelling. Vexed, the evangelist turned on Steen and cried "Don't you want to go to heaven?" Steen replied, "Aye, but I've been with these people fifty years now and I'll be happy to go wherever they do."[15]

In voluntary civic activities which appertained to a larger area than Islandmagee, Steen and Donaldson were joined by Dr. Charles Dundee who lived just across Larne Lough from Islandmagee, in the townland of Red Hall. For fifty-two years, prior to his death in an automobile accident in 1934, Dundee was the dispensary medical officer at Ballycarry, the post which served Islandmagee, and after the passing of the Local Government Act in 1898, he became the area's medical officer of health as well (both were part-time posts). His wife was an Islandmagee woman, and so although his leadership in sporting and agricultural affairs centred on Ballycarry, he always had close ties with events in Islandmagee.[16]

Now, an important point about the triumvirate of social leaders is that in addition to having considerable intelligence and a strong personality, each was an educated man. This meant that they were much more likely than the average Islander to prefer "refined" entertainments and to be acquainted with the social conventions of the outside world. Further—and this is a crucial link to my later discussion of institutional life—these men were functionaries of the most important formal institutions in Islandmagee, namely the church, the schools, and local government. Because they were civil functionaries in their professional lives, they had an investment in probity and decorum prevailing in Island life, in a way in which, say, a small farmer would not. All this helps explain why, even though it remained lively, from the late nineteenth century onwards Islandmagee's social life lost many of its rough edges and many of its distinctive local characteristics.

At its best, the system of voluntary social participation headed by local luminaries could produce civic engagement far more satisfactory than would have been given to local governmental agencies. For example, a voluntary local committee organized a dazzling celebration of Edward VII's coronation, with bonfires, entertainment, and medals for the children.[17] The same sort of committee did very well in channelling local energies into Red Cross work during World War I.[18] But when the voluntary system faltered, it fell very flat indeed. To the great embarrassment of Dixon Donaldson, the committee he headed to provide a memorial for the dead of World War I split hopelessly about the location of the memorial. Subscriptions had to be refunded,[19] and ultimately the only public monument set up for the dead of that War was a simple church tablet.

Despite the considerable evidence that the social life of Islandmagee became markedly less parochial in form in the late nineteenth and early twentieth century, one should not forget that it remained intensely local as far as the identity of the participants was concerned. This was still the age of the bicycle, the cart, the horse and trap, and "shank's mare," and even for special sports or planned recreations they generally would not go more than five miles from home. Soon this localism was to dissolve: in 1918 the first Islander bought a motorcar.[20]

(2)

Up to this point I have discussed the cultural and social life of Islandmagee without referring to the structure of formal institutions such as the churches and schools. This is not just a matter of expository convenience, but of substance. In a society such as Islandmagee, formal institutions should be discussed last because they are much less important for an understanding of how the society worked than are economic patterns, family structure, and the belief-system of the inhabitants. The formal institutions did impinge upon the communal culture, but to a remarkable extent they were shaped by the culture and assimilated by it. However, because the functionaries of formal institutions commonly leave behind copious records, historians often have taken the path of least resistance and given primacy to administrative material about the formal institutions—especially churches and schools—and implied that these agencies by themselves formed the local culture. I hope that in my describing these agencies as they operated on Islandmagee, it is clear to the reader that they performed only subsidiary roles in a very complex cultural and social system.

Even so, let me begin discussing formal institutions by mentioning those that were least important: voluntary associations such as lodges and orders. In practice, the voluntary formal social groups were three: the Loyal Orange Institutions, the Masonic Order, and the Order of Good Templars. None of them was very powerful.

Predictably, the Orange Order was not strong. It was an institution with a twofold purpose, neither of which was relevant to Islandmagee: to bond divergent Protestant factions together and to protect Protestant interests against real or imagined threats from Roman Catholics. In Islandmagee, however, there was no need to bond divergent Protestant interests, since Presbyterianism overwhelmingly prevailed. And there were no conceivable threats from Catholics. Thus, Islandmagee did not have a lodge until 1869, seven decades after the Order's foundation. The Order here acted less like the Orange Order elsewhere than as a fraternal society of men who liked to meet with each other on a social basis. Its real strength lay in the personality of R.H. Shaw, minister of the Second Islandmagee Presbyterian Church from 1853 to 1892, who was mentioned earlier (p. 148). Shaw was an able secessionist clergyman who had been influenced in his youth by the indomitable Dr. Henry Cooke. He was called to the Second Islandmagee charge in 1853, at age twenty-seven. As a clergyman his forte was the sermon and he enjoyed public oratory. His early life in Raloo and Belfast had made him an ardent loyalist and he soon became the ornament of the Islandmagee L.O.L. no. 1962, for he was prominent in public celebrations:[21]

His services were much in demand on the anniversaries of the Battle of the Boyne. It was not unusual on such occasions, should it be sweltering sunshine, when Mr. Shaw was called upon to address the assembly, to see him step forward, calmly divest himself of collar and coat, leisurely survey the crowd until every movement had ceased and every sound had died down, and then in calm and measured accents open his theme amidst intense silence, gripping the audience as he proceeded, until, in a whirl of eloquence and flowing rhetoric, his climaxes were punctuated by unrestrainable applause.

The Order on Islandmagee was viable—it hosted the district celebrations in 1880 and 1903[22] and sent off the usual offshoots, the elite Royal Black Preceptory (no. 324)[23] and a Women's L.O.L. (no. 23),[24]—but it never became central to the local social life. There were too many competing attractions, based on kinship groups and neighbourhood, to permit its becoming very important. So it hirpled along as a fraternal body, holding its monthly meeting, hosting bazaars, and giving dinner dances.[25]

Very little information is available on the second fraternal order, the Masonic Lodge (St. John's Lodge, no. 162). It was fairly old, being reported as having twenty-five members in the late 1830's,[26] and like the Orange Order, possessed its own building. Also, like the Orange Order, it was under the leadership of respectable members of the community: the Rev. Mr. Shaw was an adept of the craft,[27] and later, Dixon Donaldson was a leading supporter and sometime master.[28] The Order was popular among seamen because it provided contacts overseas.

Markedly quixotic, or perfectly attuned to the Island's needs (depending on one's perspective), was the temperance society, the Order of Good Templars. This body was formed in the early 1870's and was chaired by the minister of the First Presbyterian Church, Rev. William Campbell.[29] In 1875 the lodge, now named the "Mariner's Hope Lodge, 102" of the Good Templars, opened its own hall.[30] When the Reverend David Steen assumed the First Islandmagee charge in 1877 he took over the temperance lodge as well. The members signed a pledge stating, "I hereby solemnly promise, God helping me, to abstain from all intoxicating liquors and beverages and to employ all proper means to discourage the use and traffic in the same." A membership campaign in 1885 produced eighty-four signatures, headed by Steen's.[31] That seems to have been the lodge's apogee. In 1906 it was down to forty-seven "brothers" and twelve "sisters."[32] The group struggled along. It held monthly meetings, and to propagate its viewpoint supported a temperance elocution contest for children,[33] lectures on the merits of water versus beer,[34] concerts, and soirees; and always the Reverend David Steen was in the van, urging upon his audience the reasons for total abstinence.[35] All to little visible effect. The lodge went temporarily defunct during the 'teens of the twentieth century and even the Reverend Mr. Steen seems to have lost hope. It was resuscitated in 1919-20, chiefly through the efforts of a layman, John Hill,[36] but never regained its vigour.

These three bodies—the Orange Order, the Masonic Lodge, and the Good Templars—had a good deal in common. For one thing, none of them was very important in determining the social and cultural configuration of Islandmagee. Indeed, it is striking how little of the Island's life revolved around structured institutions. A formal corporate life was not as necessary here as in a city or large town. Second, notice that each group came under the hegemony of an individual who took his primary authority from his professional function: the Orange Order under the Reverend Mr. Shaw, the Masons under Shaw and, later, schoolmaster Donaldson, and the Good Templars, guided by the Reverend Mr. Steen. Particularly in the case of the Orange Order and the Temperance society, the institutions were used to further the professional ends of their leaders: specifically, the Reverend Mr. Shaw's fervent Biblical Protestantism and the Reverend Mr. Steen's moralism. There is, of course, nothing unusual in strong individuals using voluntary associations to further their own ends, but it does help further to explain why the organizations were not a great success: guided for extrinsic ends, they were on the Island but not of it.

(3)

Only now is it appropriate to look at the structure of the most powerful of Islandmagee's associations, the churches. Presbyterianism was the dominant religion on Islandmagee, and the First Presbyterian Church (denoted First in the 1840's to distinguish it from the former secessional church) was the heart of Presbyterianism on the Island. By unsubstantiated tradition the clergyman who was said to be the first Presbyterian minister in Ulster, Edward Brice of Ballycarry, preached in the "Old Church" in Ballykeel, Islandmagee, in the years 1613 to 1636 inclusive.[37] The first Presbyterian minister in Islandmagee whose charge can be historically documented arrived in 1647; thereafter until the later eighteenth century religious provision was irregular.[38] In contrast, in the nineteenth and twentieth centuries clerical continuity was the keynote: John Murphy served from 1789 to 1829, William Campbell from 1829 to 1876, and David Steen from 1877 to 1931 inclusive[39]—three clergymen in 143 years! Whatever else they may have been besides durable (Murphy was a drinker and was suspended for three months for intoxication at a clerical installation)[40] they undoubtedly came to know their congregations well—and vice versa.

Church attendance is difficult to gauge accurately. For example, in the 1830's First Islandmagee held two Sunday services: a parliamentary commission reported that an average of 250 persons attended;[41] yet, reporting in the late 1830's, the Ordnance Survey stated flatly that average attendance was 500.[42] The former figure is more likely to be accurate: in 1874, the year for which the communicants' roll book became available, 165 persons participated in the communion service. These communions were held twice yearly, in May and in October or November. In May 1903 the number of communicants was 118, and in May 1919 it was 125.[43] Tied into the church was a burgeoning Sunday school, which in 1868 had approximately 250 children enrolled, [44] and in 1876 nearly three hundred.[45]

Inherent in Presbyterianism has been a seemingly irresistible propensity for schisms, and the Presbyterian Church in Ireland has had several. The one which affected Islandmagee occurred in 1746 when a secession took place from the Synod of Ulster (which is to say from the Presbyterian Church in Ireland), on the grounds that the main synod was not sufficiently orthodox. As far as Islandmagee was concerned, the theological fine points were peripheral (as was the fact that a subsequent breach within the seceders' ranks occurred in 1747, on the matter of municipal oaths, between "Burghers" and "Anti-Burghers," a rift that was healed in 1818).[46] What appears to have been relevant is that during much of the eighteenth century the Islandmagee people were badly served by the Synod of Ulster: there were gaps in the clergy provisions from 1741 to 1746 inclusive, from 1753 to 1757 inclusive, from 1767 to 1768 inclusive, and from 1778 to 1782 inclusive.[47] Thus, in 1768 the Reverend William Holmes,[48] an able secessionist minister, in addition to his own Ballyeaston charge began a missionary circuit in east Antrim which produced two local congregations, one in Larne (Gardenmore) and one in Islandmagee. The Islandmagee and the Larne seceding congregations worked closely together: the clergyman preached on alternate sabbaths at Gardenmore and Islandmagee. But sharing an overworked missionary clergyman and holding service in barns had its obvious drawbacks. In 1785 a full-time clergyman, John Nicholson,[49] was called to the Larne-Islandmagee charge, and in 1796 the seceders in Islandmagee built their own meeting house.[50] Nicholson's successor, the Rev. George McCaughey,[51] served both congregations until they were separated in 1827. Hence, in 1828, the Islandmagee seceders received their first full-time clergyman, the Reverend David Potter.[52]

During Potter's tenancy the rift between the Synod of Ulster and the Secession Synod was healed, largely because the Synod of Ulster was captured in the late 1820's by the adherents of rigid orthodoxy, who proceeded to impose standards of confession and conduct which satisfied all but the most fanatical seceders. So, in 1840 the Union occurred, forming the General Assembly of the Presbyterian Church in Ireland. At first, Islandmagee's Reverend Mr. Potter disapproved of the Union;[53] but he subsequently reconsidered, and in 1845 the Islandmagee Secession church joined the General Assembly.[54] This meant that from then onwards Islandmagee was served by two Presbyterian churches which were identical in theology and discipline. Quite rightly, they were distinguished as First Islandmagee and Second Islandmagee (the former Seceding church), for nothing but historical precedence now separated them.

The numbers of Second Islandmagee congregation were consistently smaller than those of First. The probably-inflated Ordnance Survey estimate for the 1830's was an average attendance of 300 persons a Sunday at Second as compared with 500 at First.[55] The more realistic parliamentary commission of the early 1830's estimated 130 in average attendance at Second, 250 at First.[56] In the Autumn communion of 1887 at Second, seventy-eight persons participated; in Autumn 1904, seventy-four; and in Spring 1914, seventy-five.[57] A fair estimate, therefore, is that throughout the century-and-a-quarter under study, the former Seceding congregation was about three-fifths of the original orthodox congregation.

With nothing fundamental to distinguish them after 1840, the First and Second congregations simply became different branches of the same organization. Probably fortuitously, they adopted some of the same administrative patterns, especially in the retention of their clerical personnel. First Islandmagee's record of three clergymen in 143 years was beyond reach, but Second Islandmagee came close, three in 103 years: David Potter, 1828-1853, Robert

H. Shaw, 1853-1891,[58] and Henry H. Macready, 1891-1930.[59] Both First and Second Islandmagee Presbyterian Churches took part enthusiastically in the movement usually known as the Great Revival of '59. Both ministers, the Reverend Mr. Campbell (First) and Mr. Shaw (Second), participated and appear to have cooperated happily with each other. The scenes were striking. A Day of Humiliation was scheduled for Wednesday, the eighth of June preparatory to a communion taking place the coming Sunday in First Church. No sooner had the penitential service started than a young lady was dramatically "smitten down." The hysteria spread, and when on the succeeding Sunday the planned communion was held it was "such a solemn communion the members of the congregation never experienced on any former occasion." On the following Monday evening a prayer meeting was held at which hundreds attended and many were "convicted." Then, on Wednesday, four clergymen (including the two Islandmagee Presbyterian ministers) held an evangelical service in which several were "striken down" and hundreds remained in a religious fervour until the sunrise. Next day, the Second Islandmagee Presbyterian Church was full to overflowing at a service presided over by its minister, aided by the clergyman from the First and by others.[60] The effects of the revival continued for months, until emotion gradually abated.[61]

Both Presbyterian Churches benefited from the revival, but the Wesleyan Methodists profited most of all. Their chapel became a centre for revivalist activity and many of those taken by spiritual enthusiasm joined the Methodist community. These adhesions often were not permanent, however, because the Methodists on Islandmagee did not have a pastor. From 1800 until 1903, when the Reverend Richard Cole took the joint charge of Whitehead and Islandmagee, the Wesleyans were served by a combination of occasional itinerant preachers and lay leaders.[62]

An interesting point about Islandmagee Methodists is how well they and the Presbyterians got along. When the

Methodists built a chapel of their own in 1829, the Presbyterians gave them support and the neighbouring farmers carted the building material free of charge. Similarly, in the latter half of the century, when special social occasions occurred or missionary activities were scheduled, the Methodists and Presbyterians worked smoothly together.[63] Some of the explanation for these happy relations lies in the Methodists never having been a large enough minority to threaten the Presbyterian clerical interests (the Wesleyans had an estimated 25 members in the late 1830's, and even that estimate may have been high).[64] To some extent, the common evangelical Protestantism was responsible. And besides, in the early years of the twentieth century, the Methodist Chapel was the sole church to hold evening services: young men of all faiths flocked to it because it was the only place you could meet a girl.[65]

Relations between Anglicans and Presbyterians were more complicated, and for a time, less cordial. As the Ordnance Survey reported of the Islandmagee people, they were "rather hostile to episcopacy."[66] In part this was a response to the unabashedly Catholic element in the Anglican Church, a communion which claimed roots both Catholic and Reformed. Further, as far back as the early seventeenth century, there was a tradition of tension between the two faiths stemming from rivalry in attempts to define religious spheres of influence. In addition, until the mid-1820's, the vestries of the Church of Ireland had minor civil functions. As discussed in Chapter Eight, these civil functions were abolished in the 1820's and 1830's and that improved relations. And in the first third of the nineteenth century the Anglican Church became animated by evangelical influences that brought its tone and theology more into line with Presbyterian predilections.

Two major sources of tension remained between the Presbyterians and the Episcopalians: the Church of Ireland still was the Established Church, and its clergymen were supported by tithes, a tax on the entire community, paid by

Anglican and non-Anglican alike. The tithe grievance was slightly alleviated in 1838 under an arrangement whereby the landlord was made responsible for the tithe charge, but it was not until January 1871, when the Church of Ireland was disestablished and the church-tithe was no longer payable, that the last grievance disappeared.[67] Thereafter the two denominations had no cause for disharmony.

Despite having the deepest historical roots of any church on Islandmagee—its present church building on the Island was built in its basic elements in the first decade of the seventeenth century[68]—the Anglican church was numerically weak: the parliamentary investigation of the mid-1830's found that average attendance was fifty.[69]

The reason for the Church of Ireland's scant attendance rested partly on ethnic factors (the dominant culture of Islandmagee was Scottish and predisposed to Presbyterianism), but that was not the whole story. Until 1839 Islandmagee was very badly served by the Established Church, and even thereafter its local organization was in frequent flux. During the early years of the Reformation the tithes and advowson of Islandmagee fell into secular hands. In 1609, however, most of the ecclesiastical rights to the Island were joined by Royal charter in a united benefice, as a rectory, with Carrickfergus, Ralloo, Inver, and Mollusk. These parishes formed the corps of the deanery of Connor.[70] (Certain residual tithe and patronage rights seem to have been held by Lord Chichester until the mid-1630's, when he surrendered them in return for patronage of Shankill, Belfast.)[71] Now, the deanery of Connor was a most idiosyncratic office. There was no cathedral (the parish church at Lisburn was used as a putative cathedral). Yet, there was a chapter, consisting of a dean, a chancellor, a precentor, a treasurer, and four prebendaries! The dean and chapter had no revenues in their corporate capacity.[72] Instead, they took the tithes and revenues from the several parishes under their charge. The dean of Connor, with five parishes under his charge, lived near Carrickfergus and appointed two curates to do his work. Since in the 1830's only two of the five parishes, Carrickfergus and Islandmagee, had parish churches, and each had a curate, the dean must have lead a remarkably indolent life.[73] In these years the dean drew a total of £860 per annum and paid each of the curates who performed the pastoral work only £75.[74]

In 1838 the dean of Connor, Henry Leslie, found an even more desirable ecclesiastical plum in England and resigned his charge.[75] During the succeeding year, Islandmagee was made into an independent rectory, unattached to any other benefice.[76] Not that the clergy suffered by this new policy: in the mid-1830's the annual tithes were set at £400 a year,[77] a very gentlemanly sum indeed. The rectory was in crown patronage, and when Dean Leslie left for his English benefice the Islandmagee curate, James Smith,[78] became the incumbent. He in turn was replaced, in 1849, by William King Lynar,[79] who resigned in 1870 and retired to Whitehead. Upon Lynar's leaving, the Islandmagee parish was united with that of Templecorran and Kilroot, under the Reverend George Sayers,[80] which is to say Islandmagee was united with Ballycarry and Whitehead. In 1876 Sayers resigned to take the vicarage of Ballinderry, and the Kilroot-Templecorran-Islandmagee charge went to the Reverend Joseph J.H. Bennett.[81] But soon after Bennett took up his benefice, it was reorganized: in 1879 Islandmagee was broken off and restored to its former status as a separate charge, under the Reverend James Milner.[82] Then, in 1902 it was reunited with Kilroot and Templecorran under the Reverend Mr. Bennett, who was succeeded by James Richardson (1915 ff).[83] In obvious contrast to the Presbyterian, the Anglican church in Islandmagee was in a state of flux that was tantamount to confusion. Clergymen came and went relatively quickly, and the parish boundaries were altered time and time again. This kind of fluidity precluded development of the deep roots that were necessary if the church were to prosper in the conservative rural environment of Islandmagee.

In contrast to the Anglican Church, which was over-administered, the Roman Catholic Church had no institutional presence whatsoever. Islandmagee's handful of Catholics were included in a united parish that covered a large area—from Carrickfergus to Larne—and comprised three chapels, at Larne, Ballygowan, and Carrickfergus. A parish priest and a curate served the parish.[84]

How much were the Islanders willing to pay for the religious services with which they were provided? This question cannot be answered comprehensively, because of the scarcity of records. The best indication comes from First Islandmagee Presbyterian Church. The chief year-to-year expenditures were for payment of clergy. In the late 1830's and early 1840's, the church was paying a total of £75 to two clergymen, one retired, receiving £50, the other, his assistant and designated successor, receiving £25. This amount was fully covered by the Regium Donum, a government grant to the Presbyterian clergy, so that the congregation did not have to make any sacrifice at all for the payment of the clergy.[85] Nevertheless, in 1841 the congregation raised an additional £129 7s and 6d in subscriptions and pew rents (at four shillings a sitting). This from 230 individuals.[86] Given that the typical real income for a farmer of five to fifteen acres was about £93 at this time (see Chapter Three), the voluntary contribution of roughly ten shillings a subscriber represents approximately .5 per cent of real income.

Until the Regium Donum was discontinued in 1871, the First Presbyterian Church had few financial worries, and even thereafter it fared comfortably: in 1875 the church's income was £144, of which £91 10s went to clergy salaries.[87] Well could the congregation afford to put money into capital projects. The original church had been built in 1737 and had been roofed with thatch.[88] This was replaced by slate in the 1830's, at a cost to the congregation of about £100. Another stint of renovating in the 1840's cost £155, and an addition to the early 1870's cost £332.[89] Finally, in 1900, the congregation opened an imposing new structure whose awkward bulk hinted equally of prosperity and vulgarity.[90] The costs for this project were borne easily by the congregation (I have not been able to find the costs, but they must have been well into four figures). They soon made improvements to the new church, such as fitting it with acetylene lamps,[91] and in 1921 installing a new organ.[92] So, the Islanders who attended First Islandmagee Presbyterian quite adequately provided for their own religious needs. But note that they gave less to missions and to the Presbyterian Church's general sustenation fund than was considered their fair share by church authorities: this earned them a rebuke in 1902 from the Carrickfergus Presbytery.[93]

Comparable data for the other churches (Second Islandmagee Presbyterian, the Methodist Chapel, and the Anglican Church) are lacking, but the data we do have indicate that they share generally in the following pattern: (1) intense localism in expenditure of church revenues, with only a small portion going for missions and extra-Island denominational projects; (2) a fairly low level of personal sacrifice by each adherent, probably under one-half of one per cent of real annual income; (3) and due to the general prosperity of Islandmagee, even this fairly low level of personal sacrifice resulted in adequate provision of religious buildings and comfortable stipends for the clergy. I would speculate that because of their having smaller congregations, the members of Second Island Presbyterian and the Wesleyan Methodists contributed somewhat more per head than did those of First Presbyterian. On the other hand, the position of the Church of Ireland until 1871 as the Established Church, probably meant that its adherents contributed less per head than did those of the other faiths: until the abolition of compulsory tithes, lay contributions were not nearly as necessary as they were for other churches, and so the habit of regular giving to the church was not deeply ingrained. Taken together, these speculations imply that the case of the First Presbyterian Church, the one on which we do have accurate data, probably provides a representative picture.[94]

The next question that should be asked about the denominational pattern is: were there social or occupational cleavages between the various faiths? Yes, to some extent, although once again the data are more suggestive than definitive. Simply stated, it appears that the Presbyterian churches contained a larger-than-average proportion of substantial tenant farmers, and that the Episcopal Church had an excessively large proportion of labourers and artisans. This conclusion stems from an examination of baptismal and marriage registers. Thirty-three per cent of the fathers of persons married in First Islandmagee Presbyterian Church, 1845 to 1867 inclusive, were farmers;[95] thirteen per cent of the children baptized in the Church of Ireland, Islandmagee, 1879 to 1917 inclusive, were offspring of farmers.[96] The dangers of overreading such data are too obvious to need comment, but one can at least tentatively accept the generalization that the Presbyterians were somewhat better off financially than were the Anglicans.[97]

The final point to be made about the religious structure of Islandmagee is that the polity of all of the churches on the Island involved a remarkable degree of lay participation in their government. In the Presbyterian churches, the local kirk session chose its own elders and ministers. Each local church belonged to a presbytery, an intermediate body of mutual self-regulation, and each session sent delegates to the General Assembly.[98] The Methodist polity involved even greater lay participation, for throughout the nineteenth century it was primarily a lay-church, with no permanent minister.[99] And, after disestablishment became effective in 1871, laymen of the Anglican communion acquired a representative system similar to that of the Presbyterians, and obtained the dominant power in the choice of clergy and bishops.[100] This emphasis upon equality and upon representative government in church matters meshed well with the Islanders' social structure and culture, for the society was instinctively and structurally equalitarian, and perforce, democratic.

(4)

The modern educational history of Islandmagee breaks cleanly into two parts: before and after the introduction of the national system of education in the 1830's and '40s. Prior to the introduction of the national system, the Island was dotted with schools run as private money-making ventures by educational entrepreneurs. Elsewhere in Ireland, such schools were known as "hedge schools," being associated with the penal era when Roman Catholics had to conduct clandestine schools in hedges and fence rows because of governmental persecution. Not surprisingly, the hedge schools have been romanticized.[101] So, too, did Islandmagee's historian, Dixon Donaldson, romanticize the entrepreneural schools of Islandmagee.[102] Actually, in Islandmagee and throughout Ireland, these pre-state efforts were at best educationally haphazard.

In the mid-1830's there were ten private-venture schools in Islandmagee, each enrolling between six and sixty pupils. Five were taught by men, five by women. Only two teachers taught anything beyond basic literacy. The fees charged varied greatly, from 8s 8d to 10s per annum.[103] The Ordnance Surveyer calculated in the late 1830's that the proportion of children on the school books to total population was 16.7 per cent.[104] This compares to an all-Ireland figure, for the mid-1830's, of 6.58 per cent, to 9.35 per cent for the Anglican ecclesiastical province of Armagh, and to 9.11 per cent for the diocese of Connor (in which Islandmagee was located).[105]

But although better-provided than most of Ireland, Islandmagee's educational situation nevertheless was backward. As mentioned earlier (Chapter Nine), the illiteracy rate was surprisingly high, probably as high as forty to fifty per cent in the 1820's and '30's. Also, the teachers were far from impressive: the Ordnance Surveyer adjudged only one of the ten schoolmasters capable of teaching grammar, geography, or mathematics adequately.[106] What a mixed bag these pre-national system teachers were! One of them,

Thomas McCartney, insisted on living in a cave on Blackhead. During the summer months he kept his school open until six o'clock in the evening and just before dismissing it had all his pupils simultaneously recite their lessons for the day at the top of their lungs; it is said that the noise was used as a time-signal by workers to indicate that the day's work was done. Another, John Houston, taught from 1821 into the early 1840's and then decided to become a professional proselytizer. His local admirers thought so well of his potential as a preacher that they outfitted him with a donkey, harness, and trap. Some of the teachers were connected with people of substance. For example, John Montgomery (born 1783, the earliest firm dating for any of the entrepreneurial teachers mentioned herein), was the son of the manager of Islandmagee's only large farm, that of Malcolm McNeill at Brownsbay, and Montgomery himself served for a time as a Justice of the Peace. James Flack, who began a day school in 1820, came of an Islandmagee farming family of about twenty-five acres; he served as choirmaster of the Secessionist church, and as church warden of the Anglican church as well. William Blair claimed the courtesy title of "doctor," allegedly acquired during a sojourn in the United States. A mixed, but intriguing lot.[107]

Given the supposed enthusiasm of the Scots-Presbyterians for schooling, one would have expected that when the national system of education was created in 1831 they would have joined with alacrity. They did not, however, because the Presbyterian leaders became convinced (wrongly) that the new system was an attack on Biblical Christianity and an encouragement to Romanism. Throughout Ulster meetings were held, national schools were defaced and burned, and clergy and laymen who were disposed to accept the government's new system were intimidated. Finally, in 1840, the Dublin officials surrendered and modified their rules; immediately the Presbyterians became enthusiastic adherents of the national school system.[108]

Interestingly, the Islanders acted with typical independence in putting one of their schools into connection with the national system well before the Presbyterian authorities gave their official approval: in 1836 the Secessionist congregation joined the national system. Significantly, the patrons of this school were not only the Secessionist clergyman, but the Rector of the Anglican Church and the retired minister of the Orthodox Presbyterian congregation.[109] This Mulloughboy National School had fifty-seven boys and twenty-nine girls in 1839, and received £10 a year from the Dublin administration towards the teacher's salary.[110] When, in 1840, the Dublin Castle officials came to terms with the Orthodox Presbyterians, four more Island schools quickly joined (Brownsbay, Kilcoan Upper, Kilcoan Lower, and Mullaghdubh); in 1842 these four enrolled between thirty-six and 114 pupils each, and were receiving annual grants between £8 and £11 towards teachers' salaries.[111] With minor changes (the Methodists started their own school at Ballymoney in 1862)[112] this school system served the Island until the Ulster school system was taken over in the 1920's by the ministry of education of the newly-established government of Northern Ireland.

It is significant that the new educational system was introduced smoothly into the Island society (I am here talking about administrative matters; the relation of the curriculum to the Island's culture was discussed in Chapter Nine). Notice, first, that four of the five masters of the schools newly associated with the national system of education had been conducting local schools on their own initiative.[113] This may not speak highly for the standards of the national system in its early years, but it meant that the new system meshed more easily with the parochial culture than if the commissioners of national education had demanded that strangers be appointed. Second, unlike the people in most of Ireland, the Islanders preferred co-educational schools. Thus, in the 1890's, the Reverend David Steen, minister of the First Presbyterian Church, was merging Islandmagee's two sexually segregated schools (the two Kilcoan schools) into a single institution;[114] in contrast, the Roman Catholic Church in Ireland soon was pronouncing sexually mixed schools to be morally dangerous.[115] The co-educational pattern fitted with the familial-sexual patterns of Islandmagee much more closely than would have the single-sex schools that were coming to dominate the sexually repressed Catholic portions of the country. A third point: the Islandmagee national schools were community organizations. Granted, like the overwhelming majority of national schools they were under the managership of clergymen: four of them (Mullaghdubh, Brownsbay, and the two Kilcoan schools) under the minister of the First Presbyterian Church, one of them (Mulloughboy national school) under the Second Islandmagee Presbyterian clergyman and one (Ballymoney) under Methodist clergy.[116] But this was not evidence of a clerical dictatorship of education, although the clergyman did have the undeniable right of selecting the teacher; the position of the clergy in Island society was not such as to allow the clergyman to impose his will on anyone. Under the polity of the various Island churches, he was selected by the laymen of the respective denominations, and his position depended on his ability to lead, for he had no power to coerce. As evidence that the Islandmagee schools were communal projects and not just clerical jurisdictions, note: that the Larne poor law union to which Islandmagee belonged was one of seventy-seven (of 163) unions which voluntarily voted a rate to raise teachers' salaries under the National School Teachers (Ireland) Act, 1875;[117] that in 1911 the parents and citizens conducted a drive to clear the debt incurred by adding a new cookery room to the Kilcoan school, and to "harmonize its equipment with the latest ideas of the National Education Board";[118] that in 1913 the people of the area raised enough money to qualify for a government grant to erect a new building for Mullaghdubh school.[119]

The result of the school system's fitting so well with Island social patterns was that the Island children went to school. That sounds obvious, but the percentage of children on the rolls who actually attended schools is the primary indicator of institutional efficiency. Thus, whereas at the turn of the century the national average for daily school attendance was sixty-two per cent of the number of children on the rolls,[120] the Islandmagee average was seventy-eight per cent.[121] Doubtless, the schools had their flaws, but obviously the people in the Islandmagee community believed in them.

(5)

The key to understanding the position of formal institutions in Islandmagee society, and the institutions' influence upon the Island's culture, is to recognize both the institutions' importance and their *un*importance. Yes, the churches had the allegiance of most Islanders, but the clergy had a license to operate only within boundaries set by communal consent, Yes, the various lodges had adherents, but as voluntary bodies they were open to continual scrutiny. And, yes, by turning the Island population into an overwhelmingly literate one the schools affected the Island's culture, just as, being public institutions, they affected the Island's social life. But (as discussed in the preceding chapter) the curriculum was so flexible that it was moulded to local needs, while the institutional structure of the schools fitted very well with the Islanders' social predilections.

Thus, the Islanders' culture, their social patterns, their economic structure, and their institutions were in harmony. This made for a society that was markedly successful, but essentially conservative.

Chapter Eleven. A Cohesive Culture—III. Conclusion

This book began by posing what, superficially at least, is a political question: why were the Islanders revolutionaries in 1798 and counter-revolutionaries in 1920? But although the question is political in form, knowledge of mere politics makes scant contribution to the answer. As established in Chapter Eight, the substance of local government was largely a redundant overlay on the Island's familial-kinship arrangements. Similarly, for most of the nineteenth century, national politics were distant from the Islanders' concerns. In part, this was because of the franchise legislation. Until the Irish franchise act of 1850, which gave the vote to £12 rated occupiers, only freeholders could vote in rural districts, and there were no freeholders in Islandmagee save the Marquis of Donegall. Even after 1850, the franchise was limited to substantial farmers, and it was not until the "mud cabin franchise" act of 1884 that most males acquired the vote. In the 1906 election, 424 Islanders voted.[1]

Islandmagee became politicized—as distinct from becoming merely political—in 1912-14, during the passage of the third home rule bill. Significantly, the activities on Ulster Day, when the Covenant was signed, were presided over by the Reverend David Steen, minister of the Island's largest church, and by virtue of his long tenure in his charge, a venerated, almost patriarchial figure. The day's ceremony began with a religious service, Steen preaching an appropriate sermon, followed by the singing of psalms. At the close of the service the congregation filed into a large ante-room and one by one the men signed the Covenant and the women the Declaration.[2] Whether the Islanders were right or wrong in feeling that their society was threatened by the home rule movement is irrelevant. What is relevant is the fact that here something was taking place that was more than simple politics: it was a ritual expression by the local society of their intense commitment to preserving their culture.

Not surprisingly, the Islanders, in conjunction with the residents of the nearby town of Whitehead, formed a company of the Ulster Volunteer Force ("D" Company, 3rd Batallion, Central Antrim Regiment), the entire regiment being under the command of Major McCalmont, the local Member of Parliament.[3] Loyalist fervour stayed high, and in the 1918 election the local Unionists turned out a full poll in Islandmagee, despite the fact that the Sinn Fein candidate in East Antrim had no hope whatsoever. Significantly, the Unionist organizing for the election (the first in which women could vote) was done by Mrs. Steen, wife of the Reverend David Steen,[4] once again illustrating the tie of cultural values to political behaviour. When an Islandmagee branch of the Antrim Women Unionists was formed in 1920, the clergyman's wife was elected president.[5]

Precisely when Ulstermen changed from being political radicals to political conservatives is the kind of question on which historians and political scientists waste a good deal of time. It is a misleading question because it is based on the false premise that year-in-year-out politics was important and therefore worth constant attention. But we know that for the most part, politics was *not* important to the local communities of Ulster, and that during the nineteenth century most election results were vapours, having little to do with the fundamental concerns of the society. Most elections, like most political events, should be given decidedly peripheral attention. One can profitably deal with politics only on those occasions when the issues of politics intersect in some way the fundamental configurations of the culture one is studying.

The significant political questions that must be answered are: (1) *when* did an event or series of events occur which politicized the community being studied? (2) *what* was the nature of the social, economic, and cultural structure which *predisposed* the society to act in a given way, when eventually it did become politicized? and (3) *at what point,* approximately, did the given society adopt this fundamental predisposition?

In the case of Islandmagee, we have already answered the first question: the Island became politicized in 1912-14, following the introduction of the third home rule bill (not, as in some other parts of Ulster, in 1886 or 1893, when the first and second home rule bills were framed).

The answer to the second question comprehends all the data presented in the body of this study, but it can be compacted into a single phrase: as a society Islandmagee worked. It worked in the sense that economic patterns, social structure, religious beliefs, social customs, superstitions, and institutional arrangements fitted well, one with the other. And underlying their relationship was a strong economy, one which had to support only a limited population.

The answer to the third question I can only guess at, and suggest that 1850 is a sensible rough date. I suggest this date, first, because the national system of education was by then having a considerable effect. The first generation of pupils who had undergone the West British influences of the national schools were now adults and coming to influence the local society. Second, and more important, although Islandmagee did not experience the Famine, the Islanders can only have been highly conscious of how fortunate they were to have escaped its ravages, and they must have become aware of the comparative virtues of their society. Third, from mid-nineteenth century onwards, the maritime industry of Belfast expanded rapidly, providing a large variety of opportunities which Islanders were well-prepared to take. I am speculating that, say, in 1840, the average Islander would have been at least marginally predisposed to view radical political change as something that might improve his life; in, say, 1850, he would have tipped the other way, and viewed abrupt political change as more apt to do him harm than good.

But is not all this a bit too pat? Does it not imply that there exists some invisible "index of success" for any society, and that below a certain line the society will be predisposed to revolution or radical political change, while above the line it will be conservative or counter-revolutionary? No, I am not being so simple-minded, although I do think that the most important determinants of any society's stance on critical political issues are that community's degree of economic efficiency and its degree of success in integrating its culture, economy, and social structure. There is also that elusive, but real, matter of cultural self-assertion. A striking characteristic of the Protestant-dominated northeastern portion of Ireland is that it has been as assertive of its cultural identity as have the regions of the rest of Ireland, indeed perhaps more so (why this assertion has received so little attention as a cultural—as distinct from a constitutional—phenomenon in itself is an interesting question in Irish historiography). By 1800 the northeast had become a coherent regional culture embodying distinct material forms, as well as linguistic and other non-material attributes. This culture was a hybrid, incorporating native Irish and imported English and Scottish components, but dominated by the Scottish elements.[6]

(Incidentally, I hope that no reader thinks I have latched on to the thesis that the Protestant ethic made for prosperity in the northeast and that Roman Catholicism in the south had the opposite effect. Those hypotheses are too simplistic to permit meaningful examination, much less to warrant respect. In each case religion was demonstrably part of the complex web of culture, religion, and economics, but that religion caused the strikingly divergent economic patterns to develop is patently untenable.)

The compactness and coherence of the Islandmagee culture have already been discussed in detail, but the dominance of Scottish elements requires comment. The first post-reformation settlers of Islandmagee, followers of the English adventurer Sir Moyses Hill, were English, [7] but by roughly 1630, Scots prevailed: of the 377 British adult males on Islandmagee in that year, 333 were of Scottish origin.[8] The exodus of the original Magees, who were of Scottish-Catholic descent from Islay, began before 1600, and accelerated during the wars of the 1640's, the remnant settling along the northern coast of Antrim.[9] Despite the Scottish predominance, native Irish elements remained, and in addition new English migrants subsequently arrived. Thus, if we take a representative time in the nineteenth century—the 1834 tithe applotment provides a good opportunity—we find a significant non-Scots input. Of the 115 family names on the 1834 applotment for which ethnic origins can be determined, fifteen were unambiguously Irish in origin, another fifteen Irish or Scottish (the names are common to both cultures), and one either Irish or English. Twenty-four of the 115 identifiable names were clearly English in origin, eight were either English or Scottish, one either English or Irish, and the rest pure Scottish. Corollating for the ambiguous items, one can estimate that the ethnic origin of Islanders was one-fifth Irish, one-quarter English, and just over a moiety Scots.[10]

Islandmagee, despite the diversity of ethnic origins, was not a pluralistic culture. It was a single culture, and in that culture the Scottish influence dominated. Mr. and Mrs. S.C. Hall, acute observers of the Irish scene, described the Islanders as thoroughly "Scotch" in dialect, manners, and customs;[11] and the Ordnance Surveyer, writing at roughly the same time, pointed out that all the Islanders' recreations were Scottish in character.[12] The best indication of Scottish prepotence in the cultural amalgam is found by comparing religious statistics (given in Chapter Nine), with the estimate of ethnicity. Specifically, note that the Presbyterian percentage of the population (eighty-six per cent in 1834) greatly exceeded the proportion (slightly above one-half) of family names of Scottish origin. Next, notice that on Islandmagee Catholics in 1834 constituted only two per cent of the population, even though roughly twenty per cent of the family names were of native Irish origin. We can surmise, therefore, that the Catholic population of the Island was small not merely because of their spatial displacement in the early days of British settlement, but as a result of cultural subsummation by the Protestant population. In the matter of religious identity, most of the Islanders of native Irish descent opted to accept the outlook of the majority culture, rather than to maintain their separate religious identity. Perhaps this choice was prompted by fear of the Protestant majority, but it is significant that the same thing happened to those of English extraction and Anglican origin. Whereas approximately a quarter of the Islandmagee families were of English origin, only nine per cent in 1834 belonged to the Established Church. Thus, on the pivotal issue of religion, the English Anglicans, no less than the Irish Catholics, were subsumed by the Scots Presbyterians. Undeniably, both English and Irish elements were incorporated in the culture as a whole, but the dominant tone was Scots.

What does this have to do with explaining why the Islanders were revolutionary in 1798 and counter-revolutionary in 1920? It relates to the concept of cultural self-assertion. The areas in northeast Ireland that were most revolutionary in 1798 were those areas in which the process of acculturation—that is, the process of establishing a distinct and coherent regional culture—had proceeded furthest.[13] This was not accidental, for in addition to being a response to specific economic and social grievances, the rebellion in the north was implicitly an affirmation of the integrity of the Ulster-Scots regional culture against incursions by external agencies. Similarly, the Unionist counter-revolutionary activity of 1912-20 was, among many other things, a defence of a culture against a much-feared onslaught from the rest of Ireland.

So, to respond to the question originally posed in Chapter One, concerning Islandmagee's contrasting behaviour in 1798 and 1920, we can put forward a simple two-part explanation: (1) that whereas in the 1790's certain grievances inclined the Islanders to radicalism, during the succeeding century-and-a-quarter the Island society operated so successfully that the inhabitants became predisposed to conservatism; and (2) that in both instances the Islanders were so sure of their cultural identity that they did not hesitate to assert themselves when they felt that culture threatened.

Within the context of Irish historiography the value of studying a community such as Islandmagee is that it presents a pure case in which we can isolate the characteristics of Presbyterian rural people, uncomplicated by sectarian fissures and urban dislocations. Most explanations of the behaviour of Ulster Protestants in the nineteenth and twentieth centuries quite correctly introduce as explanatory factors the general influence of industrialization and the specific phenomenon of the growth of Belfast; the rise of Orangeism; and the parallel rise of evangelical religion. Notice, however, that these factors did *not* radically change the life of the Islandmagee people. They remained completely rural in residence and overwhelmingly agrarian in employment. The Belfast shipbuilding industry gave the seamen among them opportunities to become long-distance sea captains, but this only confirmed, not altered, an existing maritime orientation among the Islanders. As for the Orange Order, as discussed in earlier chapters it was of minimal importance socially and politically on Islandmagee. And except for the revival of 1859, the Islanders kept to the traditional, staid forms of Presbyterianism.

Nevertheless, the Islandmagee people in the twentieth century adopted the same loyalist political and constitutional attitudes taken on by Protestants in communities that had felt the impact of Orangeism, evangelicalism, and urbanisation. The Islanders acted as loyalists simply as an assertion of their own cultural identity. What this *suggests* (not proves—suggests) is that during the nineteenth and twentieth centuries a rugged spine of attitudes came to underly Ulster Presbyterian actions, a spine that enhoused reflexes instinctively conservative socially and inevitably loyalist constitutionally. In all probability, even without the rise of Belfast, without Orangeism and without evangelicalism, the Ulster Scots would still have violently opposed their own inclusion in a new Irish state.

Notes.

Chapter One

1. For a more detailed description of the muster see Dixon Donaldson, *Historical, Traditional, and Descriptive Account of Islandmagee* (Whitehead: "The Whitehead News and Ballycarry and Islandmagee Reporter," 1927), pp. 56-57.
2. On Orr's early political beliefs see Donald Harman Akenson and W.H. Crawford, *Local Poets and Social History; James Orr, Bard of Ballycarry* (Belfast Public Record Office of Northern Ireland, 1977, pp.6-8, 10-17.
3. The letting notice, from the *Belfast News-Letter* of 6 March 1770, is reprinted in Donaldson, pp. 50-51.
4. W.E.H. Lecky, *A History of Ireland in the Eighteenth Century* (London: Longmans, Green and Co., New Impression 1913), vol. II, pp. 50-51.
5. Donaldson, P.52. Four hundred and thirty-seven signatures were affixed, but the proportion from Islandmagee is not known.
6. The address, published in the *Belfast News-Letter*, 21 April 1772, is quoted in Donaldson, p. 52. He includes the entire list of subscribers (p. 53).
7. Lecky, vol. II, p. 51. For a study of emigration over a longer period of time, see R.J. Dickson, *Ulster Emigration to Colonial America 1718-1775* (London: Routledge and Kegan Paul, 1966).
8. Donaldson, p. 55.
9. For a discussion of the Volunteers see Lecky, vol. II, pp. 222 ff.
10. Lecky, vol. II, p. 51.
11. For a general discussion of Ulster emigrant letters, see E.R.R. Green, "Ulster Emigrants' Letters" in E.R.R. Green (ed) *Essays in Scotch-Irish History* (London: Routledge and Kegan Paul, 1969), pp. 87-103.
12. Donaldson collected the ballad in the late nineteenth or early twentieth century from "an aged friend who had learned [it] from her grandmother, who, in turn, was a young woman at the time of the episode" (p. 54).

Donaldson's account of the battle, besides suffering from severe typographical errors, requires corrections, as found in Samuel Eliot Morison's *John Paul Jones, a Sailor's Biography* (Boston: Little Brown & Co., 1959), pp. 138-163.

13. I am grateful to W.H. Crawford, Assistant Keeper of the Public Records of Northern Ireland, for communicating to me the results of his research on the social characteristics of the areas in Ulster in which the United Irishmen were influential. An important background article is Crawford's "Economy and Society

in South Ulster in the Eighteenth Century," *Clogher Record* (1975), pp. 241-258. For an important discussion of the complex nature and uneven distribution of Presbyterian radicalism see A.T.Q. Stewart, *The Narrow Ground. Aspects of Ulster, 1609-1969* (London: Faber and Faber, 1977), pp. 101-110.

14. See Lecky, vol II, p. 395 on the "deterioration" of the volunteers after 1784. I am grateful to Dr. A.T.Q. Stewart of The Queen's University of Belfast for his suggestions concerning the evolution of the United Irishmen.

15. On McClelland see Donaldson, pp. 50, 58-59.

16. [Whitehead Extra-Mural Study group], *Ordnance Survey Memoir for the Parish of Templecorran* (Belfast: The Queen's University of Belfast, 1972), p. 23. Templecorran was the legal name of the parish, but in contemporary local usage it almost always was called "Broadisland."

17. James Orr, "Donegore Hill," in *Poems on Various Subjects* (Belfast: Smyth and Lyons, 1804, reprinted, Belfast: Wm. Mullan and Son, 1935), p. 33.

18. Donaldson, p. 57.

19. George Casement to George A. McCleverty 20 July 1798, reproduced in W.H. Crawford and Brian Trainor (eds.), *Aspects of Irish Social History, 1750-1800* (Belfast: HMSO, 1969), p. 186.

20. Ibid.

21. Donaldson, p. 58.

22. Orr, "Donegore Hill," pp.34-35.

23. Donaldson, p. 58.

24. Recent accounts of the battle are found in Charles Dickson, *Revolt in the North. Antrim and Down in 1798* (Dublin: Clonmore and Reynolds, 1960) and Thomas Pakenham, *The Year of Liberty. The Story of the Great Irish Rebellion of 1798* (London: Hodder and Stoughton, 1969).

25. Donaldson, p. 58.

26. Orr, "Donegore Hill," p. 35.

27. Dickson, p. 126.

28. Donaldson, pp. 58-59. Information on the size of McCleliand's farm is found in "Applotment of Tithes in the Parish of Isle of Magee, Diocese of Connor and County of Antrim, by William Burleigh, Tithe Commissioner 1834," Public Record Office of Northern Ireland (hereafter PRONI), Fin V/159, part 1.

29. This, largest possible, estimate comes from noting that the maximum size of McClelland's band was sixty, from assuming that the other Islandmagee group that mustered at Redhall was the same size, and from assuming that the sixty Islandmagee pikemen reported to be drawn up opposite Larne did not include members of the other two groups.

30. For obits of those who died in service, see Donaldson, pp. 146-154.

Chapter Two

1. See "Memoir of the Parish of Islandmagee," in the Royal Irish Academy, Dublin, Ordnance Survey, Box 11, Antrim XI, VI, Islandmagee parish, vol. I, pp. 1-3, for an excellent contemporary description. The survey memoir, done by James Bovle in the late 1830's and completed in 1840, is found in edited transcript in the Public Record Office of Northern Ireland (no catalogue number), in "Transcript of Extracts of O.S. Memoirs." At the time of writing members of the Whitehead Extra-Mural Study Group are editing the memoir for publication.

I have made corrections to Boyle's elevations, from Ordnance Survey of Northern Ireland, Mid-Antrim Sheet Three, one inch series, published 1960.

For brief nineteenth century topographical accounts of Islandmagee see Samuel Lewis, *A Topographical Dictionary of Ireland* (London: S. Lewis, 1837), vol. II, pp.

27-28; and *The Parliamentary Gazetteer of Ireland* (Dublin: A. Fullarton, 1846), vol. II, p. 329.

2. "Memoir of the Parish of Islandmagee," p.24.

3. Ibid., unnumbered page [=45].

4. Ibid., [p. 46]. By Irish standards the clearing of Islandmagee occurred very early: in 1598 Dean Dobbs of Carrickfergus wrote that it was "without any wood—very fertile." Quoted ibid., p.10.

5. *Census of Ireland for the Year 1851, Part I, Showing the Area, Population, and Number of Houses* . . . Vol. III, pp. 8-9, H.C. [1565], 1852-53, xcii.

6. As early as 1683 it was estimated that ninety percent of the Island was "fit for fork and scythe . . . ." The estimate is found in Richard Dobb's unpublished *A Brief Description of the County of Antrim (1683)*, quoted in George Hill, *An Historical Account of the MacDonnells of Antrim: including Notices of some other Septs, Irish and Scottish* (Belfast: Archer and Sons, 1873), p. 379.

7. For a learned study of the geology of Ulster see H.E. Wilson, *Regional Geology of Northern Ireland* (Belfast: HMSO, 1972). A less technical survey is J.K. Charlesworth, "Geology," in *Belfast in its Regional Setting. A Scientific Survey* (Belfast: British Association, 1952), pp. 29-39. See also, "Geology and Physiography," in Leslie Symons (ed), *Land Use in Northern Ireland* (London: University of London Press, Ltd., 1963), pp. 59-74.

8. For a discussion of soil classification see "Land Classification" by Leslie Symons and J.G. Cruickshank in Symons, pp. 109-113.

9. For a more detailed geological account see Dixon Donaldson, *Historical, Traditional, and Descriptive Account of Islandmagee* (Whitehead: "The Whitehead News and Ballycarry and Islandmagee Reporter," 1927), pp. 6-7.

10. "Memoir of the Parish of Islandmagee," vol. I, p. 22.

11. Nicholas Stephens, "Climate," in Symons, p. 79.

12. Douglas A. Hill, "Climate and Soils," in *Belfast in its Regional Setting*, p. 42.

13. T.W. Freeman, Ireland. *A General and Regional Geography* (London: Methuen & Co., third edition, 1965), p. 45.

14. Hill, p. 40.

15. Freeman, p. 45.

16. Hill, p. 41.

17. Like any area, Islandmagee was subject to meteorological accidents, such as the tornado of 1775. See Donaldson, p. 49.

18. For etymological interpretations of the townland names—some more convincing than others—see Donaldson, pp. 9-13.

The acreage of the individual townlands was as follows:

	acres	roods	perches
Balloo	341	3	15
Ballycronan-beg	264	0	0
Ballycronan-more	356	3	22
Ballydown	210	1	8
Ballyharry	224	2	25
Ballykeel	381	3	20
Ballylumford	264	0	10
Ballymoney	328	0	22
Ballymuldrogh	168	1	23
Ballyprior-beg	241	2	6
Ballyprior-more	253	0	22
Ballystrudder	255	2	32
Ballytober	249	3	31
Carnspindle	217	3	6
Castletown	347	3	39

Cloghfin	357	3	28
Drumgurland	199	2	8
Dundressan	255	2	35
Gransha	638	3	22
Kilcoan-beg	164	2	23
Kilcoan-more	339	3	6
Mullaghboy	251	2	28
Mullaghdubh	283	1	0
Portmuck	235	1	25
Temple Effin	203	2	10
Total	7,036	2	26

Source: *Census of Ireland for the Year 1851, Part I, Showing the Area Population, and Number of Houses....* vol. III, pp. 8-9.

During the last quarter of the nineteenth century, portions of Castletown were carved out of Islandmagee to form part of the new town of Whitehead.

19. On the various ancient monuments, see: "A.M.P.," "Ancient Cemetery, in Islandmagee, County of Antrim," *Ulster Journal of Archaeology,* I ser., vol. VI (1858), pp. 346-350; D.A. Chart, E. Estyn Evans, and H.C. Lawlor, *A Preliminary Survey of the Ancient Monuments of Northern Ireland* (Belfast: HMSO, 1940), pp. 35-36; Dixon Donaldson, pp. 13-18, 26-27; "Memoir of the Parish of Islandmagee," passim; James O'Laverty, *An Historical Account of the Dioceses of Down and Connor, Ancient and Modern,* vol. IV (Dublin: M.H. Gill and Son., 1887), pp. 126-144. See also the successive revisions of the Ordnance Survey six inch maps of the Island.

20. "Memoir of the Parish of Islandmagee," vol. I, pp. 4-6, 12-18, 28-30, 33.

21. The reader will—or should—be relieved that I have not filled the text with the poetic effusions called forth by Islandmagee's topography. The best of these is James Orr's poem inspired by the Ballylumford megalith, entitled "Elegy, Composed in Island Magee, at the Tomb of an Ancient Chief," published in the *Belfast Commercial Chronicle,* 7 January 1809.

Rather more painful are the lines from "Larne Bay and Larne," by James White (1846), found in the P.R.O.N.I., D7946a:

"...to make a good jobb of the
  bay at the East
Undoubtedly Islandmagee was
  there planted
When it is green and gay
  and in summer away
It appears to bee desert and all
  but enchanted.

The Larne Times and Weekly Telegraph (20 June 1908) carried the following bit of anonymous doggerel:

> That is a statement which is true,
>   But of course, it is a paradox,
> That o'er in Isle Magee they've got
>   a Rocking-stone which never rocks
>
> With such-like statement I'll proceed,
>   And not for half a second falter—
> A Druid's Altar they have got
>   Which never was a Druid's Altar.

A lighthouse they have also there
But I don't think it's really light;
I'm sure "twould weigh one hundred tons
If it was weighed to-morrow night

And they have got a fog-bell too,
Which really ain't no fog-bell,
For according to the folk of Larne
It's an absolutely blankety
blank nuisance.

Chapter Three

1. R.D. Collison Black, *Economic Thought and the Irish Question 1817-1870* (Cambridge: Cambridge University Press, 1960), pp. 72-73.

2. Elizabeth R. Hooker, *Readjustments of Agricultural Tenure in Ireland* (Chapel Hill: University of North Carolina Press, 1938), p. 24.

3. The letter is quoted in Dixon Donaldson, *Historical, Traditional and Descriptive Account of Islandmagee* (Whitehead: "The Whitehead News and Ballycarry and Islandmagee Reporter," 1927), p. 34.

4. Essex's petitions for land, and the eventual grant, are discussed, together with some excerpts from relevant correspondence, in Walter B. Devereux, *Lives and Letters of the Devereux Earls of Essex, in the Reigns of Elizabeth, James I and Charles I, 1540-1646* (London: John Murray, 1853), vol. I, pp. 118-135. Essex's original grandiose scheme of land allocation is found in George Hill, *An Historical Account of the MacDonnells of Antrim: including Notices of some other Septs, Irish and Scottish* (Belfast: Archer and Son, 1873) pp. 417-420. Writing in 1683, Richard Dobbs, a prominent landowner in east Antrim, stated that he personally had seen the patent to Islandmagee which Essex had held. (Dobbs, quoted in Hill, pp. 378-379), See also Donaldson, pp. 32-34; *Dictionary of National Biography* and James O'Laverty, *An Historical Account of the Dioceses of Connor, Ancient and Modern* (Dublin: M.H. Gill & Son, 1887), vol. IV, pp. 124-25.

5. *DNB*

6. The grant was made before 1607: Donaldson (pp. 34-35) paraphrases a letter of that year from Chichester to the Earl of Salisbury expressing gratitude for the grant.

Francis Joseph Bigger, who did a good deal of research into Islandmagee history, believed that Islandmagee came into Chichester's hands before the Inquisition of 1605. Only by supposing that Chichester was at least de facto owner of the Island, Bigger argued, could one account for its being left unmolested while the surrounding area was being desolated. See Francis Joseph Bigger *Sir Arthur Chichester, Lord Deputy of Ireland* (Belfast: The Linenhall Press, 1904), pp.30-31.

On the other hand in an article in the *Newry Magazine*, vol. 3 (1817), p. 436, the great antiquarian Samuel McSkimin (writing under the initials "S.Mc.S.") said that after Essex's death in 1601, Islandmagee came into the possession of the bishop of Down and Connor, and that in 1602 it was leased by the bishop, Robert Hampton, to Sir Henry Piers and Sir Francis Annsley at an annual rent of less than seven pounds. Only thereafter did Chichester obtain it. Unhappily, when one examines the source upon which McSkimin based his argument, (Ware's *Bishops*. . .) it is found to be ambiguous: the bishop is reported to have acquired a fee-farm lease of the Island of Magee, but whether this was a fee-farm of tithes (as is the case in several similar items recorded in Ware) or of the actual leasehold of Islandmagee (as McSkimin believed) cannot be definitely decided; my reading of the documents suggests that the balance of probability is in Bigger's favour. See James Ware, *The Whole Works of Sir James Ware concerning Ireland. Revised and improved*, vol. I, *The History of the Bishops. . .*, (Dublin: printed for the author by E. Jones, 1739), p. 207.

7. See Debrett's *Peerage* and Burke's *Peerage and Baronetage*.
8. Donaldson, pp. 34-35.
9. Ibid., p. 35; Bigger, p.30.
10. Hill, p. 117 and p. 117n207 describes the Murloch Bay grant and states that these Magees had first settled in Islandmagee.

Hill also states (p. 117) that the Magees hailed from the Rhinns of Islay. However, more recent work suggests that they came not from the Rhinns but from the south ward of that Island. (See W.D. Lamont, "The Islay Charter of 1408," in *Proceedings of the Royal Irish Academy*, sect. C, vol. 60, pp. 168-169). The point is minor, however, for both the Magees of the Rhinns and those of the south ward were branches of the same family, originally from Kintyre, who had been made the administrative deputies over much of Islay during the fourteenth century.

These Magees were branches of the MacKay family and probably were descended from the MacKays of Ugadale in Kintyre (Lamont, p. 169). For an authoritative statement of the linguistic variants of the MacKay name, including Magee, see the "Macghie" entry in George F. Black, *The Surnames of Scotland* (New York: New York Public Library, 1946), p. 496.

The MacKay-Magee lands in Kintyre were granted to them by Robert the Bruce, probably between 1306 and 1309, inclusive. In the family there is a tradition that it was in a MacKay-Magee house that the famous spider preached his sermon on perseverance to the king (Hill, p. 39n55 and Lamont, p. 169).

But when did the Magees from the south ward of Islay take over the lands which came to be known as Islandmagee? The probably-accurate Magee family tradition was that they came to Ireland with their relative Sorley Boy MacDonnell to help him wrest the Route and the Glynns from the MacQuillans (Lamont, pp. 167-168). Lamont suggests (p. 170) that the head of the family took up residence in County Antrim between 1550 and 1570. If this is accurate, then the Magees were not long in control of Islandmagee. Of course, acquisition of effective control of the Island could have preceded by some time the actual move of the Magee family head from Islay to Ireland.

11. W.A. Maguire, *The Downshire Estates in Ireland 1801-1845* (Oxford: Clarendon Press, 1972), p. 2.
12. I am accepting Donaldson's suggestion (p. 32) that the initial lease to Hill probably was issued by Essex, not Chichester, because the settlement of the Island by Hill's people clearly had proceeded far by the Inquisition of 1605, and, in all probability, Chichester did not receive the freehold of Islandmagee until sometime after he assume the Lord Deputyship in 1604.

Here a crucial point should be noted about Sir Moyses Hill: that he was one of those tough west country adventurers who were more interested in acquiring land than in defending any specific principle, civil or religious. Being on the winning side, not the right side, was his aim. He came to Ireland in 1573 under the first Earl of Essex and was engaged in speculative enterprises until his death in February 1629-30 at age seventy-six.

On the one hand, Hill played the government's side, being a follower of both of the Essex Earls, and subsequently a follower of Charles Blount, Lord Mountjoy, who appointed him governor of Olderfleet Castle, Larne. As such, he was attacked by the MacDonnells and had to flee to a cave in Islandmagee until the trouble was over. In December 1603 he was knighted and became provost marshall of Carrickfergus, and in 1617 he was given a lifetime appointment as provost marshall of Ulster.

But on the other hand, Hill made marriage alliances with the contumacious MacDonnells. He married a sister of the most rebellious of the family, Sorley Boy MacDonnell, and Sir Moyses' eldest son, Peter, married Sorley Boy's only daughter. These marriages gave Hill the basis for a firm alliance with the MacDonnells should they appear likely to become victorious in the scramble for control of what is now County Antrim. And not only could Hill thus straddle the fence between government and rebels, he could do so *mutatis mutandis* on the Catholic-Protestant issue.

Because of his marriage alliances with the MacDonnells, Hill was also distantly related to the Magees of Islandmagee, who were related to Sorley Boy, with whom they had come to Ireland to subdue the Route and the Glynns.

These complex relationships throw additional light on the grant of the Murloch Bay lands to the Magees of Islandmagee by the first Earl of Antrim (Sir Randal MacDonnell) in 1620. MacDonnell, of course, was looking after a family who had been military retainers of his own family, who were blood relations (albeit distant ones), and who were fellow Catholics. But in moving the Magees he was also clearing from Islandmagee the leaders of the family whose residence most impeded the settlement of Islandmagee by the members of the Hill family—the head of which, Sir Moyses, was not only a relative of his own, but, as provost marshall of Ulster, was a civil figure with whom he naturally wanted to keep on good terms; the more so because the Earl's catholicism placed him in a highly vulnerable position concerning his own lands and titles.

On Sir Moyses Hill's family relationships, see John Lord, *The Peerage of Ireland....*, (revised by Mervyn Archdall), (London: G.G.J. and J. Robinson, 1789), vol. I, p. 201, and vol. I, pp. 320-321.

13. Maguire, p.8

14. For a diagrammatic genealogy of the Hill family, see the frontispiece to the calendar for D.778, in the PRONI.

15. Several early leases are found in the PRONI, among them: Arthur Chichester to Sir Moyses Hill, ninety-nine year lease of Islandmagee, dated 20 Sept. 1618, for consideration of £150 and annual rent of £200 (D. 77/1/1); a sixty-one year extension of the original ninety-nine year lease, for consideration of £3,000, granted to Charles O'Neill in trust for Michael Hill, deed dated 4 March 1699 (D.778/27). The extension had been agreed to in 1666 (see PRONI D. 778/208, which contains a recapitulation of the history of the leasehold.)

A new 99 year lease was dated 17 July 1769. The rent was to be paid in "good and lawful money of Great Britain." The only rights that Donegall kept were "all manner of Hawkes and Fowles," advowsons, and the right to hold a Court Leet, that is, a manorial court (PRONI D. 778/208).

16. "Mr. Skinner's Accounts with the Right Honourable Lord Viscount Dungannon for one year ending 1st November 1818." PRONI D. 1954/1/1.

17. I owe this summary of Donegall estate management to a private communication from Dr. W.A. Maguire. See his excellent article "The 1822 Settlement of the Donegall Estates," *Irish Economic and Social History*, Vol. 3 (1976), pp. 17-32.

18. Three extensions, differing slightly in detail, were negotiated in the early 1820's: 31 May 1820 (PRONI D.778/642a), 31 May 1821 (PRONI D.778/664a), and 4 June 1822 (PRONI D.778/706a). Ultimately, these extensions ended in 1882. The renewal fine paid at this time was £4,000. (O'Laverty, vol. IV, p. 125).

19. PRONI, D. 778/1096, dated 24 June 1841. The total renewal fines and costs on this extension were £2,123. See also "Donegall Estates, Determinable Leases, 1882," (PRONI, D. 835/7/1).

20. In 1840 Lord Dungannon allotted twenty pounds annually for the assistant minister of the First Islandmagee Presbyterian Church (Donaldson, p. 113).

21. In 1839 Dungannon had all the public houses in Islandmagee, fourteen in

number, broken up. As one would expect, this led to an illicit spirits trade. "Memoir of the Parish of Islandmagee," vol. I, p. 85 (Royal Irish Academy, Dublin, Ordnance Survey, Box 11, Antrim XI, VI, Islandmagee Parish). His predecessor had introduced lime kilns (Ibid., vol. I, p. 52).

22. The clearest statement of this very complicated matter is found in *The Revised Report s... Common Law and Equity...* Vol. LXIX, 1844-1846 (London: Sweet and Maxwell, 1904), pp. 137-140. See also the miscellaneous collection of Trevor Papers (PRONI, D. 1954/5/Box 1); also see executor's statement of 10 May 1839 (PRONI, D. 778/1081).

23. Judgement given by Lord Chancellor, *The Revised Reports....*, pp. 146-149.

24. How long the Islandmagee estate was held in a state of suspended animation by the surveying process is uncertain, but probably from 1849 to 1859, inclusive. One of the Trevor estates miscellaneous papers mentions a final chancery judgement of 1849 (PRONI D, 1954/5/ Box 1). Also, the last full year of rental receipts for the Island found in ["Rental of Viscount Dungannon's Irish Estates"] (PRONI D. 1954/1/31) is for 1847-48, which also implies that 1849 was the last year Islandmagee was actually held as a single leasehold. The deed that formally trisected the leasehold was dated 1 February 1859 (PRONI D. 778/1185).

25. See PRONI D. 1954/5/Box 1.

26. On the life of the third viscount, see *DNB*.

The complicated genealogy operative at this point, especially the interweaving of the Downshire-Dungannon interests, is best explained in the frontispiece to the PRONI calendar of the Trevor Papers (D. 778).

27. Unhappily, the information on the years of tripartite division is severely limited. The conveyance of 1859, however, is accompanied by the map reproduced in the text.

28. The absence of direct evidence makes it unclear precisely how Islandmagee was managed between the trisection of 1859 and the end of the leaseholds in 1890. Material in the seven manuscript notebooks giving the post-1860 re-evaluations of Islandmagee (as yet uncatalogued in the PRONI), indicate that Trevor, as holder of the Dungannon section, maintained his leasehold straddling the middle of Islandmagee, but that the two-thirds comprising the two ends of the Island passed into the hands of a Thomas Slingsby, Esq. Control of the various townlands is given in the re-evaluation notebook covering the years 1887-97 (p. 129) as follows:

Townlands under Slingsby leasehold:
Ballycronan-beg, Ballycronan-more, Ballydown, Ballykeel, Ballylumford, Ballyprior-beg, Ballystrudder, Castletown, Cloghfin, Drumgurland, Dundressan, Mullaghdoo, Portmuck, Temple Effin.

Townlands under Lord Trevor's leasehold:
Ballyharry, Ballymoney, Ballymuldrogh, Balloo, Ballytober, Kilcoan-beg. Kilcoan-more.

Townlands held in part by Slingsby, in part by Trevor:
Ballyprior-more, Carnspindle, Gransha, Mullaghboy.

Precisely when Slingsby came into control is uncertain, although the re-evaluation volume for 1863-78 indicates that some time between 1870 and 1878 he assumed the Leslie interest. I cannot find an approximation of when he acquired the Smith interest.

Of course, this uncertainty is irritating, but it does not undercut the point made in the text, that for much of the nineteenth century Islandmagee represented a situation of managerial confusion that naturally would lead to low expenditure on capital improvement.

29. U.H.H. de Burgh, *The Landowners of Ireland* (Dublin: Hodges, Foster, and Figgis, [1878]), p. 132.

30. Article "Islandmagee—Past and Present," by Francis Joseph Bigger in *Belfast News-Letter,* 30 July 1923. Considerable relevant information about the Donegall estate and Islandmagee is contained in the article. The Donegall estate's history is extremely complicated, as well as important, and merits a full-scale study.

On the Donegall genealogy, see Burke's *Peerage.* . . . The complexity indicated in the text is partly a result of both the third and fourth marquesses having been the issue of the second. In other words, the title passed twice in a single generation.

For a very useful article on the Donegall estates problem, see W.A. Maguire, "Lord Donegall and the Sale of Belfast: A Case History from the Encumbered Estates Court," *Economic History Review,* 2 ser., vol 29 (Nov. 1976), pp. 570-584.

31. See the report, "Irish Peerage Romance," In the *Larne Times and Weekly Telegraph,* 17 October 1903, taken from the *Daily Mail;* and Bigger's article in the *Belfast News-Letter,* 30 July 1923.

32. For example, in *Burke's.* . . (1956) and *Debrett's.* . . (1967).

33. *Larne Times and Weekly Telegraph,* 27 December 1919.

There is a tradition that a house still standing in Whitehead was used by the Donegall agent for collecting rents, but I could find no written confirmation of this.

34. *Abstract of Censuses and Returns under the Population Act.* . . . , p. 217, H.C. 1833 (634), xxxix.

35. Cf. the 1841 all-Ireland figures in T.W. Freeman, *Pre-Famine Ireland. A Study in Historical Geography* (Manchester: Manchester University Press, 1957), pp. 76-77.

36. Hooker, p. 27. In Ulster, landlords had been anxious to grant leases during the seventeenth and early eighteenth centuries. After approximately 1750, however, economic pressures led them to desire tenants-at-will, a trend that continued into the middle decades of the nineteenth century. See W.H. Crawford, "Landlord-Tenant Relations in Ulster, 1609-1820," *Irish Economic and Social History,* vol. II (1975), pp. 5-21.

37. W.H. Crawford and B. Trainor (eds.) *Aspects of Irish Social History 1750-1800* (Belfast: HMSO, 1969), pp. 7,16.

38. For the sake of convenience, I am listing only the PRONI serial numbers of the leases. They all are under the D. 778 rubric: nos. 255, 577, 660, 661, 695, 718, 721, 724-726, 732-747, 750-755, 758-808, 811-935, 937-964, 966-968, 972, 975-976, 983, 1023, 1242, 1244-1245.

The leases listed above were effected up to 1829. A few other leases signed in the years 1829-1840 inclusive were for lesser terms than thirty-one years, presumably in most cases to make them fall in at the same time as the thirty-one year leases formulated during the 1820's. See PRONI D.778: 1024, 1039a, 1050a, and 1060a, 1065, 1080, 1093-1094.

39. Compare the [untitled] Rent Roll of Viscount Dungannon's Irish Estates for 1828-29 (PRONI D. 1954/1/12) with the [untitled] Rental of Trevor Irish Estates for 1846-47 (PRONI D. 1954/1/31), and then juxtapose this with a comparison of the 1846-47 roll and the [untitled] Rental of Trevor Irish Estates, 1878-79 (PRONI D. 1954/1/65). Note that the leases were heritable.

40. A succinct and extremely serviceable study is W.F. Bailey's *The Irish Land Acts. A Short Sketch of Their History and Development* (Dublin: HMSO, 1917).

41. On the impact of such middlemen, see *First Report from Commissioners for Inquiring into the Condition of the Poor in Ireland. Appendix H, Part II. Remarks on Evidence.* . . *by one of the commissioners,* pp. 30-31, H.C. [42], 1836, xxxiv.

42. PRONI D. 2723/2-3.

43. PRONI, Val. IB: 118, p. 114.

44. PRONI [uncatalogued] "Valuation Revision Book, 1863-78."

45. The Islandmagee information is given in: *Returns of Agricultural Produce in Ireland in the Year 1849,* pp. 82-83 [1245], H.C. 1850, li.

Professor S.D. Clark of the University of Western Ontario, who has worked through the Irish agricultural reports, informs me that holdings were calculated by townlands. This means that if an individual held land in two townlands, his land was tallied as two separate holdings. Thus, both the Islandmagee and the national statistics somewhat understate the amount of land under the control of each farmer. Nevertheless, according to Professor Clark's redaction of the returns for several areas, the distortion is not very great, because townland boundaries usually followed natural boundaries and the incidence of holdings being in two separate townlands was not frequent.

The national pattern is documented in: P.M. Austin Bourke, "The Agricultural Statistics of the 1841 Census of Ireland. A Critical Review," *Economic History Review,* 2 ser. vol. XVIII, no. 2 (1965), p. 377.

46. This is clearly indicated by there being in 1849 only one agricultural holding under one acre.

47. There are five possible sources available for the delineation of inheritance patterns, none of them adequate. The first, the landlords' rolls, is not sufficient because the rolls are incomplete. The second source, valuation records, is complete, but does not indicate the relationship of individuals holding land to those who held it previously, even if they shared a family name. The third source, census records, is not available on individual families except for 1901 and 1911, and thus is too limited to provide definitive information, and the fourth source, church records, is extremely incomplete.

Most disappointing, the fifth source, the wills of the Islanders, either registered or probated, proves inconclusive. At first impression one would think that such wills would answer one's questions about inheritance patterns. However, a search through probate records for the years 1857-1910, inclusive, of all wills made by Islanders of £20 valuation or above, was extremely disappointing. To begin with, it is clear that only a small minority of the Islanders (even in this relatively high social stratum) made wills. Further, there is no indication that these wills were a representative sample of the inheritance patterns of the entire community or even of their own social level. The arrangements described are eccentric and form no pattern at all. Indeed, one suspects that wills were made chiefly in deviant cases and represent everything except the local norm!

Finally, as a cautionary note to anyone working with these wills as a form of social information, one should note that they consistently underrepresent the economic worth of the individuals involved, largely because each agricultural holding was reported at its valuation level rather than at the capitalised value of the leasehold.

For the Islandmagee wills on which I have based the preceding points, see PRONI: T. Bel 1/1, pp. 809 (McCrea); T. Bel. 1/2, pp. 64-65 (McClelland); T. Bel 1/3, pp. 14-15 (Nelson; T. Bel 1/4, p. 129 (Hill); T. Bel 1/4, pp. 538-539 (Laverty); T. Bel 1/4, pp. 671-672 (Laird); T. Bel 1/8, pp. 794-795 (Nelson); T. Bel 1/10, pp. 71-72 (Smiley); T. Bel 1/43, pp. 28-29 (Hill); T. Bel 1/53 (Fullerton); T. Bel 4/29, p. 307 (Tweed); T. Bel 4/44, p.2 (Holmes); T. Bel 4/49 (Browne).

Also see PRONI, Probate, Belf. D.R.: 28 Sept. 1860 (Hawthorne); 1891/1-536 (Hill); 1891/11-22 (Meneilly); 1894/1-340 (Kane); 1894/II-246 (Magill); 1899/II-318 (Wilson); 11 June 1902 (Templeton); 21 Sept. 1906 (Browne); 5 Aug. 1908 (Donnan).

48. See for example, the Dungannon rent roll for 1828-29 and for 1847-48 (PRONI D. 1954/1/12 and D. 1954/1/32).

On the Trevor portion of the estate, the prejudice against granting directly small individual holdings was somewhat relaxed later in the century. For example, in

1888-89, ten of 138 individual leasings on Trevor's portion were for less than one acre. See Trevor rent roll (PRONI D. 1954/1/75).

49. The compilation is made from the "Valuation Revision Book, 1863-78"

50. The sample lease on page 40 makes this clear for the 1820's onwards, but Islandmagee must have been part of the money—as distinct from barter—economy from much earlier times (I suspect for the entire eighteenth century). In any case, the leases that fell due in the 1820's had been preceded by money-payment leases. (John Dubourdieu, *Statistical Survey of the county of Antrim*. . . . [Dublin: Royal Dublin Society, 1812], p. 151.) Further, the fact that the renewal of more than one hundred leases that fell open in 1770 was advertised in the *Belfast News-Letter* clearly implies that the Island at that date was part of the money economy.

51. Patrick Lynch and John Vaizey, *Guinness's Brewery in the Irish Economy 1759-1876* (Cambridge: Cambridge University Press, 1960), p. 29.

52. W.H. Crawford of the PRONI, an expert in Ulster social history, tells me that the acquittances on Islandmagee were noteworthy and not, thus far, known elsewhere in Ulster. I suspect that "acquittance" was a pompous term for quit-rents, meaning an annual charge that arose either as commutation for certain supposed feudal services or for liabilities owed the Crown after the 1641 Rebellion. Neither the acquittances nor the two-days-work-for-a-man-and-a-horse provision should be taken as survivals of medieval or early modern practices, but as practices that were revived, and not for their original intent but to raise revenue.

53. Notice that in setting the payment dates as 1 November and 1 May, the estate managers were being quite businesslike, for it meant the abandonment of the traditional late-September and late-March dates associated with the Feast of St. Michael the Archangel and the Feast of the Annunciation of the Blessed Virgin Mary. I have found one lease of the period (PRONI 778/577) which required payment on these time-honoured days.

It is unfortunate that the available Donegall estate papers contain no Islandmagee leases, as I suspect that sometime in the late nineteenth or early twentieth century, the payment dates were changed. The *Larne Times and Weekly Telegraph* of 27 December 1919 carries a notice to the Islandmagee tenants stating that their rent must be paid to the Donegall agent, who will be at the King's Arms Hotel, Larne, on 6 and 7 January.

54. The figures for 1818-19 to 1847-48, inclusive, are derived from the rent rolls of the entire estate. For the remainder of the century, only the rolls for the Trevor third of Islandmagee are available. This "sampling" does not distort the validity of the pounds-per-acre ratio, as a comparison of rents of the Trevor portion with those of the entire Island for earlier years indicates that the Trevor portion was representative of the whole.

The rent rolls used are found in the PRONI, D. 1954/1/1, D. 1954/1/12, D. 1954/1/22, D. 1954/1/32, D. 1954/1/42, D. 1954/1/43, D. 1954/1/65, D. 1954/1/75.

In the 1890's the estate was under the fair rent provision of the 1881 land act. I estimate that the average rent per acre under the 1881 act was 12 shillings, four pence. The estimate is made from information given in advertisements in the local paper, offering to sell tenancies and specifying the judicial rent involved. The limits of this method are obvious, but the figures nevertheless are considerably better than none at all. The advertisements were taken from the *Larne Times and Weekly Telegraph,* issues of: 12 March 1898, 28 October 1899, 26 January 1901, 12 January 1907, 29 August 1908, 24 October 1908, 2 October 1909, 22 January 1910, 5 November 1910, 17 August 1912, 12 April 1913, 19 April 1913, 26 April 1913, 20 March 1915. 20 October 1917, 9 March 1918, 13 April 1918, 11 January 1919,

18 January 1919, 22 March 1919, 10 May 1919, 25 October 1919, 6 December 1919, 3 April 1920, 19 March 1921, 26 March 1921, 20 August 1921, 24 September 1921, 12 November 1921.

For three cases of the actual judicial reduction of rent, see the following files: PRONI, FIN 23/2/1A, Records Nos 3260, 4048, and 4223.

55. Maguire, pp. 63-64.
56. PRONI D. 2723/2-3.
57. Mr. and Mrs. S.C. Hall, *Ireland: Its Scenery, Character, etc.* (London: Jeremiah How, 1843), vol. III, p. 124n.
58. Ibid.
59. PRONI Val. IB:118.
60. *The First Report from Commissioners for Inquiring into the Condition of the Poor in Ireland. Appendix H. Part II. Remarks on Evidence. . . by one of the Commissioners* (p. 36) gives several examples, ranging from £13 for seventy-six acres to £170 for six acres. With the one exception, however, the examples were all under £20 an acre, and most well under £10.
61. "The price of tenant-right frequently amounts to £10, £12, £20, or £25 per acre and that sometimes as much as forty years purchase of the rent is paid for it." *Digest of Evidence taken before Her Majesty's Commissioners of Inquiry into the State of the Law and Practices in Respect to the Occupation of Land in Ireland* [The Devon Commission] (Dublin: Alexander Thom, 1847), part I, p. 290.
62. I suspect that these sums were raised on the Island itself, by farmers from their own and their relatives' savings, and by loans from the more prosperous farmers. That large sums were available is indicated by the case of Robert Thomas Arthurs, of an Islandmagee farming family, whose personal estate was probated in 1923 at £44,800 (Source: Clipping Collection in possession of Mrs. Eleanor Holmes, "Ivyhill," Islandmagee, vol. I).
63. Sean O'Faolain, *The Irish. A Character Study* (New York: Devin-Adair Co., 1956), p. 92.
64. Opportunities for purchase existed under the following United Kingdom land acts: 1870, 1881, 1885, 1887, 1888, 1889, 1891, 1896, 1903, 1907, and 1909. They also occurred under Northern Ireland acts of 1925 and 1929.

The fact that the Donegall estates were in trusteeship for a minor from 1904 to 1924 complicated matters, but it did not make it impossible for the tenantries to buy out the family. Rather, as F.J. Bigger noted, it was the tenants' refusal to take the opportunity which accounts for the land remaining so long in Donegall hands ("Islandmagee—Past and Present," *Belfast News-Letter*, 30 July 1923).

65. Even so, the Donegall estate was able to keep, as designated "building sites" a considerable amount of land. I know of one instance in the 1930's wherein a thirty-two acre field which had been kept by the estate as a building site, was sold for £900. Clearly this was agricultural, not building land.
66. For a useful contemporary example of such an hypothetical account, see the Devon Commission Digest, part I, p. 3.

For an earlier example from County Antrim, see William S. Mason, *A Statistical Account or Parochial Survey of Ireland* (Dublin: Faulkner Press, 1819), pp. 37-38.

67. The Devon Commission Digest (p. 3), gives two estimates of 10 shillings, and 13 shillings, per acre of land. Assuming that instead of buying all of his seed the farmer uses some of his own seed (or, more likely, that he trades seed with a neighbour, to avoid degeneration in quality), then the smaller figure is justified.
68. The cess figures are for 1836, and are the closest I could find to 1851. PRONI, VAL IB:118.
69. Tithe composition for Islandmagee was set at £400 a year, and remained at that level until raised to £445 in 1861. See "Applotment of tithes in the Parish of Isle of Magee, Diocese of Connor and County of Antrim by William Burleigh, Tithe Commissioners, 1834," PRONI FIN V/159.

70. This is a purely arbitrary—but not unrealistic—figure. It is based on the assumption that the farmer had a cart worth £10, a plow worth £3, various small tools worth another £10, and miscellaneous improvement expenses of £7. This totals £30, and assuming that the devices had a life of ten years, represents the straight-line depreciation. For costs of farm machinery in County Antrim early in the century (before the long nineteenth century deflation began), see Dubourdieu, pp. 156-157. On Islandmagee plow prices see "Memoir of the Parish of Islandmagee," vol. I, p. 54.

71. This item probably represents the largest single overestimate in the cost analysis, since a fifteen acre farmer probably would not have kept a full-time labourer, although he almost certainly would have bought labour services. I take the rate from the "Memoir of the Parish of Islandmagee," vol. I, p. 89. The survey stated that annual wages for a male farm servant, other than a skilled ploughman, were between six and seven pounds annually, plus food. Skilled workers received more. In 1868, a "cattleman" for a large farmer received nine shillings a week and a free house (*Larne Weekly Reporter and Northern Counties Advertiser*, 26 December 1868). As late as 1909 young farm labourers were receiving only twelve pounds a year (*East Antrim Times*, 24 August 1973).

72. Again, this is an arbitrary figure, and is probably too high. It covers things such as cartage of goods to markets, veterinary costs and breeding fees for work-animals, and the like.

73. I have excluded from the calculation crops that were of minor importance to the Islanders (barley, peas, turnips) and have rounded the figures for simplicity of presentation. For the precise figures see, *Return of Agricultural Produce in Ireland in the Year 1849*, p. 83 [1245], H.C. 1850, li.

For comparisons with other regions and with the national situation see the following: *Return of Agricultural Produce in Ireland, in the Year 1847* [923], H.C. 1847-48, lvii; *Return of Agricultural Produce in Ireland in the Year 1848* [1116], H.C., 1849, xliv; *Return of Agricultural Produce in Ireland in the Year 1850* [1404], H.C. 1851, 1.

74. *Return of Agricultural Produce in Ireland for the Year 1856*, p. xxvi, [2249], H.C. 1857-58, lvi. The specific calculation is as follows:

wheat, 1½ acres: 5.7 barrels per acre of 20 stones each = 2,394 lbs. oats, 8 acres: 7.7 barrels per acre of 14 stones each = 12,073.6 lbs. beans and peas, 2 acres: 27.9 bushels per acre of 60 lbs. each = 3,348 lbs. potatoes, 2½ acres: 42.6 barrels per acre of 20 stones each = 29,820 lbs.

The reader should be wary of comparing the production statistics given in the text with those for other parts of Ireland. The measures of produce varied greatly throughout the country and calculations of comparison should be made only by persons in strong physical and emotional health. Still, if this particular dementia must be indulged, the following sources are a considerable aid: *Agricultural Statistics, Ireland* [2245], H.C. 1857, xlii, pp. 4-5; Austin Bourke, "Notes on some Agricultural Units of Measurement in Use in Pre-Famine Ireland," *Irish Historical Studies*, vol. XIV, no. 55 (March 1965), pp. 236-245; Edward Wakefield, *An Account of Ireland, Statistical and Political* (London: Longman, Hurst, Rees, Orme, and Brown, 1812), vol. II, pp. 199-202.

75. The prices for wheat, oats, and potatoes are the average prices for Ulster for 1851 and are found in *Return showing the Average Prices of Agricultural Produce ... In Ireland during the Years 1849, 1850, and 1851*, p. 2. H.C. 1852 (307), xlvii. The beans price was not reported in that year. The best approximation I have been able to find came from the *Larne Weekly Reporter and Northern Counties Advertiser* (11 March 1865). At that time wheat and oat prices were within a shilling of the 1851 prices, so probably the beans price was comparable as well.

The specific calculation is as follows:
wheat: at 8 shillings per cwt. of 112 lbs. =   £ 8 11s

oats: at 5 shillings 7½ pence per cwt. of 112 lbs. = £25 6s 5d
beans and peas: at 7 shillings per cwt. of 112 lbs. = £10 9s
potatoes: at 3 shillings 7¾ pence per cwt. of 112 lbs. = £48 6s 2d

For agricultural prices in Ireland at other times during the century, see: Wakefield, II, pp. 203-208; *Corn. An Account of the Quarterly Average Prices of corn . . . for the 15th August 1804 to 15th May 1813*, H.C. 1812-13 (295), vi; *Wheat and Oats, Ireland*, H.C. 1837-38 (177), xlv; *Wheat, Oats and Barley (Ireland)*, H.C. 1852 (316), xlvi; *Agricultural Prices in Ireland, 1881-1918*, H.C. 1919 (201), li.

For local prices see the *Larne Times and Weekly Telegraph* for the 1890's onwards, as it regularly carried Larne, Ballymena, and Belfast market reports.

76. As mentioned earlier in the text (p. 43) it was usually the tenant farmers, not the landlords, who leased out small cottages and gardens. The average fifteen acre tenant would have had such a cottage plot to rent. The imputed rent is taken from examples in *General Valuation of Rateable Property in Ireland and Union of Larne* (Dublin: Alexander Thom & Sons, 1861), *passim*.

77. David Bleakley, "Industrial conditions in the Nineteenth Century," in T.W. Moody and J.C. Beckett (eds.), *Ulster since 1800. A Social Survey* (London: British Broadcasting Corporation (1957), p. 124.

78. P.S. Robinson, "The Geography of South East Antrim in the mid-19th Century: A Study in Historical Geography" (unpublished B.S. thesis, the Queen's University of Belfast, 1971), p. 11.

79. "S.McS.", [Samuel McSkimin] "An Account of Islandmagee taken in 1809," *Belfast Magazine*, 31 August 1809, p. 104.

80. George H. Bassett, *The Book of Antrim* (Dublin: Sealy, Bryers, and Walker, 1888), p. 399.

81. Compiled from *Return of Agricultural Produce in Ireland in the Year 1849,* pp. 82-83 [1245], H.C. 1850, li.

82. Arthur Maltby, *The Government of Northern Ireland, 1922-72: A Catalogue and Breviate of Parliamentary Papers* (Shannon: Irish University Press, 1974), p. 36.

83. Dubourdieu, p. 22. In the Parish of Donegore, County Antrim, the rotation in the 1830's was as follows: "first potatoes, secondly oats with grass seed and clover, thirdly meadow, fourthly pasture for one and occasionally for two years—sometimes oats follow the grass." *Ordnance Survey Memoir for the Parish of Donegore* (Belfast: Department of Extra-Mural Studies, the Queen's University of Belfast and the Public Record Office of Northern Ireland, 1974), p. 13.

84. "To raise a crop of peas or beans, except in gardens, is scarcely ever attempted. . . ." Wakefield, I, p. 365.

85. "Memoir of the Parish of Islandmagee," vol. I, p. 23. For an evocative description of the state of the Islandmagee crops in mid-July of a typical year, see *Larne Times and Weekly Telegraph*, 23 July 1892.

86. Dubourdieu, pp. 163-171, 173-181, 222.

87. Mr. and Mrs. S.C. Hall, 124*n*.

88. *Larne Times and Weekly Telegraph*, 10 September 1892.

89. For a fascinating and rigorous paper, see Alan Gailey, "The Last Sheaf in the North of Ireland," *Ulster Folklife*, vol. XVIII (1972), pp. 1-33. See also, G.B. Adams, "The Chirn," *Ulster Folklife*, vol. VIII (1962), pp. 10-14.

90. "Memoir of the Parish of Islandmagee," vol. I, p. 36. MacNeill was a large farmer. His rental for 1818-19 was about £340 (Dungannon rent rolls, PRONI, D. 1954/1/1).

91. See Dubourdieu, pp. 201-205. An extensive account of potato cultivation in Ulster in the late eighteenth century is [James McCully] *Letters by a Farmer originally published in the Belfast Evening Post; with several alterations and additions* (Belfast: James Magee, 1787), pp. 77 *ff*.

92. Ibid., pp. 184-187.

93. *Larne Times and Weekly Telegraph*, 10 September 1892.

94. G.B. Adams, "The Work and Words of Haymaking," *Ulster Folklife,* vol. XII (1966), pp. 66-91; "The Work and Words of Haymaking," *Ulster Folklife,* vol. XIII (1967), pp. 29-53.

95. Questionnaire completed by Captain Forsythe contained in the archives of the Ulster Folk and Transport Museum, Cultra Manor, County Down.

96. Adams (1962), p. 30.

97. Adams (1966), p. 67.

98. Taken from *Return of Agricultural Produce in Ireland in the Year 1847, Part II. Stock,* pp. 18-19 [1,000], H.C. 1847-48, lvii. The examples in the text are derived from the livestock census of the Larne Poor Law Union, which included Islandmagee. The unions were the smallest geographic unit for which the livestock figures were given. It is not unreasonable to assume that Islandmagee comprised a representative cross-section of the Larne union.

99. See advertisement for the pure bred Clydesdale "Sir Colin" to do stud at Brown's Bay, Islandmagee, for 2s. 6p. first service and £1 when the mare proved to be with foal (*Larne Weekly Report and Northern Counties Advertiser,* 9 June 1866).

100. Dubourdieu, p. 326.

101. Avy Dowlin (ed.), *Ballycarry in Olden Days* (Belfast: Graham and Heslip Ltd., 1963), p. 91.

102. Questionnaires completed by Captain Forsythe, Miss Ellen L. Miller, and Mrs. Eleanor Holmes, in archives of Ulster Folk and Transport Museum.

103. Dubourdieu, p. 181.

104. A. Atkinson, *Ireland Exhibited to England in a Political and Moral Survey of her Population....* (London: Baldwin, Cradock and Joy, 1823), vol. II, p. 102.

105. [Whitehead Extra-Mural Study Group], *Ordnance Survey Memoir for the Parish of Templecorran* (Belfast: the Queen's University of Belfast, 1972), p. 14. The dates given are 21 June, 20 August, 21 October, and 11 November.

106. *Report of the Commissioners appointed to Inquire into the State of the Fairs and Markets in Ireland,* p. 60, [1562], H.C. 1852-53, xli. The dates given are 21 June, the "second Friday after 11 August," and 31 October. The fairs were held under a patent given by Charles I, of his fifth regnal year.

107. William Heggan, "The Fairs," in Dowlin (ed.), pp. 81-82.

108. T.W. Freeman, "The Irish Country Town," *Irish Geography,* vol. III, no. 1 (1954), p. 6.

109. *Report of the Commissioners appointed to Inquire into the State of the Fairs and Markets in Ireland,* p. 43.

110. Questionnaire by Mrs. Eleanor Holmes, in archives of Ulster Folk and Transport Museum.

111. Questionnaire by Captain Forsythe in archives of Ulster Folk and Transport Museum.

112. "Memoir of the Parish of Islandmagee," vol. I, pp. 30-32, 53, 89. See also the transcript on PRONI, pp. 28-30.

I have not found any detailed description of the technology of fishing practiced by the Islanders. The Ordnance Survey says that they used drift nets for herring fishing, and larger-mesh drift nets for salmon and large fish. Probably, also, they jigged for herrings with a bare hook, a singular practice still employed in the 1970's (See *Fishing News* 16 August 1974, for a report of Islandmagee practices based on information provided by John Henshaw, D.S.M., of the *Elizabeth,* Whitehead).

The annual *Report of the Inspectors of Irish Fisheries in the Sea and Island Fisheries of Ireland....* provides scanty information (see, for example, that for 1874, [C.1176], H.C. 1875, xvii). A fascinating general account is Wallop Brabazon, *The Deep Sea and Coast Fisheries of Ireland, with Suggestions for the Working of a Fishing Company* (Dublin: James McGlashan, 1848).

113. *Report of Inquiries held by the Inspector of Irish Fisheries into an Alleged Decrease in the Supply of Fish Off Certain Parts of the Coast of Ireland...*, p. 6, [C. 5839], H.C. 1889, xxii.

114. *Larne Times and Weekly Telegraph*, 12 August 1905: Donaldson, pp. 49-50.

115. T. Egerton and F.J. Bigger, *A Local Illustrated, Historical and Antiquarian Guide for Tourists in connection with Kilroot, Templecorran, Whitehead, Islandmagee, and the District between Carrickfergus and Larne* (Belfast N.P. [1906]), p.25.

116. *Belfast Telegraph*, April 1959 (Holmes clipping collection, vol. III).

117. The accounts of voyages and the crew lists of the *Volante* are found in PRONI, Trans. 2a, nos: 15/166a, 15/166b, 17/124a, 17/124b, 18/114a, 18/114b, 19/125v, 19/125a, 21/108a, 21/108b, 22/82a, 22/82b, 23/80a, 23/80b, 24/77a, 24/77b, 26/77a, 26/77b, 28/42a, 28/42b, 29/48b, 30/43a, 30/43b, 31/39a, 31/39b, 32/33a, 32/32b, 33/35a, 33/35b, 35/20a, 35/20b, 36/21a, 36/21b, 37/17a, 37/17b, 38/13, 39/11a, 39/11b, 40/11a, 40/11b, 41/9a, 41/9b, 43/6a, 43/6b, 44/5a, 44/5b, 45/7a, 45/7b, 46/7a, 46/7b.

118. "S.M.S." in *Belfast Magazine*, 31 August 1809, p. 105.

119. "Memoir of the Parish of Islandmagee," vol. 1, pp. 65-66.

An archtypical story of the Islanders' acquisitiveness in harvesting the sea concerns the wreck of the steamship *Peridot* off Skernaghan Point on 26 November 1905. The 240 ton ship had been making for the shelter of Larne harbour, but, came upon the Islandmagee rocks instead. Nine seamen were lost. Nearly the entire population of Islandmagee quickly flocked to the disaster. Up to this point the story is circumstantially reported in the local newspaper (*Larne Times and Weekly Telegraph*, 2 December 1905).

The unreported part is that in their scavenging activities, the Islanders did not merely plunder the sea: the nine dead men were lined up on the beach, like cod, and a tarpaulin was placed over them for the night. The next morning the first visitors discovered that the tarp had been stolen. That is mere gossip, and of course I do not believe a word of it; there are, however, Islanders alive today who claim to know who took it.

120. "Memoir of the Parish of Islandmagee," vol. I, pp. 28-30.

121. Ibid., pp. 31-33, 52-53, 59-62. Apparently, the Dungannon introduction of lime at the end of the eighteenth century was the second attempt. Previously, in 1779, Lord Dungannon had tried to encourage the tenantry to lime their lands, by erecting a kiln and selling the lime at a reduced price. Most of the tenants refused this offer, the lime slackened in the kilns, and eventually broke down the kiln walls. See "S.Mc.S." in *Newry Magazine*, vol. 3 (1817), p. 507*n*

122. Donaldson (pp. 77-79), discusses the lime quarries and kilns but with very vague dating. He seems not to have known of the 1837 chancery suit.

123. Dubourdieu, p. 573; "S.M.S.," in *Belfast Magazine*, 31 August 1809.

124. Egerton and Bigger, p. 13.

125. Bassett, p. 339.

126. On Wise's plans for the cliff walk, which in fact never was completed as far around the Island as he wished, see J.R.L. Currie, *The Northern Counties Railway* (Newton Abbot: David and Charles, 1973), vol. I, pp. 225-252.

127. The path remained open until 1940. Then it was closed until 1951, when the Ulster Transport Authority re-opened it. Finally, in 1961, it was abandoned. Currie, vol. II, pp. 38-39.

128. The late Mrs. Margaret McBride (nee Maggie Walsh) generously gave me this material from the charming book she wrote for her grandchildren, entitled "Green Pastures." The quotation is from p. 20. For an obituary of Mrs. McBride, see *East Antrim Times*, 29 August 1975.

129. *East Antrim Times*, 17 May 1974.

130. *Larne Times and Weekly Telegraph*, 25 March 1904.

131. Samuel Clark, "The Political Mobilization of Irish Farmers," *Canadian Review of Sociology and Anthropology*, vol. 12 (November 1975).

Chapter Four

1. K.H. Connell, "The Population of Ireland in the Eighteenth Century," *Economic History Review*, vol. XVI (1946), p. 123.

2. This estimate is most tentative. I have made it by multiplying the number of houses reported on the 1669 hearth tax rolls as found in Dixon Donaldson, *Historical, Traditional and Descriptive Account of Islandmagee* (Whitehead: "The Whitehead News and Ballycarry and Islandmagee Reporter," 1927), p. 41, by a factor of six. This factor is the highest reasonable estimate of the number of persons per taxed house in Ireland, as derived in 1687, that being the earliest date for which national data are available. The reasons for using this factor are found in Connell's article, cited above.

One should be cautious of the final estimate for two reasons. The first and obvious one is that the final estimate is a derived, not a direct figure. Second, the reader may legitimately note that in the text I am arguing that Islandmagee did not conform to national population patterns, while in making the 1669 estimate I am mixing local data with the national index of people-per-taxed-house and I am thus making a methodological error. There are two possible responses to this second objection. The first is that Islandmagee probably conformed to the national population pattern in the late seventeenth and eighteenth centuries, although it deviated therefrom in the nineteenth. Hence, for the period that it conformed (such as 1669) relevant national material can be introduced. A second response would be to admit that the 1669 estimate is methodologically suspect and therefore just to forget it. The central argument in the text regards the nineteenth and early twentieth centuries, for which the data are sufficiently strong to support the conclusions advanced irrespective of the vexed matter of seventeenth century data. The reader may take his choice.

As for the derivative nature of the final estimate, I too am sceptical, but still believe that it is better than no estimate at all.

3. *Abstract of the Answers and Returns made pursuant to an Act of the United Parliament entitled "an Act to provide for taking an account of the population of Ireland...,"* p. 236, H.C. 1824 (577), xxvi.

There was also a government enumeration of 1813 which reported that there were 1,090 persons on Islandmagee, a figure much too low to be at all credible. For the figures, see "M.Mc.S" [Samuel McSkimin], "A Statistical account of Islandmagee," *Newry Magazine*, vol. 3 (1817), p. 395.

4. *Comparative Abstract of the Population in Ireland as taken in 1821 and 1831*, p. 30, H.C., 1833 (23), xxxix. It is generally thought that the 1831 census erred by way of over-numeration of the population (Connell, "The Population of Ireland in the Eighteenth Century," p. 113). This may be true, but if we assume that similar errors were made in the national estimate and in the Islandmagee segment, then any inferences drawn concerning growth rates are not invalidated.

5. *Census of Ireland for the Year 1861*, part I, vol. III, p. 9 [3204], H.C. 1863, lv.

6. The classic explanation is found in K.H. Connell, *The Population of Ireland 1750-1845* (Oxford: Clarendon Press, 1950). See also, K.H. Connell, "Some Unsettled Problems in English and Irish Population History 1750-1845," *Irish Historical Studies*, vol. VII, no. 28 (September 1951), pp. 225-234.

7. For example, Michael Drake has argued in "Marriage and Population Growth in Ireland, 1750-1845," *Economic History Review* vol. XVI, no. 2 (December 1963), pp. 301-313, that the marriage age was not dropping and that

marital fertility was not rising. Rather, the death rate was dropping, due to improved nutrition. He agrees with Connell in seeing the potato as the *urcause* of the population explosion, but views the intermediate mechanism differently.

A more radical criticism is made by L.M. Cullen in "Irish History Without the Potato," *Past and Present,* no. 40 (July 1968), pp. 72-83. He argues that the potato did not become the major item in the Irish diet until the late eighteenth or early nineteenth century and therefore its adoption cannot be used as the dominant factor in explaining a population boom that began long before that period. If Cullen is right (his argument is impressive, but his evidence far from comprehensive), then we are left with his conclusion, that changing diet and marriage patterns having been ruled out as primary causes of population growth, the causes of the growth in Ireland need be no different from those that operated at the same time in other countries in north and west Europe, which have still to be satisfactorily explained (p. 82).

8. S.H. Cousens, "The Restriction of Population Growth in Pre-Famine Ireland," *Proceedings of the Royal Irish Academy,* vol. 64, sec. c, pp. 94-95.

9. "Memoir of the Parish of Islandmagee," vol. I, p. 95, Royal Irish Academy, Dublin, Ordnance Survey, Box 11, Antrim XI, VI, Islandmagee Parish, vol. I. Contrast this statement about sub-division with the conclusion of the 1835 commission, that most witnesses agreed "that conacre has a direct tendency to increase population and encourage early and improvident marriages...." *First Report from Commissioners for Inquiring into the Condition of the Poor in Ireland, Appendix H., Part II Remarks on Evidence... by One of the Commissioners,* p. 6 [42], H.C., 1835, xxxiv.

10. Ibid., I, p. 95.

11. [Whitehead Extra-Mural Study Group], *Ordnance Survey Memoir for the Parish of Templecorran* (Belfast: The Queen's University of Belfast, 1972), p. 45.

12. Actually, if the county-wide data for Antrim are applicable to Islandmagee, then the degree of natural population increase is considerably reduced. Cousens' research (p. 96) reveals that the pre-Famine growth of population in County Antrim to a large extent was due to immigration into the county. This means that the degree of population immigration was even greater than the census data suggest.

13. The national figures are conveniently available in several places, for example, T.W. Freeman, *Ireland. A General and Regional Geography* (London: Methuen and Co. Ltd., third edition, 1965), p. 120.

A revealing Ulster study is James H. Johnson, "The Population of Londonderry during the Great Irish Famine," *Economic History Review,* 2 ser. vol. X, no. 2 (December 1957), pp. 273-285.

14. *Census of Ireland for the Year 1861,* part I, vol. III, p. 9.

15. Ibid., p. 9; *Census of Ireland for the Year 1871,* part I, vol. III, p. 118 [C. 964], H.C. 1874, lxxiv; *Census of Ireland for the Year 1881, areas, houses and population,* p. 21 [C. 3204], H.C. 1882, lxxviii.

16. Freeman, *Ireland. A General and Regional Geography,* p. 120.

17. Ibid., p. 120; *Census of Ireland for the Year 1891,* part I, vol. III, p. 21 [C. 6626], H.C. 1892, xciii; *Census of Ireland for the Year 1901,* vol. III, p. 2 [Cd. 1123], H.C. 1902, cxxvi; *Census of Ireland for the Year 1911... Province of Ulster,* p. 42 [Cd. 6051], 1912-13, H.C. cxvi; *Census of Northern Ireland, 1926,* p. 36.

18. An anthropological study of how marriage patterns and agricultural practices were tied together is *Family and Community in Ireland* by Conrad M. Arensberg and Solon T. Kimball (Cambridge: Harvard University Press, 1968). The field work was done in the 1930's, but can safely be projected backward in time.

The complexity of the various regional sub-patterns is analysed in "Population

Trends in Ireland at the Beginning of the Twentieth Century,'. by S.H. Cousens, *Irish Geography*, vol. V, no. 5 (1968), pp. 387-401.

For a brief revisionist discussion of post-Famine marriage patterns, see Joseph Lee, *The Modernisation of Irish Society 1848-1918* (Dublin: Gill and MacMillan, 1973), pp. 1-9.

19. See K.H. Connell, "Catholicism and Marriage in the Century after the Famine," in *Irish Peasant Society. Four Historical Essays* (Oxford: Clarendon Press, 1968), p. 113. The second set of figures was compiled only from those first marriages for which both partners specified their ages.

20. K.H. Connell, "Peasant Marriage in Ireland: Its Structure and Development since the Famine," *Economic History Review*, 2 ser., vol. XIV, no. 3 (April 1962), p. 502.

21. See K.H. Connell, "Catholicism and Marriage in the Century after the Famine," pp. 113-161.

22. K.H. Connell, "Illegitimacy before the Famine," in *Irish Peasant Society. Four Historical Essays*, pp. 82-83.

23. "Memoir of the Parish of Islandmagee," vol. I, p. 86.

24. As is the case for most of Ireland, there is not a complete set of parish registers for Islandmagee, and so the statement about pre-Famine sexual behaviour cannot be statistically verified. As for the post-Famine situation, the material is also limited. The only statistical material comes from the records of the First Islandmagee Presbyterian Church, in the custody of the Rev. R.S. Ferguson.

Of the 200 women married in the church between 1845 and 1867, inclusive, twenty-seven bore children before nine months were up.

25. The health-endangering aspects of the Roman Catholic familial-sexual code are discussed in Donald Harman Akenson, *The United States and Ireland* (Cambridge: Harvard University Press, 1973), pp. 151-167 and in Donald Harman Akenson, *A Mirror to Kathleen's Face: Education in Independent Ireland 1920-60* (Montreal and London: McGill-Queen's University Press 1975), pp. 135-142

The arguments in those books pertain specifically to the period 1920-60, but apply even more strongly to the years 1850-1920.

26. See the essays in *Belfast. The Origin and Growth of an Industrial City*, edited by J.C. Beckett and R.E. Glasscock (London: British Broadcasting Corporation, 1967). Unfortunately there are no statistics for the migration of population within the County Antrim-Belfast region, and so the argument for Islandmagee is necessarily inferential.

27. The agricultural changes as well as the seafaring opportunities discussed in the text are documented in detail in Chapter Three.

A relevant and important article is James H. Johnson's "Rural Population Changes in Nineteenth-Century Londonderry," *Ulster Folklife*, vols. XV and XVI (1970), pp. 119-136. County Londonderry experienced the effects of the potato famine to a greater degree than did Antrim, but even so Johnson concludes that the Famine cannot be used as a single-factor explanation of that county's population decline. He concludes that, "indeed, there is more than a suspicion that Londonderry was undergoing the normal process of rural depopulation found throughout Britain in the second half of the nineteenth century. The population of Londonderry would have begun to decrease even if the potato failure had not occurred, although the precise turning point in the county's demographic history might have been delayed a few years." (p. 134).

Also germaine is "The Drift from the Land" by Ronald H. Buchanan, *Ulster Folklife*, vol. VI (1960), pp. 43-61. This is a review essay centering on John Saville's *Rural Depopulation in England and Wales, 1851-1951*, with parallels drawn concerning Northern Ireland. The article is useful, but is marred by Buchanan's failure to distinguish between Famine-induced population decline and the quite different process of rural depopulation stemming from economic causes common to Great Britain and Northern Ireland.

Chapter Five

1. Redcliffe N. Salaman, *The History and Social influence of the Potato* (Cambridge: Cambridge University Press, 1949), Appendix I. See also, *Second Report from the Select Committee on the State of the Labouring Poor, in Ireland*, H.C. 1829, (347), iv.

2. This second mortality crisis of 1849 often is ignored. See S.H. Cousens, "The Regional Variation in Mortality during the Great Irish Famine," *Proceedings of the Royal Irish Academy*, vol. 63, sec. C., p. 127.

The two standard histories of the Famine are: R. Dudley Edwards and T. Desmond Williams (eds), *The Great Famine. Studies in Irish History 1845-52* (Dublin: Browne and Nolan Ltd., 1956); and Cecil Woodham-Smith, *The Great Hunger* (New York: Harper and Row, 1962).

3. I am grateful to Dr. Karen Logan for providing me with a copy of her unpublished paper, "County Antrim, 1830-1860. An Uncommon Irish County," from which the general remarks about the county are drawn.

Despite its title, there is very little observation of any value in A.S. Adair's, *The Winter of 1846-7 in Antrim, with Remarks on Out-Door Relief and Colonization* (London: James Ridgway, fifth edition, 1847).

4. P.S. Robinson, "The Geography of South East Antrim in the mid-19th Century: A Study in Historical Geography," (Unpublished B.S. thesis, the Queen's University of Belfast, 1971), p. 34.

5. S.H. Cousens, "The Regional Pattern of Emigration during the Great Irish Famine, 1846-51," *Transactions of the Institute of British Geographers*, 28, p. 121.

6. Compare the Dungannon rent roll for 1846-47 and that for 1847-48, PRONI, D. 1954/1/31 and D. 1954/1/32.

7. Cousens, "The Regional Pattern of Emigration during the Great Irish Famine, 1846-51," pp. 122-123.

8. *Distress (Ireland). Second Report of the Relief Commissioners*, pp. 24-25 [819], H.C. 1847, xvii.

9. *Distress (Ireland). Third report of the Relief Commissioners*, p. 31 [836], H.C. 1847, xvii.

10. "Larne Board of Poor Law Guardians, report from 4 August 1840 - 9 September 1848," PRONI, BC 17/A/4.

For interesting material on the work of Poor Law Guardians elsewhere in County Antrim, see *The Great Famine in Antrim, Randalstown and Districts. Extracts from the minute books of the Board of Guardians of Antrim Poor Law Union, 1844-1846, 1851-1853* (Belfast: Public Record Office of Northern Ireland, [1972]).

Chapter Six

1. Mr. and Mrs. S.C. Hall, *Ireland: Its Scenery, Character, Etc.* (London: Jeremiah How, 1843), p. 123*n*.

2. See *General Valuation of Rateable Property in Ireland ... Union of Larne* (Dublin: Alexander Thom and Sons, 1861), pp. 107, 108, 111, 113.

3. Ibid., pp. 103-116.

The first comprehensive valuation of Ireland was done in the 1830's. It is of less value than it might be, because it was made by townlands, not individual holdings. Up to 1836 all buildings of £3 or more were valued, but an act of 1836 raised the minimum to £5. Fortunately, the 1859 valuation included all buildings and gives the names of individual holders.

Under the procedure set in the 1830's, agricultural land was valued as though let by a fair landlord to a respectable tenant on a twenty-one year lease. Strict tables, ranging from one penny to thirty shillings per statute acre, were employed, and so it was the national-standard table, not the local market value of a tenancy, which determined its rating. (See *Valuation Records* published by the PRONI).

It is useful to compare the acreage of the various townlands to their 1830's assessed value, because this gives an indication of the quality of farm land.

The following table is derived from: *Census of Ireland for the Year 1851,* Part I, pp. 8-9 [1565], H.C. 1852-53, xcii; *General Valuation of Rateable Property in Ireland . . . Union of Larne,* pp. 103-116.

Townland	Acreage (to nearest whole acre)	1830s valuation (nearest £)	1859 valuation (nearest £)
Balloo	341	293	347
Ballycronan-beg	264	260	295
Ballycronan-more	357	372	376
Ballydown	210	232	277
Ballyharry	225	263	316
Ballykeel	381	407	418
Ballylumford	264	262	279
Ballymoney	328	285	333
Ballymuldrogh	168	155	184
Ballyprior-beg	242	307	327
Ballyprior-more	253	277	286
Ballystrudder	256	280	332
Ballytober	250	279	348
Carnspindle	218	256	285
Castletown	348	374	419
Cloghfin	358	319	373
Drumgurland	200	198	222
Dundressan	256	263	274
Gransha	639	675	747
Kilcoan-beg	165	195	212
Kilcoan-more	340	419	448
Mullaghboy	252	250	281
Mullaghdubh	283	261	296
Portmuck	235	248	265
Temple Effin	204	219	252
Total	7,037	7,349	8,192

4. *Abstract of Censuses and Returns under the Population Acts. . . .* p. 218, H.C., 1833 (634), xxix.

5. "Memoir of the Parish of Islandmagee", vol. I, p. 91. Royal Irish Academy, Dublin, Ordnance Survey, Box 11, Antrim XI, VI, Islandmagee Parish, vol I.

6. John Dubourdieu, *Statistical Survey of the County of Antrim. . . .* (Dublin: Royal Dublin Society, 1812), pp. 144-145.

7. Derived, with arithmetical corrections, from: *Census of Ireland for the Year 1851. Part I. Showing the Area, Population, and the Number of Houses, by Townland and Electoral Divisions. Vol. III Province of Ulster. County of Antrim,* p. 380 [1565], H.C. 1852-53, xcii; *Census of Ireland for the Year 1851,* Part VI, p. xxxiv [2134], H.C. 1856, xxxxi.

An interesting reference to a one-roomed house in Islandmagee that has remained occupied to the present day is found in "The Housing of the Rural Poor in Nineteenth-Century Ulster," by Alan Gailey in *Ulster Folklife,* vol. 22 (1976), pp. 34 and 40.

8. Caoimhin O'Danachair (Kevin Danaher), "Traditional Forms of the Dwelling House in Ireland," *Journal of the Royal Society of Antiquaries of Ireland,* vol. 102, part I (1972), p. 77. The author included windows in the side, not gable walls, as a basic characteristic, but this did not hold for Islandmagee, where windows in the gable end were common.

9. The distinction between the two basic house types was first drawn by Ake Campbell, in "Notes on the Irish House," *Folkliv,* vol. I (1937), pp. 207-234.

There is an impressive literature on the domestic architecture of the North of Ireland, most of it published in *Ulster Folklife.* In addition to articles cited elsewhere in these notes, see: E. Estyn Evans, "The Ulster Farmhouse," *UFL,* vol. I (1955), pp. 27-31; E. Estyn Evans, *UFL,* vol. III (1957), pp. 14-18; George Thompson, Desmond McCourt, and Alan Gailey, "The Magilligan Cottier House," *UFL,* vol. X (1964), pp. 23-24; E. Estyn Evans, "Some Cruck Roof-Trusses in Ulster," *UFL,* vol. XII (1966), pp. 35-40; Alan Gailey, *Rural Housing in Ulster in the Mid-Nineteenth Century* (Belfast: HMSO, 1974).

10. The specific example is found on the farm of A. Brown Esq., Ballykeel, Islandmagee. I am grateful to the Browns for help in examining this cottage.

11. Alan Gailey, "The Thatched House of Ulster," *Ulster Folklife,* vol. VII (1961), pp. 16-17.

12. Ibid., pp. 15-16, describes these jamb walls and shows their provincial distribution.

13. Ibid., p. 14, reports evidence in the archives of the Ulster Folk and Transport Museum indicating that the outshot once was found in Islandmagee.

For a description of the artifact, see Desmond McCourt, "The Outshot House-Type and its Distribution in County Londonderry," *Ulster Folklife,* vol. II (1956), pp. 27-34.

On traditional houses in Islandmagee see questionnaires completed by Captain Forsythe and by Miss Geraldine McIlwaine in the archives of the Ulster Folk and Transport Museum.

14. Gailey, "The Thatched Houses of Ulster," p. 13.

15. Ronald H. Buchanan, "Stapple Thatch," *Ulster Folklife,* vol. II (1957), p. 19.

On thatching, see also, A. Fenton, "Clay Building and Clay Thatch in Scotland," *Ulster Folklife,* vols. XV/XVI (1970), pp. 28-51.

16. Dubourdieu, p. 145.

17. O'Danachair, "Three House Types," p. 24. See also, Desmond McCourt, "The House with Bedroom over Byre: A Long-house Derivative?" *Ulster Folklife* vols. XV/XVI (1970), pp. 3-19.

18. This example is found on the Brown farm, Ballykeel.

19. The material in this paragraph is taken from questionnaires on the hearth completed by Captain Forsythe and by Miss Ellen L. Miller in the archives of the Ulster Folk and Transport Museum.

20. See questionnaires completed by Miss Ellen L. Miller and by Mrs. Eleanor Holmes, in the archives of the Ulster Folk and Transport Museum.

An excellent general survey is Alan Gailey's, "Kitchen Furniture," *Ulster Folklife* vol. XII (1966), pp. 18-34. For comparisons, see F.G.A. Aalen "Furnishings of Traditional Houses in the Wicklow Hills," *Ulster Folklife* vol. XIII (1967), pp. 61-68.

21. Mrs. Margaret McBride (*nee* Maggie Welsh), "Green Pastures," p. 2. See Chapter Three, note 128

22. "Memoir of the Parish of Islandmagee," vol. I, pp. 91-92.

23. Ibid., vol. I, pp. 91-92.

24. Questionnaire completed by Mrs. Eleanor Holmes, in archives of the Ulster Folk and Transport Museum.

Inferentially, Mrs. McBride's autobiography is important, because it indicates that by the turn of the century the salt fish diet no longer predominated.

25. "Memoir of the Parish of Islandmagee," vol. I, p. 92.

26. Questionnaire completed by Mrs. Susan E. Hay, Ballycarry, from information given by an Islandmagee resident, in archives of Ulster Folk and Transport Museum.

Chapter Seven

1. A valuable summary of road legislation is Alan McCutcheon, "Roads and Bridges," *Ulster Folklife,* vol. X (1964), pp. 73-81. Also useful is Ivor J. Herring, "Ulster Roads on the Eve of the Railway age, c. 1800-40," *Irish Historical Studies,* vol. II, no. 6 (September 1940), pp. 160-188. A well-illustrated article is "Road Planning in Ireland before the Railway Age," by J.H. Andrew, *Irish Geography,* vol. V, no. 1 (1964), pp. 17-41. Also relevant is J.T. Fulton, "The Roads of County Down, 1600-1900," (unpublished Ph.D. thesis, The Queen's University of Belfast, 1972). For general background, see "Communications," by Kevin B. Nowlan in *Ulster since 1800: Second Series,* edited by T.W. Moody and J.C. Beckett (London: British Broadcasting Corporation, 1957), pp. 138-147.

The Grand Jury presentments for County Antrim are found in the Linen Hall Library, Belfast.

2. Herring, p. 176.

3. "Memoir of the Parish of Islandmagee," vol. I, p. 37. Royal Irish Academy, Dublin Ordnance Survey, Box 11, Antrim XI, VI, Islandmagee Parish, vol. I.

4. Ibid., vol. I, pp. 38-40.

5. [Whitehead Extra-Mural Study Group]. *Ordnance Survey Memoir for the Parish of Templecorran* (Belfast: The Queen's University of Belfast, 1972), p. 18.

6. See McCutcheon, pp. 75, 76, 79.

7. The map is derived from information provided on: Estate Survey Map of Islandmagee, c. 1770, PRONI, D. 835/1/3, p. 41; the 1832 Ordnance Survey Map, PRONI, OS 6/1/47/1 and OS 6/1/41/1; the 1857-58 Ordnance Survey revision map, PRONI, C.L. 2/1/41 and C.L. 2/1/47; the Ordnance Survey, 1902 revision, Antrim, sheets 41 and 47.

8. *Second Report of the Commissioners appointed to consider and recommend a General System of Railways for Ireland. Appendix,* p. 33, H.C. 1837-38 (145), xxxv. The coaches were able to carry sixteen passengers, although ten to twelve was the average. One service cost 2½d per mile for inside seats and 1½d for outside; the other charged 3d per mile for inside, and 2d for outside seats.

9. *Vice-Regal Commission on Irish Railways. Fifth and Final Report,* vol. VI, p. 4 [Cd. 5247], H.C. 1910, xxxvii.

10. R.G. Morton, *Standard Gauge Railways in the North of Ireland* (Cultra: Ulster Folk and Transport Museum, third impression, 1972), p. 11.

11. Brendan Pender and Herbert Richards, *Irish Railways Today* (Transport Research Associates, 1967, place of origin unspecified), p. 132.

12. A valuable history of the nineteenth century railroad which affected Islandmagee is J.R.L. Currie's *The Northern Counties Railway* (Newton Abbot: David and Charles, 1973), two volumes.

For material on the affairs of the line see the *Larne Weekly Reporter and Northern Counties Advertiser,* 8 September 1866, 25 April 1874, 9 May 1874, 15 August 1874, 22 January 1876, 27 April 1878, 27 May 1876, 4 August 1877, 3 June 1878, 29 July 1876.

13. Pender and Richards, pp. 28-29. Prior to 1877, the Whitehead station was considerably farther to the south and not readily accessible to the people of Islandmagee.

14. H. Fayle, *Narrow Gauge Railways of Ireland* (East Ardsley, Yorkshire: S.R. Publishers Ltd., originally published, London: Greenlake Publications Ltd., 1946), pp. 13ff. See also, D.B. McNeill, *Ulster Tramways and Light Railways* (Cultra: Ulster Folk and Transport Museum, 1956), esp. pp. 7, 15, and Plate VII.

15. Dixon Donaldson, *Historical, Traditional, and Descriptive Account of Islandmagee* (Whitehead: "The Whitehead News and Ballycarry and Islandmagee Reporter," 1927), pp. 23-24.

16. "Memoir of the Parish of Islandmagee," vol. I, pp. 41-43.

17. *Larne Times and Weekly Telegraph,* 25 June 1910.

18. Donaldson, pp. 49-50.

19. O.B. McNeill, *Coastal Passenger Steamers and Inland Navigations in the North of Ireland* (Cultra: Ulster Folk and Transport Museum, 1960), pp. 8-9.

20. A.W.H. Pearsall, *North Irish Channel Services* (Cultra: Ulster Folk and Transport Museum, 1962), p. 31.

21. Ibid., p. 30.

22. Ibid., p. 30.

23. Ibid., pp. 20-23. For early descriptions of the service see *Larne Weekly Reporter and Northern Counties Advertiser,* 10 August 1872 and 18 July 1874, and Boyd's *Pictorial Guide to Larne and the Antrim Coast...,* p. 43.

24. Pearsall, p. 9. In 1873, the price for a Larne-New York ticket (on the Glasgow-New York run) was as follows: steerage, six guineas; second class, nine guineas; and cabin class, fifteen guineas, maximum, *Larne Weekly Reporter and Northern Counties Advertiser,* 7 June 1873).

Chapter Eight

1. E.R.R. Green, "The Great Famine," in T.W. Moody and F.X. Martin (eds.), *The Course of Irish History* (Cork: Mercier Press, 1967), p. 263.

2. *Return for each County in Ireland of the portion of such county ... under the Peace Preservation Act,* pp 4-5, H.C. 1877 (167), lxix.

3. *Offenses, Ireland,* pp 2, 8, 11, H.C. 1833 (80), xxix.

4. *Stipendiary Magistrates (Ireland),* pp 6-8, H.C. 1844 (131), xlii.

5. Ordnance Survey, "Memoir of the Parish of Islandmagee," vol. I, p. 65, Royal Irish Academy, Dublin, Ordnance Survey, Box 11, Antrim XI, VI, Islandmagee Parish, vol. I.

6. Samuel Lewis, *A Topographical Dictionary of Ireland* (London: S. Lewis, 1837), vol. II, p. 28; "S.Mc.S." (Samuel McSkimin), "A Statistical Account of Islandmagee," *Newry Magazine,* vol. 3 (1817), pp. 436-437.

7. Dixon Donaldson, *Historical, Traditional and Descriptive Account of Islandmagee* (Whitehead: "The Whitehead News and Ballycarry and Islandmagee Reporter," 1927), pp 74-75. On the manor courts generally, see *Report from the Select Committee on Manor Courts, Ireland,* H.C. 1837-38 (648), xvii; *Return of the Name of each Seneschall or Steward of a Manor in Ireland...,* p. 3., H.C. 1842 (35), xxxviii; R.B. McDowell, *The Irish Administration, 1801-1914* (London: Routledge and Kegan Paul, 1964), pp. 117-118.

8. *Return of the Names of the Several Petty Session Districts into which each County in Ireland is divided under the "Petty Session (Ireland) Act, 1951"...,* p. 1, H.C. 1856 (12), liii.

9. *Larne Weekly Reporter and Northern Counties Advertiser,* 3 June 1865.

10. Ibid., 9 February 1867 and 23 February 1867.

11. *Report from the Select Committee on Manor Courts, Ireland,* p. 140.

12. *Larne Times and Weekly Telegraph,* 18 October 1902.

13. Ibid., 18 October 1902.

14. Ibid., 1 July 1899.

15. Ibid., 8 July 1899.
16. Ibid., 26 July 1913. I can find no indication of a final judgement having been rendered.
17. For general discussion of the structure of the Irish court system see McDowell, pp 104-134. For early in the nineteenth century see Edward Wakefield, *An Account of Ireland, Statistical and Political* (London: Longman, Hurst, Rees, Orme and Brown, 1812), vol. II, pp 342ff.
18. *Larne Weekly Reporter and Northern Counties Advertiser*, 25 March 1865.
19. Ibid., 1 July 1865.
20. On the fights, see [Whitehead Extra-Mural Study Group], *Ordnance Survey Memoir of the Parish of Templecorran* (Belfast: The Queen's University of Belfast, 1972), pp. 15 and 28.
21. *Larne Times and Weekly Telegraph*, 16 March 1912.
22. Ibid., 1 August 1896.
23. Note, however, that protection of the person was a privilege accorded fully only to adults and merely in part to children. In 1901 a pupil at the Mullaghdubh National School summoned the master, Thomas Dowther, before the Carrickfergus session for assault. The boy, thirteen years of age, had been severely struck on the hand for singing too loud during the music lesson and had lost the use of the thumb. The court decided that the punishment had not been too severe and dismissed the case *(Larne Times and Weekly Telegraph,* 7 December 1901).
24. *Larne Times and Weekly Telegraph*, 31 August 1912, 5 October 1912, 19 October 1912 and 15 March 1913.
25. "Memoir of the Parish of Islandmagee," vol. II, pp 84-85.
Lest one think that as an alien to the community the Ordnance Surveyer was inclined to exaggerate the locals' vices, it is worth noting that a sympathetic observer familiar with the community, the distinguished Carrickfergus antiquarian Samuel McSkimin, reported the same things in an article he wrote in 1817:

    All classes are truly industrious and shrewd in their common dealings, taking pride in making a "hard bargain," and an equal care against dry bargains, whiskey being an indispensable requisite on all such occasions: from which practice and similar traits of what is called goodfellowship, a propensity to drinking spirits has increased much within the last thirty years...

    Dances are pretty frequent.... Spirituous liquors are introduced at all those meetings and paid for by the men; the women pay the music.... Much junketing takes place during the winter, at all of which a plentiful use is made of spirits, it being the alpha and omega of every meeting.

From "S.Mc.S.", "A Statistical Account of Islandmagee," *Newry Magazine,* vol. 3 (1817), pp. 434 and 435.
26. Ibid., vol. I, p. 85.
27. *Larne Weekly Reporter and Northern Counties Advertiser*, 20 May 1876.
28. *Larne Times and Weekly Telegraph*, 29 September 1894.
29. *East Antrim Times* (1969), Holmes Clipping Collection, vol. VI.
30. "Memoir of the Parish of Islandmagee," vol. I, p. 75.
31. *First Report from Commissioners for Inquiring into the Condition of the Poor in Ireland,* Appendix C, parts I and II, pp 113-115 [35], H.C. 1836, xx.
32. See the church records cited in Chapters Nine and Ten. The role of the churches in distributing charity is very difficult to determine precisely, largely because most of the churches' charitable work went unrecorded. Also some of it was extra-local, as when the Church of Ireland parish gave £30 to the Protestant Orphan Society *(Larne Times and Weekly Telegraph,* 25 April 1903).
33. *First Report from Commissioners for Inquiring into the Condition of the Poor in Ireland and Appendix A, with Supplement,* [Supplement], p. 274, H.C. 1835 (369), xxxii.

Campbell's testimony of the 1830s tallies with that of Samuel McSkimin, who found that even in the particularily difficult year of 1817 there were only twelve persons in need of community assistance and that in most years the numbers rarely exceeded six. "A Statistical Account of Islandmagee," p. 437.

34. *A Return giving the Date of the Formation of each Union under the Poor Relief Act. . .*, p. 3, H.C. 1843 (627), xlvi.

35. On the poor law see R.D. Collison Black, *Economic Thought and the Irish Question, 1817-1870* (Cambridge: Cambridge University Press, 1960), pp 86-133.

36. "Electoral Divisions of the Larne Union," in PRONI, BG XVII/EA/1.

For the obit of a long-time Islandmagee guardian, William McFerran of "Druid's Cottage," Islandmagee, see *Larne Weekly Reporter and Northern Counties Advertiser,* 5 December 1874.

37. *Poor Rates, Ireland,* p. 1, H.C. 1849, (608), xlvii

38. *Appendix to the Report of the Commissioners appointed to inquire into the execution of the Contracts for certain Union Workhouses,* p. 92 [568], H.C. 1844, xx.

39. *A Return of the Number of Inmates . . . in each Workhouse in Ireland on the 25h day of March . . .*, 1846 (297), xxxvi.

40. *Return of the Number of Persons 18 years of Age in the Workhouses of Ireland . . .*, p. 1, H.C. 1849 (609), xlvii.

41. *Poor Relief. Ireland,* p. 3, H.C. 1851 (1), xlix.

42. *Return of each Union Workhouse in Ireland showing Number of Paupers it is Capable of Containing,* p. 2, H.C. 1878 (200), lxv.

43. Thirty-three able-bodied females, but no men, were in the Larne workhouse according to, *Return from each of the Poor Law Unions showing what kinds of employment are carried on . . .*, p. 23, H.C. 1852-53 (513), lxxiv.

44. McDowell, p. 177.

45. *Return from each of the Poor Law Unions showing what kinds of employment are carried on . . .*, p. 23.

46. *Larne Weekly Reporter and Northern Counties Advertiser,* 6 May 1865.

47. Ibid., 2 September 1876.

48. Compare, *Return of average number of Pauper Children in each Union Workhouse in Ireland . . .*, p. 2, H.C. 1878 (250), lxv, with *Return of each Union Workhouse in Ireland showing Number of Paupers it is capable of containing. . . .*, p. 2.

49. *Return showing for each Union in Ireland the number of each sex . . .*, p. 2, H.C. 1892 (360—Sess. I), lxviii.

50. *Return of the Names of the Poor Law Unions of Ireland that have put their schools in connection with the National Board,* p. 1, H.C. 1854 (206), lv.

51. *Larne Weekly Reporter and Northern Counties Advertiser,* 18 January 1868.

52. *Report from the Select Committee appointed to inquire into the Administration of the Relief of the Poor in Ireland,* p. 183, H.C. 1861 (408), x.

53. *Return of the Average Number of Children in each Union Workhouse . . .*, p. 2, H.C. 1880 (400), lxii.

54. *Report from the Select Committee appointed to inquire into the Administration of the Relief of the Poor in Ireland,* p. 564.

55. *Poor Law. Ireland,* p. 4, H.C. 1845 (351), xxxviii.

56. *Larne Weekly Reporter and Northern Counties Advertiser,* 3 March 1866.

57. Three in 1861, or approximately one per cent of the inmates. See, *Report from the Select Committee appointed to inquire into the Administration of the Relief of the Poor in Ireland,* p. 464. See also "A Statistical Account of Islandmagee," pp. 508-511.

58. *Lunatic Asylums, Ireland,* p. 2, H.C. 1850 (354), li.

59. *Return of the Average Number of Pauper Children in each union Workhouse in Ireland . . .*, p. 2, H.C. 1878 (250), lxv.

60. See, for example, *Return showing for each Union in Ireland, the number of each sex . . .*, p. 2.

61. See "Medical Book of the Committee of Management of the Ballycarry Dispensary District in the Larne Union," PRONI, BG XVII/AA/1.
62. McDowell, pp 181, 185.
63. In 1879, for example, none of the fifty-two persons receiving outdoor relief was able-bodied. *Return of Numbers in Receipt of Relief in the Several Unions in Ireland...*, p. 4, H.C. 1880 (420), lxii.
64. *Larne Times and Weekly Telegraph,* 19 February 1898.
65. *Larne Weekly Reporter and Northern Counties Advertiser,* 25 July 1874.
66. PRONI, BG XVII/EA/1 and BG XVII/EA/2. The registers overlap. The indoor relief register also is extant, but is too unwieldy to work with conveniently (PRONI, BG/XVII/6/1-19).
67. Donald H. Akenson, *The Church of Ireland. Ecclesiastical Reform and Revolution 1800-1885* (New Haven and London: Yale University Press, 1971), pp. 53 and 350n118.
68. For an indication of Islandmagee resentment against the governmental costs regendered by the new town, see *Larne Times and Weekly Telegraph,* 17 August 1907.
69. *East Antrim Times,* 21 September 1973.

Chapter Nine

1. For an essay rich in analogies to Islandmagee see "The Mind and Character of the Lowlander," in James G. Leyburn, *The Scotch-Irish. A Social History* (Chapel Hill: University of North Carolina Press, 1962), pp. 62-79.
2. For an example of field work properly used, see Conrad M. Arensberg and Solon T. Kimball, *Family and Community in Ireland* (Cambridge: Harvard University Press, second edition, 1968).
3. Ordnance Survey, "Memoir of the Parish of Islandmagee," vol. I, p. 95, Royal Irish Academy, Dublin, Ordnance Survey Box 11, Antrim XI, VI. Islandmagee Parish, vol. I.
The marriage pattern was similar in the ethnically-similar neighbouring parish: "Men particularly of the better class usually attain the age of 28 or 30 before they encumber themselves and women rarely marry before 19." Source: [Whitehead Extra-Mural Study Group] *Ordnance Survey Memoir for the Parish of Templecorran* (Belfast: The Queen's University of Belfast, 1972), p. 45.
4. As argued in Chapter Four, the fall in Islandmagee's population from 1881-1911 is best explained by reference to competing economic opportunities for the young, not to any new impediment to marriage.
5. Derived from, *Abstract of the Answers and Returns made pursuant to an Act... to provide for taking an account of the Population of Ireland,* p. 236, H.C., 1824 (572), xxii; *Census of Ireland for the Year 1871,* Part I, *Area, Houses and Population...,* vol. III, *Province of Ulster, County of Antrim,* p. 118, H.C. [C.964], 1874, lxxiv; *Census of Ireland for the Year 1881, Area, Houses and Population... Ulster, County of Antrim,* p. 118, H.C. [C.3204], 1882, lxxviii.
6. Derived from the manuscript census forms for 1911, Public Record Office, Dublin. County of Antrim, Census 1911/131.
7. Ibid.
8. See Arensberg and Kimball, passim.
9. "Memoir of the Parish of Islandmagee," vol. I, p. 95.
10. *Ibid.,* vol. I, p. 86.
11. See the courting behaviour described in Alan Dent, *Burns in His Time* (Edinburgh: Nelson, 1966), pp. 35-37.
12. "Baptism Register, 1854-present, Second Islandmagee Presbyterian Church," in possession of William McCalmont, Esq., Clerk of Session.

13. *Supplement to the Seventeenth Report of the Registrar-General*, p. 13 [C.4153], H.C. 1884, xx.
14. K.H. Connell, *Irish Peasant Society. Four Historical Essays* (Oxford: Clarendon Press, 1968), p. 82.
15. "Memoir of the Parish of Islandmagee," vol. I, p. 86.
16. Derived from "Register of Marriages, 1845-67," in the possession of the Rev. R.S. Ferguson, of the First Presbyterian Church, Islandmagee.

In compiling these figures I gave three weeks' margin to allow for possible prematurity. Thus, the figures probably slightly understate the incidence of premarital pregnancy.

17. "S.M.S.," "An account of Islandmagee taken in 1809," *Belfast Magazine*, 31 August 1809, p. 104.
18. Cited in Richard Hayward, *In Praise of Ulster* (Belfast: Wm. Mullan & Son, 1938), pp. 84-85.
19. "Register of Marriages, 1845-67," in the possession of the Rev. R.S. Ferguson.
20. "Register of Marriages" in the possession of the Rev. Canon Bourns, St. Patrick's Church, Whitehead.
21. "Register of Marriage, Islandmagee Methodist Chapel," in possession of the Rev. J.F. Little, Whitehead.
22. Compare the lists in Dixon Donaldson's *Historical, Traditional and Descriptive Account Of Islandmagee* (Whitehead: *The Whitehead News and Ballycarry & Islandmagee Reporter*, 1927) pp. 40 and 50-51.
23. Compare the list in Donaldson, p. 41 with PRONI, Fin V/159, Parts I and II, "Applotment of tithes in the Parish of Isle of Magee, Diocese of Connor and County of Antrim by William Burleigh, Tithe Commissioner, 1834."
24. "Memoir of the Parish of Islandmagee," vol. I, p. 103.
25. *First Report of Commissioners of Public Instruction . . . Ireland*, p. 220 [46], H.C., 1835, xxxiii. The 3.3 per cent was defined as "other Protestant." On Islandmagee, this meant Methodist.
26. "Memoir of the Parish of Islandmagee," vol. I, p. 83.
27. For example, the Islandmagee clergy never tried to enforce the rule against riding or driving to church. See questionnaire completed by G.V. McIlwaine, in archives of Ulster Folk Museum.
28. "Memoir of the Parish of Islandmagee," vol. I, p. 84.
29. Mrs. Margaret McBride (nee Maggie Welsh), "Green Pastures," p. 38.
30. "Memoir of the Parish of Islandmagee," vol. I, p. 81.
31. The full list of leases from which this figure is derived is found in Chapter Three, Note 38.
32. *Census of Ireland, 1901*, Part II, *General Report with illustrative maps, etc.*, p. 527 [Cd. 1190], H.C. 1902, cxxix.
33. "Memoir of the Parish of Islandmagee," vol. I, pp. 56, 69-70.
34. The earliest national school rolls for Islandmagee in the Public Record Office of Northern Ireland are for Mullugdubh for 1863-1908 (SCH 89/1-1 and SCH 89/1/2) and for Kilcoan for 1856-1862 (SCH 46/1/1 and SCH 46/1/2).
35. *Census of Ireland for the Year 1881, Area, houses and population . . . Ulster, County of Antrim*, p. 131 [C. 3204], H.C. 1882, lxxviii. *Census of Ireland, 1901*, Part II, *General Report with illustrative maps, etc.*, p. 527.
36. For a discussion of the national schools, see Donald H. Akenson, *The Irish Education Experiment, The National System of Education in the Nineteenth Century* (London: Routledge & Kegan Paul, and Toronto: University of Toronto Press, 1970).
37. "Memoir of the Parish of Islandmagee," vol. I, p. 70.
38. T. Egerton and F.J. Bigger, *A Local Illustrated Historical and Antiquarian Guide for Tourists in connection with Kilroot, Templecorran, Whitehead, Islandmagee*

and the district between Carrickfergus and Larne (inclusive) (Belfast: N.P. [1906]), p. 25.

39. "Memoir of the Parish of Islandmagee," vol. I, pp. 104-105.

40. Donaldson, pp. 135-136. See also items in Holmes Clipping Collection, vol. I.

41. The letters are found in the PRONI, D. 2723/1-38. Various logs and ship's papers are PRONI D.2723/2-3.

John Gamble, Esq. of Emerald Isle Books, Belfast, kindly showed me Smiley's atlas: *The English Pilot. The Fourth Book* (Dublin: Boulter Grierson, 1767). This is a very rare book. Two copies only are known: one in the Library of Congress, Washington D.C., the other in Gamble's possession.

Its bibliographic value aside, one can only be amazed that a ship's master in the 1850's was sailing with charts drawn in the 1760's.

42. In 1959, long after the high noon of Islandmagee sea-faring, there still were about twenty retired sea captains living on Islandmagee. *Belfast Telegraph,* April 1959 (Holmes Clipping Collection, vol. III).

43. *Northern Star,* 25 April 1796, quoted in Donaldson, p. 5.

44. See Chapter Three, pp. 60-62.

45. On the interraction of tourists and Islanders, Mrs. McBride's "Green Pastures" is especially revealing.

46. The witchcraft story is very fully documented. See: Donaldson, pp. 43-48; *A Narrative of some strange events that took place in Island Magee and Neighbourhood, in 1716, in consequence of which several persons were tried and convicted at Carrickfergus, for Witchcraft, "By an Eye Witness,"* (Belfast: Joseph Smith, 1822); Classon Porter, *Witches, Warlocks, and Ghosts* (Reprinted from "the Northern Whig," 1885).

The tenaciousness of the Islandmagee witches story in oral tradition is amazing. I heard a version of it from the Canadian novelist the late Dennis T. Patrick Sears in 1973. Mr. Sears lived all his life in Canada and though of Irish extraction, had no connections with Islandmagee.

47. "Memoir of the Parish of Islandmagee," vol. I, p. 98.

48. Questionnaires completed by Captain Forsythe and Miss Ellen Miller in archives of Ulster Folk Museum. A general discussion is J.G. Dent, "The Witchstone in Ulster and England," *Ulster Folklife,* vol. X (1964) pp, 46-48.

49. Donaldson, p. 22.

50. Ibid., p. 22.

51. Ibid., pp. 23-23.

52. Reported in questionnaire completed by Mrs. Susan E. Hay, archives of the Ulster Folk Museum.

53. Compare the description of the funeral in James Orr's "The Irish Cottier's Death and Burial," (originally published, Belfast, 1817, and reprinted, Belfast, 1935), with the description of wakes that follows in the text.

54. The description of turn-of-the-century funeral customs comes chiefly from questionnaires completed by Mme. Ellen Miller, and Geraldine V. McIlhraine, and by Captain Forsythe, in the archives of the Ulster Folk Museum. See also, "Ballycarry Fifty Years Ago," by Eileen Bartley in *Ballycarry in Olden Days* edited by Avy Dowlin (Belfast: Graham and Heslip Ltd., 1963), p. 101. A revealing denunciation of alcoholic excesses at wakes is found in the *Larne Weekly Reporter and Northern Counties Advertiser,* 19 February 1876.

A turn-of-the-century wake story, from Captain Forsythe: An old rustic, Richard Flynn, on his way to pay respects at an old friend's wake, called on a local poteen distiller. Says Richard, "I want a quart of whiskey, Willie."

Says Willie, "I did not get paid for the last quart you got."

Says Richard: "You say nothing, Willie, and neither will I."

55. Donaldson, pp. 76-77.

56. Samuel McSkimin, *The History and Antiquities of the County of the Town of*

Carrickfergus . . . (Belfast: T. Smyth, second edition 1823), pp. 44ff.

57. "Memoir of the Parish of Islandmagee," vol. I, p. 103.

58. Donaldson, pp. 37-40, 72-73.

59. Lord Killanin and Michael V. Duignan, *The Shell Guide to Ireland* (London: Norton, second edition, 1967), p. 313.

60. The discussion of the mummer plays is drawn from the pioneering work of Alan Gailey: "The Rhymers of South-East Antrim," *Ulster Folklife*, vol. XIII (1967), pp. 18-28; *Irish Folk Drama* (Cork: Mercier Press, 1969), esp. pp. 43-50; and an article in *The Education Times*, 20 December 1973. A description of the Islandmagee plays is found in a questionnaire completed by Mrs. Eleanor Holmes, in archives of the Ulster Folk Museum.

61. Questionnaires completed by Miss Ellen Miller, Mrs. Eleanor Holmes and Captain Forsythe, in archives of Ulster Folk Museum; Donaldson, p. 22.

62. From questionnaires completed by Miss Ellen Miller and by Captain Forsythe in the archives of the Ulster Folk Museum.

63. Donaldson, p. 19.

64. Ibid., p. 20.

Chapter Ten

1. Ordnance Survey, "Memoir of the Parish of Islandmagee," vol. I, pp. 95, 96, Royal Irish Academy, Dublin, Ordnance Survey, Box 11, Antrim XI, VI, Islandmagee Parish, vol. I.

2. Ibid., vol. I, pp. 96-97.

3. *Larne Weekly Reporter and Northern Counties Advertiser*, 25 June 1870.

4. Ibid., 1 April 1876.

5. *Larne Times and Weekly Telegraph*, 11 February 1893.

6. Ibid., 2 April 1910.

7. Ibid., 20 September 1902, 21 July 1906, 20 July 1907.

8. Ibid., 10 June 1911, 29 July 1911.

9. Ibid., 21 August 1909.

10. Ibid., 7 August 1909, 3 July 1910.

11. Ibid., 31 March 1906.

12. Ibid., 27 February 1904, 8 February 1908.

13. Victor Glenn (ed.), *History of Islandmagee, by Dixon Donaldson* (privately printed 1968), pp. 87-89; Holmes Clipping Collection, vol. II.

14. Career information from clergy file of the Presbyterian Historical Society, Belfast.

15. The story is from Dr. Hugh Calwell, The Promenade, Whitehead.

16. Glenn, p. 77; Holmes Clipping Collection, vols. I and II.

17. *Larne Times and Weekly Telegraph*, 14 June 1902, 28 June 1902.

18. Ibid., 22 July 1916.

19. Letter by Dixon Donaldson, Ibid., 1 May 1920.

20. Questionnaire completed by G. McIlwaine, in Archives of Ulster Folk Museum.

21. Dixon Donaldson, *Historical, Traditional and Descriptive Account of Islandmagee* (Whitehead: "The Whitehead News and Ballycarry and Islandmagee Reporter," 1927), p. 122.

22. *Larne Times and Weekly Telegraph*, 10 July 1903.

23. Ibid., 9 February 1921.

24. Ibid., 9 July 1921.

25. Ibid., 18 August 1894, 23 September 1899, 2 February 1901, 8 May 1920, 24 July 1920; see also Holmes Clipping Collection, vol. VI.

26. "Memoir of the Parish of Islandmagee," vol. I, p. 100.

27. T. Egerton and F.J. Bigger, *A Local, Illustrated, Historical and Antiquarian Guide for Tourists in connection with Kilroot, Templecorran, Whitehead, Islandmagee and the District between Carrickfergus and Larne (inclusive)* (Belfast: n.p., [1906]), p. 27.

28. Holmes Clipping Collection, vol. II. See also *Larne Times and Weekly Telegraph*, 21 February 1903, 6 January 1906.

29. *Larne Weekly Reporter and Northern Counties Advertiser*, 8 June 1872.

30. Ibid., 13 November 1875.

31. "Roll and Records, Islandmagee Total Abstinence and Prohibition Society," in the possession of the Reverend R.S. Ferguson, First Presbyterian Church, Islandmagee.

32. *Larne Times and Weekly Telegraph*, 3 March 1906.

33. Ibid., 25 April 1908.

34. Ibid., 28 March 1908.

35. Ibid., 22 February 1908, 5 February 1910.

36. Ibid., 31 January 1920.

37. In my view it is profitless to argue whether or not Brice actually was a genuine Presbyterian. Donaldson argues the case against Brice's Presbyterianism at considerable length (pp. 100, 104-106). A discerning discussion of the complicated early origins of Presbyterianism in Antrim, including a specific discussion of Brice, is "The Coming of Presbyterianism in Ulster," by H.G. Calwell, in *The Non-Subscribing Presbyterian*, no. 837 (Sept. 1976), pp. 163-169.

38. Donaldson, pp. 106-111; see also clergy list in Presbyterian Historical Society, Belfast.

39. John Murphy. Born 1756, the son of a schoolmaster of Cairncastle, licensed by Templepatrick Presbytery 1786. Ordained to Islandmagee 15 August 1789. Married Jane Brown "who was skilled in medicine." Suspended for three months in 1824. Retired in 1828. Died 12 July 1842.

William Campbell. Born (n.d.) Killyleagh. Educated at Old College, Belfast. General Certificate 1825. Licensed by Dromore Presbytery November 1827. Ordained to Islandmagee 14 April 1829. Married in 1844 to A. Nelson, of Islandmagee. Died 17 August 1876.

David Steen. Born near Limavady (n.d.). Educated at Queen's College Belfast and Assembly College Belfast. Received B.A. (Queen's) 1875. Licensed by Belfast Presbytery 1875. Ordained to First Islandmagee 14 August 1877. Married 1897.

Source: MS "Irish Presbyterian Church Fasti." Presbyterian Historical Society, Belfast.

40. Donaldson, p. 111.

41. *First Report of Commissioners of Public Instruction in Ireland*, p. 221a, H.C. 1835 (46), xxxiii.

42. "Memoir of the Parish of Islandmagee," vol. I, p. 77.

43. "Communicants Roll Book for First Presbyterian Church" [1874-1904]; "Communicants Roll Book for First Presbyterian Church, Islandmagee" [1914-1965], in possession of the Reverend R.S. Ferguson, Islandmagee.

44. *Larne Weekly Reporter and Northern Counties Advertiser*, 8 August 1868.

45. Ibid., 26 August 1876.

46. The standard history of the Seceders is David Stewart, *The Seceders in Ireland, with Annals of their congregations* (Belfast: Presbyterian Historical Society, 1950).

47. Card file list of First Islandmagee clergy in Presbyterian Historical Society, Belfast.

48. William Holmes. Born Ramelton, Co. Donegall (see Donaldson, p. 118), 1739. Educated in Scotland. Licensed by Moira and Lisburn Anti-Burgher Presbytery. Ordained, Rashee, Anti-Burgher 29 June 1768. Removed with his congregation to new church at Ballyeaston in 1787. Also in charge of Larne and

Islandmagee. Retired 1813. Died at Whitehouse, Islandmagee, 31 November 1823. Source: MS "Irish Presbyterian Church Fasti," Presbyterian Historical Society, Belfast.

49. John Nicholson. Born Dumfries, Scotland, 1761. Ordained Larne Anti-Burgher Church (Gardenmore) 10 August 1785. Resigned charge to take Berry Street, Anti-Burgher Church, Belfast 30 August 1799. Died 10 March 1814. "A liberal minded and accomplished man, an excellent Hebraist and a first rate classical scholar" (*Belfast News-Letter,* 15 March 1814).

50. Donaldson, pp. 119-120; Stewart, pp. 249-250.

51. George McCaughey. Born Portglenone 1770. Licensed Templepatrick and Ahoghill Anti-Burgher Presbytery. Ordained Larne (Gardenmore) 8 July 1800. Retired 1838. Died 7 February 1841. Source: MS "Irish Presbyterian Church Fasti," Presbyterian Historical Society, Belfast.

52. David Potter. Licensed Tyrone Seceding Presbytery, 1820. Ordained Islandmagee 22 April 1823.

53. Stewart, p. 249.

54. MS "Irish Presbyterian Church Fasti," Presbyterian Historical Society, Belfast.

55. "Memoir of the Parish of Islandmagee," vol. I, p. 77.

56. *First Report of the Commissioners of Public Instruction in Ireland,* p. 221a.

57. Taken from session book of the Second Islandmagee Presbyterian Church, in the possession of William McCalmont, Esq., Clerk of Session.

Second Islandmagee also had a vigorous Sunday school, although I have been unable to determine numbers enrolled. See *Larne Weekly Reporter and Northern Counties Advertiser,* 6 July 1872, 8 August 1874.

58. Robert H. Shaw, Born Cairncastle. Educated at Royal Belfast Academical Institution. General Certificate 1844. Licensed at Carrickfergus Presbytery 1852. Ordained to Second Islandmagee 29 June 1853 (Donaldson, p. 123). Died 27 January 1892. Source: MS "Irish Presbyterian Church Fasti," Presbyterian Historical Society, Belfast.

59. Henry H. Macready. Born Castlerock (n.d.). Education Magee College, Derry. Licensed Coleraine Presbytery 1890. Ordained Second Islandmagee 17 March 1891. Retired 1930. Source: MS "Irish Presbyterian Church Fasti," Presbyterian Historical Society, Belfast.

60. Ian R.K. Paisley, *The 'Fifty-Nine Revival. An Authentic History of the Great Ulster Awakening of 1859* (Belfast: Free Presbyterian Church, 1958), pp. 52-53.

As far as Islandmagee is concerned this source is more accurate than one might expect. The Islandmagee material is taken directly from the virtually-unobtainable, *The Revival in Islandmagee* (London: 1860), by William Campbell.

61. For a general history see John T. Carson, *God's River in Spate, The Story of the Religious Awakening of Ulster in 1859* (Belfast: Presbyterian Church in Ireland, 1958).

62. Donaldson, pp. 130-132.

Richard Cole. Born Durrus, Co. Cork 22 June 1847. Entered probationary ministry 1870. Ordained 1874. Londonderry Circuit 1874-76, Lurgan 1876-79, Ballymena 1879-1882, Larne 1882-85, Glenavy 1885-88, Banbridge 1888-1891, Belfast (Falls Road) 1891-1894, Armagh 1894-97, Banbridge 1897-1900, Carrickfergus 1900-1913, Whitehead and Islandmagee 1903-1913. Retired 1913. Died 1925. Source: Donaldson, p. 132.

63. Donaldson, p. 130.

64. "Memoir of the Parish of Islandmagee," vol. I, p. 78.

65. Interview with the Reverend Mr. McLeer, retired Methodist minister, Whitehead.

As a footnote, it is worth noting that the Methodist chapel in Islandmagee is one of only two in Ireland called a chapel rather than a church. This is English rather than Irish nomenclature, for in Ireland "chapel" is usually reserved for Roman Catholic churches, not Protestant dissenting meeting places. It is indicative of the security of the Protestant position on Islandmagee that the Methodists could take up the normally-Catholic designation without causing comment.

66. "Memoir of the Parish of Islandmagee," vol. I, p. 100.

67. See Donald H. Akenson, *The Church of Ireland: Ecclesiastical Reform and Revolution 1800-1885* (New Haven and London: Yale University Press, 1971), passim.

68. Not, as is sometimes stated, in 1596 (Donaldson, p. 99).

69. *First Report of the Commissioners of Public Instruction in Ireland*, pp. 220a-221a.

70. *Report of His Majesty's Commissioners of Ecclesiastical Inquiry, Ireland*, pp. 400-401, H.C. 1831 (93), ix.

71. William Reeves, *Ecclesiastical Antiquities of Down, Connor and Dromore* (Dublin: Hodges and Smith, 1847), p. 272.

72. *Second Report from His Majesty's Commissioners into the Union of Parochial Benefices in Ireland*, pp. 20, 31, H.C. 1834 (406), xxiii.

73. *First Report of Commissioners of Public Instruction in Ireland*, pp. 220a-221a.

74. *Third Report of Commissioners of Ecclesiastical Revenue and Patronage in Ireland*, p. 300, H.C. 1836 (246), xxvi.

75. Donaldson, p. 100.

76. "Memoir of the Parish of Islandmagee," vol. I, p. 76.

77. *Third Report of Commissioners of Ecclesiastical Revenue and Patronage in Ireland*, p. 300.

78. James Smith. Born Dublin, 1799. Educated Trinity College, Dublin, B.A. 1821, M.A. 1832. Ordained curate of Islandmagee 1826. Became rector of Islandmagee 1839. Resigned 1849. Died 26 February 1865. Source: Donaldson, pp. 100-101.

79. William King Lynar. Born Dublin 1818, the son of a captain in the 18th Royal Irish regiment. Educated Trinity College Dublin, B.A. 1844, M.A. 1860. Ordained curate of Lisburn 1848. Incumbent of Islandmagee 11 April 1849. Resigned 1870. Died 1873. Source: Donaldson, pp. 102-103.

80. George Brydges Sayers. Born 1831 Limerick, the son of a physician. Educated Trinity College Dublin, B.A. 1853, Divinity Testimonium 1854. Ordained 1854. Held curacies in Dunluce, Donaghmore, and Ballywillan. Became Vicar of Templecorran and Kilroot in 1869, to which was attached Islandmagee on 11 June 1870. Resigned to become Vicar of Ballinderry, 1876. Died 15 June 1903. Source: Donaldson, p. 103.

81. Joseph John Hamilton Bennett. Born 1845, the son of an Anglican clergyman of County Cork. Educated Trinity College Dublin, B.A. 1866, Divinity Testimonium 1870. Ordained as Curate of Glenavy. Rector of Kilroot-Templecorran-Islandmagee 1876. Islandmagee separated from this united benefice 1879. Islandmagee reunited 1902. Died 10 October 1915. Source: Donaldson, p. 103.

82. James Milner. Curate for Islandmagee 1876-78. Rector of Islandmagee 1879-1902. Retired 1902. Died 22 October 1916. Source: Donaldson, pp. 103-104.

83. James Richardson. Educated Portora Royal School and Trinity College Dublin, B.A. 1901, M.A. 1907. Ordained curate of Willowfield, Belfast 1901, curate of Layde 1903, of Cushendall 1903, and of Ballinderry 1904. Rector of Stoneyford 1908. Rector of Kilroot-Templecorran-Islandmagee 1915ff. Source: Donaldson, p. 104.

84. *Appendix to the First Report of the Commissioners of Public Instruction in Ireland*, p. 44; "Memoir of the Parish of Islandmagee," vol. I, p. 78.

85. "Memoir of the Parish of Islandmagee," vol. I, p. 77.
86. "Committee Book, First Presbyterian Church, Islandmagee," [1831-1897] in possession of the Reverend R.S. Ferguson, Islandmagee.
87. Ibid.
88. "Memoir of the Parish of Islandmagee," vol. I, p. 26.
89. Donaldson, pp. 112-114.
90. On the opening, see *The Witness,* 19 October 1900.
91. *Larne Times and Weekly Telegraph,* 1 February 1913.
92. *The Witness,* 11 March 1921.
93. *Larne Times and Weekly Telegraph,* 10 May 1902.
94. I infer that Second Islandmagee Presbyterian congregation must have given more per capita than the First from the fact that although it had only about three-fifths the number of members, in the late 1803's it was providing its clergyman with a £105 annual stipend, £30 of which came directly from the congregation; whereas First gave their clergy only the £75 Regium Donum ("Memoir of the Parish of Islandmagee," vol. I, pp. 77-78) Also, until 1900 when the new First church was erected, the Second church was superior to the First. And in 1891 the Second Presbyterian congregation presented their minister with a manse that even today is one of the few architecturally distinguished homes on the Island (see Donaldson, p. 124).

As for the Methodists, admittedly they did not support a full-time clergyman, but for the two dozen persons in the core congregation to have raised (even with outside help) the sum of £565 to build their chapel in 1829 bespeaks a fairly high level of financial commitment. ("Memoir of the Parish of Islandmagee," vol. I, pp. 27-28.)

95. "Register of Marriages [1845-67], First Presbyterian Church, Islandmagee," in possession of the Reverend R.S. Ferguson.
96. "Parish of Islandmagee, Register of Baptisms 1879-1917," in custody of the Reverend Canon Bourns, Whitehead.
97. Usually the landlord or his representative had a place on the Anglican vestry (see for example, Islandmagee Vestry Board, 1879-1899, PRONI, MIC 1/87). This membership was purely nominal, as the landlords were non-resident. Also, after the impoverished Marquess of Donegall took over direct landlordship in 1891, the attachment was not even profitable. An entry in the vestry book for 25 March 1892 noted that the Marquess was unable to pay his usual £30 assessment!
98. See John M. Barkley, *A Short History of the Presbyterian Church in Ireland* (Belfast Publication Board, Presbyterian Church in Ireland, 1959), pp. 64-117.
99. Donaldson, p. 129-131.
100. See Donald H. Akenson, *The Church of Ireland. Ecclesiastical Reform and Revolution, 1800-1885,* pp. 275-321.
101. For a discussion of the literature on the hedge schools, see my review article in *Irish Historical Studies,* vol. XVI, no. 62 (September 1968), pp. 226-230. The hedge schools are evaluated in my book, *The Irish Education Experiment: The National System of Education in the Nineteenth Century* (London: Routledge and Kegan Paul, and Toronto: University of Toronto Press, 1970), pp. 45-58.
102. See Donaldson, pp. 82-92.
103. *Second Report of the Commissioners of Public Instruction, Ireland,* p. 283a [47] H.C. 1835, xxxiv.
104. "Memoir of the Parish of Islandmagee," vol. I, p. 72.
105. *Second Report of the Commissioners of Public Instruction, Ireland,* pp. iv-v, xii-xiii.
106. "Memoir of the Parish of Islandmagee," vol. I, p. 70.
107. Donaldson, pp. 82-92.
108. See Akenson, *The Irish Education Experiment...,* pp. 161-187.

109. Donaldson, p. 93.
110. *Appendix to the Fifth Report of the Commissioners of National Education in Ireland,* pp. 18-19 [161], H.C. 1839, xvi.
111. *Appendix to the Eighth Report of the Commissioners of National Education in Ireland,* p. 18, [398], H.C. 1842, xxxiii
112. Donaldson, p. 98.
113. Ibid., 90-99 passim.
114. Ibid., p. 97.
115. "Statements and Resolutions of the Irish Hierarchy at Maynooth Meeting June 21," *Irish Ecclesiastical Record,* 4 ser. vol. XXVII, no. 7 (July 1910), p. 92.
116. Donaldson, pp. 93, 97-98, supplemented by *Appendix to the Fortieth Report of the Commissioners of National Education in Ireland, for the Year 1873,* p. 414 [C.965], H.C. 1874, xix.
117. *Returns of the Names of Poor Law Unions in Ireland which have Agreed to become "contributory unions" under "the National School Teachers (Ireland) Act," 1875,* pp. 3-4. For details of the Act see Akenson, *The Irish Education Experiment....,* p. 318.
118. *Larne Times and Weekly Telegraph,* 7 January 1911.
119. Holmes Clipping Collection, vol. III.
120. Akenson, *The Irish Education Experiment...,* p. 346.
121. This figure, for 1903, is derived from information in the account books of the district school inspector for Islandmagee and surrounding area. It is in the possession of Hamilton Mitchell, Esq., Islandmagee, whose father was the attendance officer.

Chapter Eleven

1. See: J.C. Beckett, *The Making of Modern Ireland, 1603-1923* (London: Faber and Faber Ltd., 1966), pp. 304, 355, 394; E.D. Steele, *Irish Land and British Politics; Tenant Right and Nationality, 1865-1870* (Cambridge: Cambridge University, Press, 1974), p. 6; Edward Wakefield, *An Account of Ireland, Statistical and Political* (London: Longman, Hurst, Rees, Orme, and Brown, 1812), vol. II, pp. 285, 301-302; Holmes Clipping Collection, vol. III.
2. *Larne Times and Weekly Telegraph,* 5 October 1912.
3. Ibid, 13 June 1914.
4. Ibid., 21 December 1918.
5. Ibid., 1 May 1920.
For a discussion of the squabble within the East Antrim Unionist Association in 1919-20, see Wayne R. Hindsley, "The Ulster Question: The Establishment of the Government of Northern Ireland, 1918-1923" (Unpublished Ph.D. thesis, Queen's University, Kingston, Ontario, 1974), pp. 26-33.
The new arrangements for the Government of Northern Ireland involved a multiple-seat, proportional representation system. The county of Antrim had seven Stormont seats, six of which in 1921 went to Unionists. Sydney Elliot, *Northern Ireland Parliamentary Election Results, 1921-1972* (Chichester: Political Reference Publications, 1973), p. 10.
6. For a compelling discussion of the development of the northeastern regional culture, see Alan Gailey, "The Scots Element in North Irish Popular Culture: Some Problems in the Interpretation of Historical Acculturation." I am grateful to Dr. Gailey for giving me a copy of this unpublished paper, which is scheduled to appear soon in *Ethnologia Europaea.*
7. Dixon Donaldson, *Historical, Traditional, and Descriptive Account of Islandmagee* (Whitehead: "The Whitehead News and Ballycarry and Islandmagee Reporter," 1927), p. 32.

8. M. Perceval-Maxwell, *The Scottish Migration to Ulster in the Reign of James I* (London: Routledge and Kegan Paul, 1973), p. 233.

9. See above, Chapter Three (p. 33) and Francis J. Bigger, *Sir Arthur Chichester, Lord Deputy of Ireland* (Belfast: The Linenhall Press, 1904), pp. 28-29.

10. Compiled from "Applotment of tithes in the Parish of Isle of Magee, Diocese of Connor and County of Antrim by William Burleigh, Tithe Commissioner, 1834," (PRONI, Fin V/159), and from the following books: Henry Harrison, *Surnames of the United Kingdom: A Concise Etymological Dictionary*, 2 vols. in one (Baltimore: Genealogical Publishing Co., 1969); Edward MacLysaght, *The Surnames of Ireland* (Shannon: Irish University Press, 1969); Clifford Stanley Sims, *The Origin and Significance of Scottish Surnames* (Baltimore: Genealogical Publishing Co., 1968). Of these, MacLysaght is much the most valuable.

The total set of names included 131 surnames, of which sixteen could not be ethnically identified.

11. Mr. and Mrs. S.C. Hall, *Ireland: Its Scenery, Character, etc.* (London: Jeremiah How, 1843), vol. III, p. 123.

12. Ordnance Survey, "Memoir of the Parish of Islandmagee," Royal Irish Academy, Dublin, Ordnance Survey, Box 11, Antrim XI, VI, Islandmagee Parish, vol. I, p. 96.

13. Gailey, pp. 11-12.

Index

Absentee landlords. *See* Landlords
Acquittances, 44, 189n52
Adams, G.B., 53
Adams, Jamie, 11
Agrarian agitation, 106
Agriculture: as primary economic sector, 39; middlemen, 41-42; costs, 46-47, 191n70-n73; yields, 47-48, 191n74; farm incomes, 46-48; crop patterns, 47, 48-51; prices, 47-48, 191n75; farming calendar, 49, 51; co-operation, 51-52; rituals, 135, 136
Aiken, James, 102
Alcohol consumption. *See* Drinking
All Hallow's Eve, 143
Amalgamation of holdings, 12-13
American influence, 14-17
Ancient monuments, 27, 182n19
Anglican Church. *See* Church of Ireland
Antrim county library system, 7
Antrim, successive Lords, 111, 185n12
Antrim town, 12, 18, 19, 20
Automobile. *See* Motorcar
Ayr, 97

Bagot, Lord Baron, 37
Ballast Board. *See* Belfast Harbour Commissioners
Ballinderry, 161
Ballycarry, 12, 17, 19, 54, 55, 104, 106, 138, 146, 150, 161. *See also* Broadisland
Ballycarry Dispensary District, 112, 116
Ballycarry station, 96, 106
Ballycastle, 96
Ballyclare, 19, 96
Ballyeaston, 156
Ballygowan, 162
Ballykeel point, 12
Ballylig lime works, 60
Ballymena, 95, 96

Ballymena and Larne Railway, 96
Ballymoney, 96
Ballymoney school, 167, 168
Bangor, 97
Beans, as distinctive crop, 52-53
Beaufort, Duke of, 37
Bed outshot, 83
Belfast, 57, 72, 95, 96, 97, 98, 105, 111, 131, 133, 152, 174, 179
Belfast Harbour Commissioners, 59
Belfast Lough, 15-16, 57, 97, 140
Belfast Naturalists Field Club, 149
Belfast and Northern Counties Railway, 60-61, 95-96
Bell, Mary Ellen, 103
Bennett, Joseph J.H., 161, 211n81
Birt, 53
Blackhead, 29, 59, 61
Blackhead regatta, 147
Blair, William, 166
Boles, 85
Box bed, 86
Brice, Edward, 132, 155, 209n37
Brice, Robert, 132
British Library, London, 8
Broadisland, 11, 17, 18. *See also* Ballycarry
Brown, Agnes, 102
Brown, Samuel, 102
Brown's Bay, 29, 93, 133, 166
Brown's Bay regatta, 147
Brown's Bay school, 167, 168
Bullet window, 83
Burial customs, 137-38

Calendar. *See* Cultural calendar. *See also* Agriculture: farming calendar
Calwell, William, 54
Campbell, William, 108-109, 153, 155, 158, 204n33, 209n39
Carnspindle Bay. *See* Mill Bay
Carrickfergus, 13, 15, 16, 32, 37, 38, 55, 57, 93, 95, 96, 98, 101, 102, 105, 134, 139, 160, 161, 162, 163

Index 215

Castle Chester. *See* Castle Chichester
Castle Chichester, 17, 29, 139
Cecil, Sir Robert, 32
Celibacy. *See* Marriage rate
Census records, 6
Charity, 108, 203n32
Cheese making, 55
Chichester, Sir Arthur, 31-34, 183n6, 184n12
Chichester, family of. *See* Donegall
Chirn. *See* Last sheaf
Christmas customs, 140-41
Christmas rhymers. *See* Mummers
Church attendance, 155-56, 157, 159
Church finance, 162-63
Church government, 164
Church of Ireland, 12, 13, 91, 115-16, 126, 159-61, 163, 164, 167, 176
Churn: plunge and barrel, 55. *See also* Last sheaf
Clark, S.D., 188n45, 195n131
Climate, 24-25
Coast guards, 59
Co-educational schools, 167-68
Cole, Richard, 158, 210n62
Colville, John and Sarah, 103
Communications, 91-98
Connor, deanery of, 160-61
Cooke, Henry, 152
Cottagers, 43, 79-80
Cove regatta, 147
Crane, 85
Crawford, W.H., 179n2, 179-180n13, 180n19, 187n37, 189n52, 189n53
Crime, 99-100
Cullen, Paul, 110
Cultural calendar, 140-43
Cultural self-assertion, 174-80
Culture, as concept, 4-5
Curry, William, 20

Dairying, 54-55
Dancing, 145-47
Delph, 85, 87

Devereaux. *See* Essex, Earls of
Diet, 76, 87-88. *See also* Potato
Dispensaries Act of 1851, 112
Domestic architecture, 4, 80-85
Donaldson, Dixon, 140, 148-49, 151, 153, 154, 165, 179n12
Donegall, successive Lords, 13, 14-15, 31-35, 37-39, 46, 101, 171, 212n97
Donnelly, James, 5n
Downshire, Marquisate of, 34. *See also* Dungannon, and Hill, Sir Moyses
Dowther, Thomas, 203n3
Drake, 15-16
Drinking, 105-106, 107, 128, 145, 203n25
Dublin, 30, 102, 103, 130, 166, 167
Dubourdieu, John, 49
Dulse, 59
Dundee, Charles, 148, 150
Dungannon, successive Lords, 12-13, 32-38, 45, 57, 59, 101, 106, 185n20, 185n21, 194n121

Earling, 56
Early marriage. *See* Marriage age
Easter customs, 142, 146
Education, formal, 129-31, 165-69, 173, 203n23
Edward VII, 151
Elizabeth I, 32
Ellis, Captain, 19
Ellison, Mary Anne, 103
Emigration, 12, 70, 77, 98, 125
Encumbered Estates Act, 37
Essex, first Earl of, 32, 183n4
Essex, second Earl of, 32, 34, 183n6, 184n12
Established Church. *See* Church of Ireland
Ethnomorphism, 2

Fairies and spirits, 135, 136-37, 139, 143
Fairs, 55-56
Fallacy of cross-grouping, 2
Falling table, 86

Family continuity, 124-25
Family formation, 121-23
Family size, 120-21
Family structure, 119-25 passim
Famine, 65, 69, 70, 71, 72, 75-77, 173-74
Farm buildings, 84-85
Farm size, 42-43
Farney, barony of, 32
Ferris point, 29, 59
Fetes, 147
Feudal service, 44
First Islandmagee Presbyterian Church, 124, 149-50, 155-57, 162-63, 164, 167, 168
Fishing. *See* Maritime activities
Flack, James, 166
Folk medicine, 88-89
Folklore, 3, 8-9, 139-50
Fornication. *See* Pre-marital sex
Forsythe, Captain, 53, 56
Freemason. *See* Masonic Order

Galway, 58
Gamble, John, 207n41
Gardenmore, 156
Geological Survey, 7
Glasgow, 58, 97, 98
Glynn, 18, 60
Gobbins, 29, 60, 61, 139-40
Gobbins hawks, 60
Gobbins Road. *See* New Road
Gos-hawks. *See* Gobbins hawks
Grand jury, 92, 116
Granny. *See* Last sheaf
Great Road. *See* Low Road
Green, E.R.R., 5, 99, 179n11, 202n1
Grey Point, 57

Hall, Mr. and Mrs. S.C., 79, 175
Hallowe'en customs. *See* All Hallow's Eve
Harris, Rosemary, 5
Harvest customs. *See* Last sheaf. *See also* Hay-making
Hawthorne, Mary, 102-103
Hay-making, 53-54
Hearth, 85-86, 87

Hearts of Steel, 14
Henshaw, John, 193n112
Hill family. *See* Dungannon
Hill, Sir Moyses, 33-34, 175, 184n12
Hill, Thomas, 102
Hill-Trevor, Lord Arthur, 37, 42, 45
Hiring fairs, 56
Holmes, William, 156, 209n39
House furnishings, 85-87
Houston, John, 166
Hoy, William, 132
Hudson, Charles, 132

Illegitimacy, 71, 122-23
Indoor relief. *See* Larne Poor Law Union
Infidelity, 71-72
Inheritance, 44-45, 188n47
Inver, 160
Irish Fisheries Board, 20, 57
Irish Folklore Commission, 8n
Irish sea, 23
Irving, John, 60

Jackson, Luke, 105
James I, 32
Jones, John Paul, 15-16

Ker, R.G., 18
Kilcoan School, 148-49, 158, 167
Kilroot, 15, 57, 161
Kilwaughter, 13
Kingsmill, Robert. *See* Robert Brice
Kinvarna, 58
Knights of St. John of Jerusalem, 27
Knowehead, 11, 17, 134

Land act of 1870, 41, 45, 46
Land act of 1881, 41, 42, 46, 72
Land tenure, 12-13, 39-41, 43-46, 125, 189n50, 190n64
Land prices, 45-46
Landlord-tenant relations, 62-63
Landlords, 31-39. *See also* Donegall, and Dungannon

Lapping hay, 53
Larne, 13, 18, 19, 39, 55, 60, 61, 95, 96, 97, 98, 101, 102, 103, 105, 106, 156, 162
Larne Harbour, 29, 61, 95, 97
Larne Lough, 11, 12, 29, 83, 89, 96, 124, 150
Larne Mendicity Society, 108
Larne Poor Law Union, 77, 109-115, 116, 168
Larne Rural District Council, 116
Larne and Stranraer Steamboat Co., 98
Last sheaf, 52
Leases. *See* Land tenure
Leasehold of Islandmagee, 34-37
Leslie, Christiana Powell, 35
Leslie, Henry, 161
Leslie, Penelope, 35
Lighthouses, 59
Lime, 59-60, 97
Linen Hall Library, 7
Lisburn, 102, 160
Literacy, 129-30, 148, 165
Liverpool, 97
Livestock, 54-55
Local government, 91-93, 95, 115-17, 171
Local Government Act of 1898, 95, 116-17, 150
Local history, 1-3
London, Jack, 123-24
Londonderry, 58
Low Road, 93
Lunatic asylum, 111
Lynar, William King, 161, 211n79
Lyon, James W., 37

McBride, Margaret, 194n128
McCalmont, Robert, 59
McCartney, Thomas, 166
McCaughey, George, 156, 210n51
MacDonnell, Sorley Boy, 184n10, 185n12
McClelland, William, 11, 17, 19, 20, 29, 60, 180n28, 180n29
McGookin, 102
McIlwaine, Thomas, 102

McKay, Mary Anne, 103
McNeill, Malcolm, 54, 166
McSkimin, Samuel, 123, 139, 183n6, 203n25, 204n33
Macready, Henry H., 158, 210n59
Magee, family of, 33, 175, 184n10
Maguire, W.A., 5, 185n17, 187n30
Manor court, 101
Mariner's Hope (temperance) Lodge, 153-54
Marital fertility, 66-67
Maritime activities, 27-30, 56-60, 72, 96-98, 174, 179, 193n112, 194n119
Maritime influence, 131-33
Markets. *See* Fairs
Marriage age, 66-67, 68, 70-71, 120, 121, 123, 205n3
Marriage rate, 70-71
Marriages with outsiders, 123-25
Masonic Order, 153-55
"Massacre" of 1642, 139-40
Mawhinney, John, 58-59
May Day, 142-43
May Eve, 136
Medical facilities, 112. *See also* Folk medicine
Merchant marine. *See* Maritime activities
Merchant Seaman's Widows Fund, 108
Methodists, 124, 126, 158-59, 163, 167, 168, 210n65, 212n94
Middle Road, 93
Midland and NCC, 133
Milking, 54-55
Mill Bay, 29, 106
Mill Road. *See* Middle Road
Milliken, James, 146
Milner, James, 161, 211n82
Ministry of education (N.I.), 167
Mogey, John W., 5
Mollusk, 160
Montgomery, John, 166
Mornington, Anne, Countess of, 35
Motorcar, 151
Mullaghboy (*var.* Mulloughboy) school, 148, 167, 168

218   Between Two Revolutions

Mullaghdubh school, 146, 167, 168
Mummers, 140-41
Murphy, John, 155, 209*n*39

National Library, Dublin, 7-8
National system of education, 166-69, 173
Neighbouring, 51-52
New Road, 93
New Year's Day, 142
Newport, 58
Nicholson, John, 156, 210*n*49
Nugent, General, 20

O'Faolain, Sean, 2
Oral history, 8-9
Orange Order, 20, 146, 147, 152-55, 179, 180
Order of Good Templars, 153-55
Ordnance survey, 5, 6-7, 17, 24, 29, 54-55, 68, 71-72, 92-93, 96, 105, 122, 127, 131, 135, 139-40, 145, 155, 157, 159, 165, 175, 180*n*1
Orr, Ann, 102
Orr, James, 12, 17-18, 19, 20, 182*n*21
Orr, Samuel, 102
Outdoor Relief. *See* Larne Poor Law Union

Para-military bodies, 14
Parish, as historical unit, 3
Parish records, 6
Pauperism, 77
Penal laws, 12
Petty sessions, 101-102, 103
Pike, 53
Pitt, William, 37
Police, 100
Political attitudes, 21-22, 171-78
Poor Jones, 53
Poor law. *See* Larne Poor Law Union
Population, 65-73, 195*n*2
Pot oven, 85
Portmuck, 20, 27, 29, 57, 60, 93, 97

Portmuck Isle, 20
Portmuck regatta, 147
Portrush, 97
Port Davy, 97
Potato failures (pre-1845), 75-76. Post-1845, *see* Famine
Potato thesis, 66, 68, 195*n*7
Potter, David, 156-57, 210*n*52
Pre-marital pregnancy, 71-72, 197*n*24, 206*n*16
Pre-marital sexual activity, 121-23, 127-28. *See also* Pre-marital pregnancy
Presbyterians, 12, 105, 126, 128, 130, 155-59, 166-67, 176, 177, 178. *See also* First, and Second, Islandmagee Presbyterian Church
Presentment system, 92-93
Property damage, 104-105
Public Record Office, Dublin, 7
Public Record Office, Northern Ireland, 6-7

Quarter sessions, 102, 103
Quiltings, 146

Railroads, 60-61, 95-96
Rainfall, 25
Raloo, 13, 152, 160
Ranger, 15-16
Recreations, 145-58
Red Hall, 11, 17, 18, 150
Regional history. *See* Local history
Regium donum, 162
Religious beliefs (general) 126-29. *See also* Church of Ireland, Methodists, and Presbyterians
Religious offerings, 162-63, 212*n*94
Rents, 43-44, 77
Revival of '59, 158
Revolution, 11-22, 171-78
Richardson, James, 161, 211*n*83
Rising of 1798, 11-21
Roads, 91-95
Roman Catholics, 71, 72, 110, 139-40, 152, 161-62, 168, 175, 176

Index 219

Ross, Robert, 58
Royal Black Preceptory, 153
Royal Irish Academy, 6
Royal Navy, 131-32
Rucks, 53
Rural depopulation, 72-73, 197n27

Sabbatarianism, 128, 206n27
St. John's (Anglican) Church. See Church of Ireland
St. John's Masonic Lodge, 153
Sayers, George, 161, 211n80
Scavenging, 59
School attendance, 165, 168-69
Schoolmasters, 129-30, 165-66, 167, 168. See also Dixon Donaldson
Schooling. See Education, and Literacy
Scobes, 85
Scollop thatch, 83
Scottish cultural dominance, 175-76
Sea captains. See Ships' masters
Seacoast, 27-30
Seafaring. See Maritime activities
Sears, Dennis T. Patrick, 207n46
Second Islandmagee Presbyterian Church, 122, 148, 156-58, 163, 168, 212n94
Sectarian relations, 12, 13, 62, 139-40, 158-60, 164
Self-binding reaper, 52
Servants, 79-80
Settle beds, 86
Shaftesbury, Countess of, 37
Shake coles, 53
Shankill, 160
Shaw, R.H., 148, 152-53, 154, 157-58, 210n58
Ships' masters, 58
Shebeens, 106
"Sitting up," 146
Slander, 103
Slaughterford, 139
Smiley, Samuel, 132-33
Smith, Lady Anne Caroline, 35
Smith, William, 37
Smuggling, 20, 59

Social control (summary), 106-107
Social structure, 24, 79-80, 128, 164
Social welfare system, 107-115
Soil quality, 24, 28
"Soirees," 146
Spirit groceries, 106
Stack garden, 53
Steen, David, 148, 149-50, 153-54, 155, 167, 171-72, 209n39
Stewart, A.T.Q., 180n14
Stranraer, 98
Straw twister. See Thrawnheuk
Sub-culture, as concept, 4-5
Sub-division and sub-letting, 40-43, 46, 67
Sunshine, 25
Superstitions, 86, 134-39
Symington, Robert, 132

Tea party, 146
Tedding, 53
Temperance. See Order of Good Templars
Templecorran, 68, 161. See also Broadisland
Tester bed, 86
Thatch, 83-84
Theft, 127
Thrawnheuk, 54
Threshing, 52
Tithes, 13, 16, 17, 20, 159-60, 161
Topography, 23-30
Tourism, 60-62, 128
Tourism: influence on culture, 133-34
Townlands, 25-27, 181n18, 186n28, 199n3
Tweed, Robert, 102
Twining, Violet, 38-39

Ulster covenant, 171-72
Ulster Folk and Transport Museum, 7, 8-9
Ulster Volunteer Force, 172
United Irishmen, 16-17

Valuation of land, 198n3

Vestry, 91, 115-116, 159
Volante, 58
Volunteer movement, 14, 17
Violence, 13-14, 100, 104, 106, 203n23

Wakes, 137-38
Weavers, 16, 17, 83
Westport, 97
Whiteboys, 13
Whitehead, 62, 96, 106, 117, 158, 161, 172
Wise, Berkeley Dean, 61, 194n126
Witchcraft and magic, 134-37
Workhouse. *See* Larne Poor Law Union
Wright, William J., 103

Yeomanry, 20

Soc
DA
990
I86
A38
1979